DATE DUE	
FEB 15 1986	
JUN 16 1986	
MAIN LIBR DATE DUE 04 29 95	
BRODART, INC.	Cat. No. 23-221

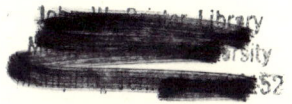

INTERPRETATION

INTERPRETATION

*An Essay in the Philosophy
of Literary Criticism*

P. D. JUHL

Princeton University Press
Princeton, New Jersey

Copyright © 1980 by Princeton University Press

Published by Princeton University Press, Princeton, New Jersey

In the United Kingdom: Princeton University Press, Guildford, Surrey

All Rights Reserved

Library of Congress Cataloging in Publication Data will be found on the last printed page of this book

Clothbound editions of Princeton University Press books are printed on acid-free paper, and binding materials are chosen for strength and durability

Printed in the United States of America by Princeton University Press, Princeton, New Jersey

CONTENTS

Preface ... ix

I. Introduction ... 3
   1. The Nature of the Problem ... 3
   2. Why Is a Conceptual Analysis of Literary Interpretation Useful? ... 10
   3. The Claims to be Defended ... 12

II. The Theory of E. D. Hirsch ... 16
   1. Hirsch's Thesis ... 16
   2. Is the Author's Intention the Only Genuinely Discriminating Norm? ... 20
   3. Is the Author's Intention an Arbitrary Criterion? ... 23
   4. Meaning and Significance: The Explanation of Interpretive Disputes ... 27
   5. Meaning and Significance: The Understanding of Literary Works ... 32
   6. Hirsch's Claim That the Meaning of a Literary Work Cannot Change ... 37
   7. Conclusion ... 42

III. Is Evidence of the Author's Intention Irrelevant? ... 45
   1. Introduction ... 45
   2. The Anti-Intentionalist Thesis ... 49
   3. Can a Speaker's Statement about His Intention Disambiguate His Utterance? ... 52
   4. Sentence-Meaning and Utterance-Meaning ... 54
   5. Allusion ... 58
   6. Irony ... 62

IV. The Appeal to the Text: What Are We Appealing to? ... 66
   1. Introduction ... 66
   2. Internal and External Evidence ... 67

Contents

	3. Interpretation and the Explanation of Textual Features	69
	4. The Role of an Author's Intention in the Explanation of Textual Features	74
	5. Can't We Dispense with the Explanation of Textual Features?	76
	6. The Complexity Criterion	81
	7. On Interpreting a Text Produced by Chance: Can It Constitute a Whole?	82
	8. Conclusion	86
V.	Context and the Rules of the Language	90
	1. What Makes the Context of an Utterance Relevant to Its Meaning?	90
	2. The Speaker's Beliefs, Personality, and Knowledge of the Language	95
	3. Speaker and Author	100
	4. Can We Exclude an Interpretation on the Basis of the Rules of the Language?	106
	5. Conclusion	112
VI.	Aesthetic Arguments and Other Aspects of Critical Practice	114
	1. Aesthetic Arguments	114
	1.1 Aesthetic Considerations as Evidence of Intention	116
	1.2 Aesthetic Considerations versus Evidence of Intention	121
	1.3 Are Aesthetic Considerations Ever Decisive?	126
	2. Intention and Awareness: Or How Much Can the Author Have Meant?	128
	2.1 Are the Meanings of Textual Details Unintended?	129
	2.2 Planning and Intending	133
	2.3 The Author's Attitudes and the Associations of the Text	135
	2.4 Paradise Lost and the Text-As-Palimpsest Thesis	138
	3. The Rejection of an Author's Statement about His Intention	140
	4. Can an Author Make His Text Mean Anything He Likes?	143
	5. Conclusion	148

Contents

VII. Life, Literature, and the Implied Author: Can (Fictional) Literary Works Make Truth-Claims? ... 153
 1. THE ISSUE ... 153
 2. THE IMPLIED AUTHOR AND THE CONNECTION BETWEEN LITERATURE AND LIFE ... 154
 3. HOW ONE MIGHT ARRIVE AT THE NOTION OF AN IMPLIED AUTHOR ... 159
 4. ASSERTION AND THE IMPLIED AUTHOR ... 163
 5. THE RELATION BETWEEN AUTHOR AND WORK: WHO IS EXPRESSING THE PROPOSITIONS EXPRESSED BY A LITERARY WORK? ... 167
  5.1 *Empson on Housman* ... 169
  5.2 *Crane on Swift* ... 175
  5.3 *Booth on Fielding and Others* ... 180
 6. THE PRESUMPTION THAT AN AUTHOR HOLDS THE BELIEFS WHICH HIS WORK EXPRESSES ... 185
 7. WHY SUPPOSE THAT A LITERARY WORK HAS AN IMPLIED AUTHOR? ... 189
 8. CONCLUSION ... 194

VIII. Does a Literary Work Have One and Only One Correct Interpretation? ... 196
 1. INTRODUCTION ... 196
 2. MULTIPLICITY OF MEANING AND INCOMPATIBLE INTERPRETATIONS ... 199
 3. POSSIBLE READINGS AND CRITICAL CHOICES ... 203
 4. CRITICAL DISAGREEMENTS AND ACCEPTABLE READINGS ... 208
 5. PARALLEL PASSAGES ... 214
 6. POETRY AND THE EXPRESSION OF ATTITUDES: CULLER'S RULE OF SIGNIFICANCE ... 219
 7. THE SURVIVAL OF LITERARY WORKS ... 224
 8. THE INEXHAUSTIBILITY OF LITERARY WORKS ... 225
 9. WHY ARE THERE SEVERAL INTERPRETATIONS FOR MOST LITERARY WORKS? ... 231
 10. CONCLUSION ... 237

APPENDIX. The Doctrine of *Verstehen* and the Objectivity of Literary Interpretations ... 239
 1. INTRODUCTION ... 239
 2. SZONDI'S CONCEPTION OF *VERSTEHEN* AND ITS ROLE IN THE VERIFICATION OF INTERPRETIVE CLAIMS ... 242

Contents

3. IS IT POSSIBLE TO ESTABLISH WITHOUT CIRCULARITY THAT A FACT IS EVIDENCE FOR AN INTERPRETATION? THE DOCTRINE OF THE 'HERMENEUTIC CIRCLE' AS A QUEST FOR CERTAINTY — 249
  3.1 *Can the Meaning of an Earlier Reading Be Objective Evidence for the Meaning of a Later Reading?* — 250
  3.2 *Can an Interpretation of a Given Passage Be Objectively Confirmed or Disconfirmed by an Appeal to Other Passages?* — 259
  3.3 *Szondi's Arguments against Beissner's Interpretation of the First Strophe of Hölderlin's "Friedensfeier"* — 268
4. THE CONCEPTUAL RELATION BETWEEN THE MEANING OF A WORK AND THE AUTHOR'S INTENTION — 279
5. THE INTERPRETATION OF FACTS AS EVIDENCE FOR AN INTERPRETATION OF A LITERARY WORK — 287
6. CONCLUDING REMARKS — 299

Bibliography — 301
Index — 323

PREFACE

THIS BOOK is an attempt to provide and defend an analysis of our concept of the meaning of a literary work. In undertaking to do this I am assuming that we in fact share one such concept, that one such concept underlies the practice of literary interpretation. Although this assumption is not unproblematical, I hope the book will bear it out.

I have made use of a wide range of examples of interpretive commentary and disagreement throughout the book. These examples are not incidental or merely illustrative. Rather, they form an integral part of my argument by helping to bring out the logical implications of the way we speak and think in practice about the meaning of literary works. Furthermore, the particular views I defend have been widely repudiated. I have been concerned therefore to show, among other things, that the intuitions and tacit assumptions which on my account form the basis of literary interpretation also underlie the practice of those critics and theorists who hold metacritical positions contrary to mine.

I should like to thank the late Edgar Lohner, who introduced me to literary theory, for his inspiration and help in my first efforts in this area. For useful and illuminating comments on earlier versions of various chapters, I am indebted to Robert Howell and S. S. Prawer, as well as to the students to whom I have had the pleasure of presenting some of this material at Oxford, Kenyon College, and Princeton. I am grateful also to Martin Steinmann, Jr., Alan Tormey, and especially Michael Hancher for many perceptive criticisms and suggestions. Warm thanks are due Sanford Thatcher of Princeton University Press who has helped me with his expert advice and who has been a pleasure to work with.

I have learned a great deal from Monroe Beardsley and E. D. Hirsch. Their penetrating studies have been a source

Preface

of innumerable ideas and have in large measure determined the direction in which my own views have developed. I hope that my criticism of some of their views will not obscure the deep respect I have for their work.

I owe a special debt to A. Peter Foulkes for his continued encouragement and support as well as for many invaluable discussions about the problems dealt with in the following pages. Finally, and above all, I want to thank my wife not only for helping on matters both of substance and style, but for enriching my life in ways which made it possible for me to write this book.

Earlier versions of Chapter IV and section 4 of Chapter V have appeared in the *Journal of Aesthetics and Art Criticism*, Vol. 36 (1978), and *Modern Language Notes*, Vol. 92 (1977), respectively. Portions of Chapters VII and VIII were read at the Center for Advanced Studies in Language, Style, and Literary Theory of the University of Minnesota, Minneapolis, in the fall of 1978. I am grateful to Yale University Press for permission to quote extensively from E. D. Hirsch's *Validity in Interpretation*.

Konstanz, July 1979   P. D. Juhl

INTERPRETATION

I

Introduction

1. The Nature of the Problem

A SIGNIFICANT PART of Western culture consists of literary works. They have become assimilated into that culture and have come to influence people's beliefs and values by being understood in a certain way. If they were understood very differently, our cultural tradition itself would be likely to be or become very different from what it is. The interpretation of literary works is thus of considerable importance in shaping that cultural tradition. It seems desirable therefore to have a general characterization of what is involved in interpreting a literary work, in saying of a particular literary work that it means so-and-so. The purpose of this book is to provide such a characterization. I shall attempt to analyze our concept of the meaning of a literary work. I want to emphasize that my purpose is not to *recommend* a certain notion of the meaning of a literary work, nor to recommend a certain way of interpreting literary works. To put it differently, I am not concerned to prescribe standards or criteria on the basis of which we *ought* to construe literary works.[1] Nor am I concerned to establish empirical generalizations as to how certain readers or groups of readers tend to interpret literary texts.[2]

I shall try to show rather what our common concept of the meaning of a literary work is. What I shall present then is

---

[1] See A. P. Foulkes' acute and helpful observations on E. D. Hirsch's theory in *The Search for Literary Meaning*, pp. 22ff.

[2] For systematic attempts to provide a basis for an empirical theory of literary interpretation, see Götz Wienold, *Semiotik der Literatur*, and Foulkes, *The Search for Literary Meaning*.

Introduction

neither an empirical theory of literary interpretation nor a "persuasive definition,"[3] but an analysis of what it is for a literary text to have a certain meaning.

In order to clarify the nature of the question which I propose to examine, as well as to provide a frame of reference for my discussion, I want to briefly mention several representative theories which offer various answers to the question.

(1) One might argue that what a literary work means depends on the reader's purpose.[4] A specialist in Elizabethan literature, for example, might be primarily interested in interpreting a literary work of that period in terms of the beliefs of its author. Another reader may prefer to construe a work in such a way that it accords as much as possible with his own views. Yet a third reader might choose that interpretation of a work which maximizes its aesthetic value. This is not, of course, to say that any interpretation of a literary work is correct provided only that it answers a reader's purpose or interest. A further condition is that the interpretation is linguistically possible—that it does not violate the relevant linguistic rules.[5] Thus, on this view, to say that a literary work has the meaning m is to say (a) that m is one of the readings in accord with the relevant rules of the language (at the time the work was written) and (b) that m answers the purpose or interest of a reader. It is obvious that, on this theory, there will be a fairly large number of equally correct interpretations of any given literary work.

(2) According to another view, similar to the first, interpretive statements are essentially normative.[6] They can be justified in terms of a particular standard or standards of

[3] See Charles L. Stevenson, *Facts and Values*, pp. 32-54.

[4] I. C. Hungerland, "The Concept of Intention in Art Criticism," pp. 738ff. Cf. also her *Poetic Discourse*, pp. 168-71, 175.

[5] Mrs. Hungerland seems to take these to be the rules of the language at the time the work in question was written. See "The Concept of Intention in Art Criticism," pp. 741f.

[6] Charles L. Stevenson, "On the Reasons That Can Be Given for the Interpretation of a Poem," pp. 127ff.

Introduction

interpretation, but the question what the *proper* standard or standards are is a genuinely normative one; that is, it calls for an implicit or explicit decision by the critic as to how a work *should* be read. Suppose a critic accepts the following criterion: 'A work means *m* if and only if that is how the author understood it.' Then he can justify a particular interpretive claim about a work by appealing to this criterion. But since, on the present theory, the criterion which a critic accepts is a normative claim as to how literary works *ought* to be read, it can in turn be justified only by considerations bearing on the latter question. One might argue, for example, that a certain standard or a certain method of interpreting literary works corresponds to "habits of mind" that *ought* "to be cultivated" or, alternatively, that a certain standard (or a particular interpretation) ought to be rejected because it is "indicative of habits of mind that no one *ought* to have."[7]

Consequently, the explicit or implicit standards which underlie claims about the meaning of a literary work function as imperatives or quasi-imperatives[8]; what a particular work means is in some measure determined by "a critic's own individuality."[9] Again, as with the first proposal, a reader cannot construe a work in any way he likes. The rules of the language in which a work is written set limits to its possible interpretations.[10] Thus, on this theory, a claim about the meaning of a literary work is, within the limits indicated, a statement about how the work in question ought to be construed; that is, it is a statement (at least in

[7] *Ibid.*, p. 135.
[8] Charles L. Stevenson, "Interpretation and Evaluation in Aesthetics," in Kennick (ed.), *Art and Philosophy*, p. 484.
[9] *Ibid.*, p. 482.
[10] See Stevenson, "On the Reasons That Can Be Given for the Interpretation of a Poem," p. 122. Stevenson discusses only a case in which we might be inclined to say that a reader is not *interpreting* a work at all, but doing something else. I assume, however, that Stevenson would also want to rule out interpretations, properly so called, which violate the rules of the language in which the text is written.

part) about the critic's personal preference based on his beliefs, attitudes, habits of mind, and so on—in short, on his "own individuality."

(3) A variant of this theory defines the meaning of a literary work as "a class of similar experiences, one or other of which those words in that order and arranged in that form, *ought* to evoke in a reader familiar with the language (or languages) in which [the work] is written."[11] As with the preceding proposal, the question what a particular literary work means calls for a decision. The main difference is that, on the present view, the "ought" in the definition calls for an "aesthetic decision"[12] while, presumably, a critic's decision as to what criteria to accept or how to construe a work need not, on the preceding theory, reflect an *aesthetic* judgment on his part.

(4) According to another theory, there are at least three different criteria which jointly determine what a literary work means.[13] The first of these, "correspondence," requires that an interpretation be based on historical knowledge of the "subject matter" dealt with in a particular work. If, for example, a poem contains a reference to a certain myth, then a critic needs to be familiar with the myth in question or the version (or versions) of that myth current at the time the poem was written in order to construe the latter correctly. (I assume that the "correspondence" criterion also excludes an interpretation which violates the rules of the language in which the text is written.) The second standard requires an interpretation to accord with what the author intended; the third that, on a given interpretation, the various parts of the work form a coherent whole. In contrast to theories (1), (2), and (3) above, an interpretation is, on

[11] Theodore Redpath, "The Meaning of a Poem," in Weitz (ed.), *Problems in Aesthetics*, pp. 368ff.
[12] *Ibid.*, pp. 371f.
[13] Ernest Kris and Abraham Kaplan, "Aesthetic Ambiguity," in Kennick (ed.), *Art and Philosophy*, pp. 419ff.

Introduction

this view, subject to these criteria regardless of (i) a critic's beliefs as to which standard or standards *ought* to be accepted, (ii) his purpose in interpreting a work, and (iii) his belief as to what interpretation maximizes the aesthetic value of a work. Although the advocates of this theory assume that in general their three standards "tend to converge,"[14] it is obvious that in any given instance they may lead to different results. When they do, a work will presumably have several equally defensible interpretations. Hence a statement about the meaning of a literary work is, according to this theory, a factual claim about the satisfaction of one or more of the above conditions.

(5) On a prominent phenomenological theory of interpretation, the meaning of a literary work is said to be determined in part by the "historical situation" of the critic.[15] The process of understanding a text involves a "fusion of horizons" (*Horizontverschmelzung*[16]) of the critic and of the text.[17] This theory is based on the so-called hermeneutic circle, the thesis that the understanding of the whole (text) depends on the understanding of the parts and vice versa.[18] It is obvious that if this thesis is correct, any sort of objective understanding of a text is in principle impossible. The only criterion for determining whether or not an interpretation is

[14] *Ibid.*, p. 421.
[15] H.-G. Gadamer, *Wahrheit und Methode*, p. 280 (English trans., *Truth and Method*, p. 263).
[16] *Ibid.*, p. 290 (*Truth and Method*, p. 273).
[17] For criticisms of Gadamer's views, see Heide Göttner, *Logik der Interpretation*, pp. 79-93, and E. D. Hirsch, "Gadamer's Theory of Interpretation." For an interesting defense of Gadamer's theory, see David Couzens Hoy, *The Critical Circle*. On Gadamer and other major figures in hermeneutics, see Richard E. Palmer, *Hermeneutics*.
[18] For a detailed application of this thesis to specific problems and methods of literary interpretation, see Peter Szondi, "Über philologische Erkenntnis." For a critical discussion of this thesis, see Wolfgang Stegmüller, "Der sogenannte Zirkel des Verstehens," and P. D. Juhl, "The Doctrine of *Verstehen* and the Objectivity of Literary Interpretations" (reprinted as the appendix to this volume).

Introduction

correct is the coherence of the various parts of the text under the interpretation in question.[19] But whereas the preceding theory (4) allows at least in principle an objective assessment of the coherence of a text under a given interpretation, the present theory precludes the very possibility of such an assessment. For, on this theory, the only constraint on a critic's interpretation of the parts is his interpretation of the whole.[20] It follows that a statement about the meaning of a work is a statement about a particular critic's subjective understanding, about his personal perspective, about his own *Vorurteile*.[21] Hence it is somewhat misleading to say that, according to this theory, it is the "historical situation" or "the whole of the objective course of history" (*das Ganze des objektiven Geschichtsganges*[22]) which determines what a work means.

(6) Perhaps the most widely held view is that the meaning of a work logically depends (i) on the rules (or "public conventions") of the language in which a text is written and (ii) on the coherence and complexity of a literary work under a given interpretation.[23] To say that a particular literary work means m is to say (a) that m is one of the linguistically possible readings of the text and (b) that, of

[19] See Emilio Betti, *Die Hermeneutik als Allgemeine Methodik der Geisteswissenschaften*, pp. 43f.

[20] See Gadamer, *Wahrheit und Methode*, pp. 253, 275, 277 (*Truth and Method*, pp. 238, 259, 261f.).

[21] See *ibid.*, pp. 250ff., 261ff. (*Truth and Method*, pp. 235ff., 245ff.).

[22] *Ibid.*, p. 280 (*Truth and Method*, p. 263).

[23] The most persuasive defense of this view is found in Monroe C. Beardsley, *Aesthetics*, pp. 24-29, 129-47, and *The Possibility of Criticism*, pp. 16-61. For a variant of this thesis, see Anthony Savile, "The Place of Intention in the Concept of Art," in Osborne (ed.), *Aesthetics*, pp. 169ff. Savile adds a condition which restricts "the correct reading of the text to one which its author could have given it, where 'could have' is taken not so much to mean 'was able to' but 'might reasonably have given in those circumstances' "—i.e., "in the intersubjectively identifiable circumstances of its production" (p. 174).

Introduction

these readings, *m* maximizes the coherence and complexity of the work. The question whether these two conditions are satisfied in a particular case is held to be, at least in principle, objectively decidable. Thus, for example, whether a word sequence has certain associations or connotations in a particular text, or whether certain possible associations or connotations of a word sequence in a text increase its coherence or the complexity, can be determined objectively; that is, it does not depend on the purpose, the subjective experience, aesthetic decision, or other normative considerations of a particular critic.

(7) Finally, there is the view that the meaning of a literary work is determined by the author's intention.[24] Usually, the qualification is added that the meaning of a work depends on the author's intention only within the limits of what the text could—given the rules of the language—be construed to mean.[25] A statement about the meaning of a work is, on this view, as on (4) and (6), an objective claim, namely, with the qualification noted, a statement about what the author intended to convey by his work.

It is clear that all of these theories have certain implications as to what kinds of facts constitute evidence for the meaning of a literary work. Much of what I shall therefore be concerned with in the following is what considerations are relevant to questions about the meaning of a work. My purpose is not, however, to settle various interpretive controversies or even to add an argument in favor of one or the other of the interpretations of a particular text. Rather, my

[24] See E. D. Hirsch, *Validity in Interpretation*, and *The Aims of Interpretation*, pp. 1-92, 146-58. See also F. Cioffi, "Intention and Interpretation in Criticism," and A. J. Close, "*Don Quixote* and the 'Intentionalist Fallacy.'" Erwin Panofsky has defended a similar view about the fine arts in "The History of Art as a Humanistic Discipline." For a discussion of Panofsky's thesis, see Richard Wollheim, *Art and its Objects*, pp. 62f.
[25] See Hirsch, *Validity in Interpretation*, p. 31.

Introduction

aim is to help clarify what such controversies are about, to shed light on the logic of interpretation by showing what a claim about the meaning of a literary work entails.

Although the theory I shall present is not an empirical but an analytical theory, it is clearly subject to empirical constraints. It must account in some plausible manner for the sorts of things critics and ordinary readers alike actually do in interpreting a work, what they take into account in arriving at an interpretation. It must be able to account for cases in which there is substantial agreement about the meaning of a work as well as for cases in which such consensus is lacking. Any theory which cannot adequately account for such facts and hence must dismiss as in principle misguided a significant part of what critics and readers do in interpreting literary works—to what criteria they appeal in practice, for example—will be suspect of offering, not an analysis of our common concept of the meaning of a literary work, but rather an implicit recommendation as to how we ought to conceive of its meaning.

2. WHY IS A CONCEPTUAL ANALYSIS OF LITERARY INTERPRETATION USEFUL?

An analysis of the concept of the meaning of a literary work does not add to our (empirical) knowledge of what a particular work means. One may wonder therefore what the value of such an analysis is, why such a theory might be worth having. The answer to this question is twofold. By providing an account of the logical structure of statements and arguments about the meaning of a literary work, such a theory makes us aware of what we as critics or readers are doing in interpreting literature. It makes us aware, in other words, of the logical commitments of our claims about the meaning of literary works.

Furthermore, a theory of this sort provides the basis for a principled acceptance or rejection of an interpretation of a literary work. Without such a theory we can accept or reject

Introduction

the practical criteria to which a critic might appeal in support of his interpretation of a work only on intuitive grounds. The theory enables us to justify the acceptance or rejection of such criteria and hence (indirectly) of the interpretations based on them.

Consider, for example, a controversy about the meaning of a text from the sixteenth century. Critic A construes the work in one way, critic B in another. Let us assume that, in support of his reading of the text, A has produced considerable evidence based on the language of the time and on the interpretation of the work by the author's contemporaries. Now B might conceivably insist that facts about the language at the time the work was written as well as the interpretation of the work by the author's contemporaries are simply irrelevant to its meaning. The meaning of a work, B might contend, is determined by our (twentieth-century) usage of the words which constitute the text. And B might be able to show that, by this criterion, his own reading is correct, whereas A's is incorrect.

It is obvious that without a theory of what it is to say that a literary work means so-and-so, we cannot decide the crucial issue between A and B as to what kinds of facts constitute evidence for the meaning of a work. We might, of course, find A's criteria more plausible; but, without a theory, we can defend our acceptance of his interpretation only on intuitive grounds. On the other hand, a well-founded theory would enable us to justify, on other than merely intuitive grounds, a claim about what kinds of facts constitute evidence for the meaning of a literary work. Consequently, we could defend our acceptance of, say, A's interpretation without begging the question whether the kinds of facts A has adduced are indeed evidence of what the work means. Furthermore, we would then be in a position to assess the relative weight of the various kinds of facts relevant to the meaning of a work. To put the point differently, we would also be able to determine what, if anything, would constitute better evidence of the meaning of the text

Introduction

than, say, facts about the language at the time the work was written.

3. The Claims to be Defended

I shall defend three main claims.

(1) I shall attempt to uphold the view that there is a logical connection between statements about the meaning of a literary work and statements about the author's intention such that a statement about the meaning of a work *is* a statement about the author's intention.

E. D. Hirsch's books *Validity in Interpretation* and *The Aims of Interpretation* present undoubtedly the most important and justly influential recent defense of a similar position. The difference is basically this. Hirsch believes that there is no logical connection between the meaning of a work and the author's intention. He holds rather that we *ought* to accept the author's intention as the decisive criterion of what a text means, since otherwise literary interpretation will be hopelessly subjective and therefore unable to provide genuine knowledge about the meaning of literary works. Whereas Hirsch is more or less explicitly offering a recommendation as to what critics *ought* to do in interpreting a text—namely, try to ascertain the author's intention—my view is that they are necessarily doing so already, in virtue of what it is for a literary work to have a certain meaning. In the next chapter I shall discuss Hirsch's theory in some detail, partly in order to differentiate more fully my own view from his and to indicate what I take to be difficulties with his position, and partly to bring out the force of one of his most valuable and important contributions to the theory of interpretation, namely, his distinction between meaning and significance.

Chapters III to VI will be devoted to the development and defense of my view concerning the connection between the meaning of a work and the author's intention. I shall examine the central aspects of the practice of literary inter-

Introduction

pretation and, in particular, the kinds of facts and criteria to which critics commonly appeal in justifying, or in attempting to rule out, a particular interpretation, such as features of the text, the coherence of a work under a certain interpretation, the nonlinguistic context of an utterance, the rules of the language, and so on. I shall try to show that an appeal to any of these involves an implicit appeal to the author's likely intention. Indeed, I shall argue that a fact will be evidence for the meaning of a literary work if and only if it is evidence of what the author intended to convey. Part of my argument for this claim will consist in contrasting statements about the meaning of a literary work created by a person with statements about the meaning of a text produced by chance, such as a computer poem.

(2) I shall try to show (in Chapter VII) that how we view the story, the situation, or events presented in a work, or what we take to be expressed or suggested by it, is determined not by our picture of the so-called implied author, but rather by our picture of the real, historical person. If a literary work conveys or expresses certain propositions, then —or so I shall argue—the real author is committed to the truth of those propositions and to the corresponding beliefs; that is, the propositions a work expresses or conveys are expressed or conveyed by, and hence attributable to, not the "implied author," but rather the real, historical author. It follows that, in an important sense, literature is not autonomous, that the connection between literature and life is a good deal closer than the implied-author doctrine, or the view that (fictional) literary works cannot make genuine assertions, would lead us to believe. I shall also suggest some reasons why the many critics and theorists who have accepted the implied-author thesis, or who have taken a similar position, have felt the need for such a notion.

(3) Chapter VIII will set out some considerations on behalf of the view that a literary work has one and only one correct interpretation. My claims here are (a) that a literary work cannot have logically incompatible meanings and (b)

Introduction

that there is reason to believe that it is in principle possible to determine the correct interpretation of a work.

Since one of the claims I shall be defending is a version of the intentionalist thesis, a word is in order on my use of the term 'intention'. In speaking of what an author intended to convey by his work, I do not mean what he *planned* to write or to convey.[26] Nor am I using the term 'intention' in the broader sense of 'motive' in which it may include, for example, his desire to achieve fame or other causal factors.[27] Nor do I mean by 'intention' the "sustained focal effect"[28] or the textual coherence of a work. Rather, I am using the term in the sense of an author's intention in writing a certain sequence of words[29]—in the sense, that is, of what he meant by the words he used. However, what an author planned to write, his motives for writing, as well as the coherence of his text under a given interpretation, may certainly constitute *evidence* of what (in the sense in which I am using the term 'intention') he intended to convey by his work.

[26] That a literary work may not mean what its author *planned* to convey would be difficult to deny. See John M. Ellis, *The Theory of Literary Criticism*, pp. 120f., and René Wellek and Austin Warren, *Theory of Literature*, pp. 148f.

[27] See G. Wilson Knight, *The Wheel of Fire*, pp. 6f., and Richard Kuhns, "Criticism and the Problem of Intention," pp. 6, 14. On the distinction between motive and intention, see Quentin Skinner, "On Performing and Explaining Linguistic Actions," pp. 15f., and "Motives, Intentions, and the Interpretation of Texts," pp. 401f., and Anthony Kenny, *Action, Emotion and Will*, Ch. 4, esp. pp. 84-99.

[28] Richard Kuhns, "Semantics for Literary Languages," pp. 101f.

[29] In his paper "Motives, Intentions, and the Interpretation of Texts" (pp. 402-404), Skinner elucidates the notion of "what . . . the writer mean[s] by what he says in his work" (p. 397). He concludes that an author's intention in writing a work is logically equivalent to what he means by the utterances which constitute the text (pp. 403f.). See also Skinner's valuable paper, "Hermeneutics and the Role of History." On the sense of 'intention' relevant to statements about the meaning of a literary work, see also Michael Hancher, "Three Kinds of Intention," pp. 830ff., and Close, *"Don Quixote* and the 'Intentionalist Fallacy'," in Newton-de Molina (ed.), *On Literary Intention*, p. 179.

Introduction

I should like to emphasize that I am not arguing for or against a certain *method* of interpreting literary works. In particular, I am not arguing for a kind of biographical approach to the study of literature. Whether or not personal events in a poet's life play an important role in his poetry is an *empirical* question and obviously cannot be settled on *a priori* grounds.[30] It may be a truism that a man's (personal) experience shapes his beliefs and values; but it evidently does not follow that a poem or a novel is about the writer's personal life or about his psychological states. Furthermore, different critical methods and approaches tend to illuminate different aspects of a work, and by and large they are not, or need not be, incompatible.[31]

It is, of course, true that the version of the intentionalist thesis I shall be defending bears on the validity of various 'methods' of interpretation; but it does so only insofar as they imply metacritical claims about the concept of the meaning of a literary work. And although the various literary-critical methods have been associated with such claims, they can with minor adjustments be usefully applied even if the respective metacritical claims are false. All that follows from my thesis is that any (and only) evidence of the author's intention is *ipso facto* evidence of the meaning of the work. But this leaves considerable room for different methods and different approaches to the study of literature.

[30] See, e.g., Northrop Frye, "The Critical Path," pp. 95-96; T. S. Eliot, "Tradition and the Individual Talent," p. 9; and Hirsch, *Validity in Interpretation*, pp. 15-16.

[31] See Jost Hermand's demand for a synthesis of methods, *Synthetisches Interpretieren*, pp. 169ff.; see also Edgar Lohner, "The Intrinsic Method."

II

The Theory of E. D. Hirsch

E. D. HIRSCH has maintained that the meaning of a literary work is determined by the author's intention. In the following, I should like to examine Hirsch's thesis and the arguments he gives in support of it. I shall also consider his distinction between the meaning and the significance of a work as well as his claim that the meaning of a work is "determinate" and hence cannot change.

1. HIRSCH'S THESIS

Hirsch formulates his principal thesis as follows:

> Verbal meaning is whatever someone has willed to convey by a particular sequence of linguistic signs and which can be conveyed (shared) by means of those linguistic signs.[1]

Hirsch offers this as a (provisional) definition of verbal meaning. What sort of definition is being propounded here? In order to answer this question, it will be useful to consider the argument which Hirsch gives in support of his definition:

> ... the only compelling normative principle that has ever been brought forward is the old-fashioned ideal of rightly understanding what the author meant. Consequently, my case rests not on the powerful moral arguments for re-cognitive interpretation, but on the fact that it is the only kind of interpretation with a determinate object, and thus the only kind that can lay claim

[1] Hirsch, *Validity in Interpretation*, p. 31.

The Theory of E. D. Hirsch

to validity in any straightforward and practicable sense of that term.[2]

One might think that Hirsch's definition is an analytic statement, a claim about our concept of the meaning of a literary work. If it were, one would expect Hirsch to argue that a critic would simply be mistaken if he construed a work not according to the author's (likely) intention but according to, say, what makes the 'best' work, or how the author's contemporaries understood the text—provided the latter differed from what the author (probably) intended. But Hirsch does not give such an argument. Instead, he contends that only the author's intention provides "a genuinely discriminating norm,"[3] that is, a criterion which would allow us, at least in principle, to determine which of the linguistically possible interpretations of any given work is correct.

It would still be possible, of course, that Hirsch is analyzing (or purports to analyze) our concept of the meaning of a literary work; in particular, this would be likely if, for example, Hirsch claimed that our notion of the meaning of a work is such that only one of the linguistically possible interpretations of a text can be correct, and hence that it precludes the possibility that the meaning of a work depends (even within certain limits) upon, say, the critic who interprets it. But Hirsch appears to hold that the rules of the language in question—what he calls "the principle of sharability"[4]—constitute the *only* constraint on how a critic or reader can properly interpret a literary work:

> Since it is very easy for a reader of any text to construe meanings that are different from the author's, there is nothing in the nature of the text itself which requires the reader to set up the author's meaning as his norma-

[2] *Ibid.*, pp. 26-27.   [3] *Ibid.*, p. 26.
[4] *Ibid.*, p. 31. Actually, Hirsch's principle of sharability seems to impose somewhat weaker constraints than the rules of the language in which the text is written; see *ibid.*, pp. 14-15, 234.

tive ideal. Any normative concept in interpretation implies a choice that is required not by the nature of written texts but rather by the goal that the interpreter sets himself. . . . Bluntly, no necessity requires the object of interpretation to be determinate or indeterminate, changing or unchanging.[5]

I take Hirsch to be saying here that our notion of what it is for a literary work to mean so-and-so does not imply a particular criterion which specifies (in general terms) which of the linguistically possible interpretations of a given work is correct. In other words, our concept of the meaning of a literary work imposes no constraints on the interpretation of a work other than those imposed by the rules of the language in question (or Hirsch's "principle of sharability"). Within those limits, the meaning of a work depends on "the goal that the interpreter sets himself." Hence as far as Hirsch's analysis of our concept of the meaning of a literary work is concerned, his theory appears to be very similar to those of Hungerland and Stevenson.[6]

Now we can see more clearly the relation between Hirsch's contention that only the author's intention provides "a genuinely discriminating norm" and his definition of verbal meaning. Hirsch begins with the assumption that any literary text can be properly construed in a number of different ways, limited only by the principle of sharability (by what can be conveyed by the text). Consequently, there will not even in principle be one and only one correct interpretation of a work. Hence if claims about the meaning of a literary work are to be objective statements, if literary interpretation is to be a science or discipline and not "just a play-

[5] *Ibid.*, pp. 24-25. See also Hirsch's article, "Three Dimensions of Hermeneutics," pp. 246-49; reprinted in Hirsch, *The Aims of Interpretation*, pp. 75-79.

[6] See Hungerland, "The Concept of Intention in Art Criticism," pp. 738ff.; and Stevenson, "On the Reasons That Can Be Given for the Interpretation of a Poem," pp. 127ff.

ground for the jousting of opinions, fancies, and private preferences, where the stake is not knowledge but the so-called higher humane values,"[7] then we need a criterion which allows, at least in principle, one and only one interpretation of a work to qualify as correct or valid. But—or so Hirsch claims—only the author's intention provides such a criterion. It follows that literary interpretation will be a science or discipline, and thus be able to yield genuine knowledge, only if we define "verbal meaning" as Hirsch suggests.

Hirsch's contention that only the author's intention provides "a genuinely discriminating norm," then, offers a reason why, given that it is desirable for literary interpretation to be a science or discipline, we ought to accept his definition of verbal meaning.

And now we can also see what kind of definition it is, namely, a stipulative definition or recommendation.[8] It amounts to the proposal that we ought to conceive of the meaning of an utterance or a literary work in terms of what the speaker or author intended to convey.[9] Consequently, the question whether Hirsch's thesis is true or false does not arise; being a proposal, it does not assert anything.

[7] Hirsch, *Validity in Interpretation*, p. 163; see also Hirsch, "Value and Knowledge in the Humanities," pp. 66-67. For some critical comments, see M. H. Abrams, "What's the Use of Theorizing about the Arts?", pp. 50-53.

[8] See Arthur Pap, "Theory of Definition," in Olshewsky (ed.), *Problems in the Philosophy of Language*, pp. 282-83; and Stevenson, *Facts and Values*, pp. 32ff.

[9] In his article, "Three Dimensions of Hermeneutics" (*The Aims of Interpretation*, pp. 77, 78, 85, 89, 90-92), Hirsch explicitly formulates his thesis as a recommendation or as, in his words, a "basic moral imperative" (p. 92; see esp. pp. 90-92). The main difference between the thesis presented in this paper and the definition given in *Validity in Interpretation* is that in the latter Hirsch rejects the argument based on the "ethics of language" (pp. 26f.) and appeals instead to the epistemological or pragmatic considerations discussed above. See also *The Aims of Interpretation*, pp. 7, 8, 135.

The Theory of E. D. Hirsch

2. Is the Author's Intention the Only Genuinely Discriminating Norm?

I want now to examine more closely Hirsch's contention that only the author's intention provides "a genuinely discriminating norm" for interpretation. I shall try to show, first, that Hirsch's claim is false and, second, that even if it were true, it would not constitute an adequate reason for adopting his recommendation.

It would be conceivable, for example, that a group of distinguished literary critics is appointed or elected to serve as arbiter in disputes about the meaning of literary works. The decision of a majority or plurality of those critics could then be taken as the criterion for determining what a literary work means. Whether or not such a quasi-legal adjudication of interpretive disagreements would be desirable, such a criterion cannot be ruled out on the grounds that it does not in principle constitute a "genuinely discriminating norm." Furthermore, such a criterion could in practice undoubtedly resolve a larger number of interpretive controversies than an appeal to the author's intention; it would be more likely, for instance, to be able to settle disputes about the meaning of anonymous works or texts for which the evidence of the author's intention is insufficient or conflicting.

In his attempt to show that various theories of interpretation do not provide a sufficiently restrictive criterion, Hirsch discusses *inter alia* the view that the meaning of a work is determined by "public consensus."[10] It is doubtful, however, whether Hirsch can in fact, on his assumptions, rule out the latter.

Consider his arguments against the following objection. Suppose a particular text could, under the rules of the language, have the meaning m_1 or the meaning m_2. Suppose further that at time t_1, when the author wrote the work, he intended to convey m_1 by it, but at some later time, t_2, he wants his work to be understood as meaning m_2. In that

[10] Hirsch, *Validity in Interpretation*, pp. 12f.

The Theory of E. D. Hirsch

case, the author's intention does not allow us, even in principle, to decide whether the text means m_1 or m_2.

Hirsch argues against this conclusion as follows. First, he maintains that what has changed in such a case is not, or not necessarily, the meaning of the text, but rather the author's response to this meaning—that is, the "significance"[11] of that meaning to the author. It may be true, of course, that the author's response to what he meant at t_1 has changed; but this is beside the point. For the assumption is not, or not just, that at t_2 the author no longer believes that what he meant at t_1 is worth expressing or that at t_2 he has a different attitude toward what he meant at t_1. Rather, the assumption is that at t_2 the author wants his work to be understood differently, namely, as meaning m_2.

Second, Hirsch claims that far from establishing that the author's earlier meaning has changed, the example shows that it has not in fact changed, for otherwise the author could not know that he no longer wants to convey what he meant at t_1.[12] It may be true, in a sense, that the *earlier* meaning has not changed, but this is irrelevant to the question whether the meaning of the text has changed, whether, that is, at t_1 it meant m_1, whereas at t_2 it means m_2. Thus in order to avoid the conclusion that the meaning of a text may change, Hirsch argues that if an author changes his mind as to what he wants to convey by his text, or how he wants the latter to be understood, then a critic would simply have to choose which text he wants to interpret. In other words, in such a case we have not one text, but two.[13]

Now Hirsch rejects public consensus as a criterion of what a text means because readers frequently do not agree about the meaning of literary works. For, in such cases, the criterion of public consensus does not allow us to decide what the text in question means. If one group of readers or critics claims that a particular work means m_1, while another group maintains that it means m_2, then the criterion cannot in prin-

[11] *Ibid.*, p. 8. [12] *Ibid.*, p. 9.
[13] *Ibid.*

ciple resolve the issue. The problem is that the solution which Hirsch adopts in the case in which an author changes his mind as to what he wants to convey by his text, or how he wants it to be understood, is clearly also open to a proponent of the public consensus criterion. If two groups of readers or critics disagree about the meaning of a work, then we can say, just as in the analogous case involving Hirsch's criterion, that we have two texts (or works) instead of one.

Hence it seems that Hirsch cannot reject public consensus as an interpretive norm on the grounds that it does not provide a criterion which can in principle decide any interpretive dispute. One could, of course, modify Hirsch's criterion such that only the author's intention at the time he wrote the work in question counts in determining what it means. In that way we could avoid the complication which arises if an author later changes his mind about how he intends his text to be understood. But it is possible—and not uncommon—that an author's intention changes in the course of his writing a particular work. In that case the modified criterion will also be insufficient. We could then narrow the possibilities even further and say that only the author's final intention at the time he wrote the work counts.

One might contend, however, that even if an author's intention does not in principle allow us to resolve every controversy about the meaning of a work, it nevertheless enables us to decide a significantly larger number of disputes than the criterion of public consensus. But this seems doubtful. For if there is a logical connection between an author's intention and the meaning of his work, as I shall argue, then it would seem to be unlikely that a considerable number of persisting interpretive disagreements can be resolved by an appeal to the author's intention. Furthermore, a somewhat more refined application of the criterion of public consensus[14] might very well reveal (or produce)

[14] See Hans Glinz, *Sprachwissenschaft heute*, pp. 106-108, and "Methoden zur Objektivierung des Verstehens von Texten," pp. 75-107.

The Theory of E. D. Hirsch

significantly greater agreement in the interpretation of literary works than might at first sight appear to exist (or appear likely to be reached).

3. Is the Author's Intention an Arbitrary Criterion?

I have so far argued that the author's intention, if it is a "genuinely discriminating norm," is not the only criterion which satisfies this condition. I want to suggest now that even if Hirsch's claim were true, it would not constitute an adequate reason for accepting his recommendation.

If the crucial question in assessing the adequacy of a theory of interpretation or of an interpretive criterion were whether or not it provides a genuinely discriminating norm, then we would be justified in adopting, for example, the following proposal: A literary work means m if and only if m is the (linguistically possible) reading which a specified critic, to be selected at random, likes least. When the first critic chosen dies, a successor is selected (also at random). We postulate further: Any given critic selected determines the meaning only of works which have not already been interpreted by one of his predecessors. If a chosen critic cannot in a particular case make up his mind about which of the linguistically possible readings of a text he likes least, then the correct interpretation is determined by lot.

This criterion certainly constitutes a genuinely discriminating norm. Yet to adopt it would be absurd. It is unacceptable, not because it fails to provide a means for deciding in principle what any given work means, but because it does not even remotely correspond to our notion of what it is for a literary work to mean so-and-so. To adopt this criterion would in effect be to sacrifice the subject matter of literary interpretation for the sake of objectivity. Hence Hirsch's claim that only the author's intention provides a genuinely discriminating norm would not, even if it were true, constitute by itself an adequate reason for accepting his proposal. Clearly, the question whether a theory of interpretation provides a genuinely discriminating norm is neither the only nor the most important consideration in assessing its adequacy.[15] A much more basic consideration would seem to be whether the proposed theory corresponds reasonably well to the way in which we in fact construe literary works—whether, that is, it constitutes a reasonably close approximation to our concept of what it is for a literary work to mean this rather than that. The question which now arises is this: What reason do we have for supposing that Hirsch's definition, unlike the above criterion, satisfies this condition?

Hirsch notes that

> ... in legal questions, changed interpretations can be institutionalized by a pronouncement from the highest court. But in the domain of learning such pronouncements cannot carry authority. No one, for example, would hold that a law means "what the judges say a law means" if there were not a supreme tribunal to decide what, after all, the judges say. There could never be such arbitrary tribunals in the domain of knowledge and scholarship.[16]

It is not obvious, however, that the author's intention is not an equally arbitrary criterion. Nor does Hirsch give any arguments to show that it is not. What he does argue is that the author's meaning is "determinate," "sharable," and allows us to decide which of the possible implications of a text are or are not in fact implications of the latter[17]; that is, he argues that the author's intention provides "a genuinely discriminating norm." But it is not clear how this bears on the question whether or not the author's intention is an arbitrary criterion.

Hirsch may have had this sort of objection in mind when

---

[15] For a related point, see Noam Chomsky, *Aspects of the Theory of Syntax*, p. 20.
[16] *Validity in Interpretation*, p. 123n.
[17] *Ibid.*, pp. 27, 31-67.

The Theory of E. D. Hirsch

he claimed that "there exists only one norm"—the author's intention—which is "universally compelling."[18] However, Hirsch also holds that there is no general consensus about the meaning of most literary works and that this is the result of the banishment of "the original author as the determiner of meaning."[19] But if this is true, then it would appear that there is a considerable number of readers and critics— namely, those who reject interpretations based on the author's intention—to whom Hirsch's criterion seems less than compelling.

It will not do to object here that if a text does not mean what its author meant by it, then it cannot have a determinate meaning.[20] For this simply leads us back to the claim that only the author's intention constitutes "a genuinely discriminating norm." Furthermore, it is rather unlikely that those critics who hold, for example, that the meaning of a literary work is what it "means to different sensitive readers"[21] will find Hirsch's appeal to objectivity very persuasive.

This last point need not, of course, be very disconcerting if Hirsch were to show that the meaning of a literary work is, and is necessarily, determinate—in virtue of our notion of what it is for a text to have a certain meaning. But to take this view would be inconsistent with Hirsch's basic premise,

---

[18] *Ibid.*, p. 25.

[19] *Ibid.*, p. 5; see also p. 13 and his article, "The Norms of Interpretation."

[20] See Hirsch, *Validity in Interpretation*, pp. 5, 45f., 249. Hirsch claims that an "indeterminate meaning is not sharable" (p. 45). Surely it is possible to convey to someone the meaning of a word (or sentence) which *in abstracto* is ambiguous and hence may on different occasions of its use have different meanings. If this is so, then the meaning of such a word (or sentence) is "sharable." Hence even if a literary work, like an ambiguous word taken *in abstracto*, has more than one meaning, it does not follow that its meaning is not sharable.

[21] T. S. Eliot, "The Frontiers of Criticism," p. 113. Eliot, for example, quite explicitly rejects the view "that there must be just one interpretation of [a] poem as a whole, that must be right" (*ibid.*).

namely, that our concept of what it is for a text to have a certain meaning does not imply a particular criterion or standard which specifies (in general terms) which of the linguistically possible interpretations of a work is correct. On Hirsch's view, a reader or critic is justified in choosing any criterion or standard of interpretation he likes; for, in Hirsch's words, "any normative concept in interpretation implies a choice that is required . . . by the goal that the interpreter sets himself."[22]

It follows that regardless of what criterion a reader chooses to accept, or what goal he decides to set himself, his interpretation of a particular work will be 'correct' provided only that his reading is possible under the rules of the language in which the work was written—that is, provided only that it satisfies Hirsch's condition of "sharability." Let us suppose that Hirsch is right in maintaining that what a work means depends on the reader's purpose or goal and that a "reader can [justifiably] adopt or reject any norm."[23] Then to say that henceforth an interpretation of a literary work—which satisfies Hirsch's principle of sharability—will be correct if and only if it corresponds to what the author intended would in effect be to rule out by fiat an indefinitely large number of what are, *on Hirsch's premise*, perfectly legitimate interpretations. To put the point another way, if Hirsch's assumption about our concept of the meaning of a literary work is correct, then his definition would distort the meaning of literary works no less fundamentally than the proposal I outlined above. This would surely be too high a price to pay for objectivity. I do not want to say that so radical a proposal could not be justified. I am claiming rather that Hirsch's contention (that only the author's intention provides a genuinely discriminating norm), even if

[22] Hirsch, *Validity in Interpretation*, p. 24. On this point, see also Jack Meiland's perceptive criticism of Hirsch, "Interpretation as a Cognitive Discipline," pp. 34f.
[23] *Validity in Interpretation*, p. 26.

The Theory of E. D. Hirsch

it were true, would not constitute an adequate reason for accepting his definition.

4. MEANING AND SIGNIFICANCE: THE EXPLANATION OF INTERPRETIVE DISPUTES

In his arguments against the claim that the author's intention does not provide a criterion which can in principle decide any interpretive dispute, Hirsch introduces a distinction between the meaning and significance of a text. Since this distinction is extremely important and valuable, I want to examine it more closely. In order to appreciate its value fully, however, it will be useful to indicate what the distinction will not be able to do for us.

Hirsch formulates his distinction as follows:

> *Meaning* is that which is represented by a text; it is what the author meant by his use of a particular sign sequence; it is what the signs represent. *Significance*, on the other hand, names a relationship between that meaning and a person, or a conception, or a situation, or indeed anything imaginable.[24]

Interpretive disagreement frequently arises, according to Hirsch, because critics often fail to distinguish between meaning and significance: between, for example, their own response—one kind of significance—and the meaning to which they are responding.[25]

One problem with Hirsch's explanation is that it begs the crucial question what the meaning of a literary work is. For suppose a critic disagrees with Hirsch about the meaning of a particular literary work. Suppose further that the critic offers an existentialist interpretation of the work, whereas

[24] *Ibid.*, p. 8. See also pp. 62f., 140-44; and *The Aims of Interpretation*, pp. 2f., 79-81, 85-88, 146.
[25] *Validity in Interpretation*, pp. 38f., 63, 214f.

the author intended something very different. I take it that this would be a case of confusing meaning with subject matter.[26] Now if, invoking his distinction, Hirsch contested the critic's interpretation, the latter would presumably not admit that he is saying something about the significance, rather than the meaning, of the work. The critic would probably simply deny that Hirsch had correctly understood the work, and he would no doubt also reject Hirsch's criterion. Clearly, Hirsch could not justifiably reject the critic's interpretation unless he could show that what a work means *is* what the author intended.

Hirsch wants to say that the critic in our example is not construing the meaning of the work but rather commenting on its significance. Hence if the critic claims that his interpretation corresponds to the meaning of the work, he is simply mistaken. The problem with this claim is that it presupposes that the meaning of a work *is* as a matter of fact (or rather of logic) what the author intended to convey. It presupposes, that is, a definition different in kind from the one which Hirsch appears to be defending, namely, a recommendation. It is perhaps not surprising that Hirsch does not offer much in the way of argument for the thesis that there is a logical connection between the meaning of a work and the author's intention; for it is inconsistent with Hirsch's basic assumption, that our concept of what it is for a literary work to have a certain meaning does not require that meaning to be "the stable and determinate meaning of an author."[27]

But let us suppose that the meaning of a literary work *is* what the author intended to convey. Can we then explain interpretive disagreements (which are not disputes about what the author intended) in terms of Hirsch's distinction between meaning and significance? Hirsch claims that "the two kinds of significance that have been most often confused with verbal meaning" are "symptomatic meaning" and

[26] See *ibid.*, pp. 57-61.   [27] *Ibid.*, p. 24.

The Theory of E. D. Hirsch

"subject matter."[28] Let us first take a simple case of confusion between verbal meaning and subject matter. Suppose a boy writes a little poem about a child who loses his way in a forest; he describes the child's loneliness and fear. Let us presume the boy wanted to convey just this, the fear and loneliness of a child having lost his way in a forest. This, then, is the meaning of the poem. Now a critic might say: 'That is not what the lines mean at all. The child is not simply a child but stands for man in general, utterly lost in an alien and cruel world; the child's fear and loneliness represent man's universal condition, his existential anxiety and loneliness.' In such a case it might seem plausible to say that the critic is relating the meaning of the poem to an existential symbolism in terms of which he interprets it.

One could, however, raise the following objection to the view that the critic is, strictly speaking, relating the *meaning* of the poem to something else. If the critic asserts that the child stands for man in general, then, since the (imaginary) referent (or designatum) of the word 'child' cannot be identified with its meaning,[29] the critic is not relating the *meaning* of 'child' to something else (his existential symbolism) but rather its (imaginary) referent. Alternatively, if we deny that the word 'child' (and its synonyms) in the poem has a referent at all, one could argue that it is the *word*, but not its meaning, that is being interpreted in terms of (or related to) an existential symbolism.

Let us consider another case. Suppose the poem just mentioned was written by a man who intended just what the

[28] *Ibid.*, p. 63.
[29] See Gottlob Frege, "Über Sinn und Bedeutung," in *Funktion, Begriff, Bedeutung* (ed. Günther Patzig), p. 41. Frege's famous example is "Abendstern" and "Morgenstern"; the meaning of these words is different, yet their referents are identical. See also W.V.O. Quine,. who gives as an example "creatures with a heart" and "creatures with a kidney" ("Two Dogmas of Empiricism," in Olshewsky [ed.], *Problems in the Philosophy of Language*, p. 406).

29

critic said it means. The symbolic interpretation now represents the meaning of the poem. Suppose another critic maintains that the poem is merely a portrayal of man's anxiety and loneliness in modern society; on this interpretation, the poem does not depict the human condition in general but only in a particular society. In this case the second critic is not relating the meaning of the poem (represented by the first critic's interpretation) to something else; he could at most be described as interpreting the literal meaning of the poem symbolically. But that is, on our present assumption, not what it means. Hence the distinction between meaning and significance does not accurately describe the disagreement just considered.

In fact, it is doubtful whether any interpretive disagreement can be accurately described in terms of the meaning-significance distinction. For consider a simple ambiguous sentence, such as 'I saw the shooting of the hunters.'[30] Suppose one person claims that a particular utterance of this sentence means 'I saw the hunters shooting' while another takes it to mean 'I saw the hunters being shot.' Now regardless of whether the speaker meant the former or the latter, the alternative interpretation cannot be regarded as relating what the speaker *meant* to something else (in this case, ordinary English); what is being related (interpreted) here are words (terms, symbols), not their meanings.

As far as "symptomatic meaning" is concerned, it is again not what the speaker (consciously) *meant* that is being interpreted in terms of some symbolic system (or related to something else), but rather the words he used. Suppose (to vary one of Hirsch's examples[31]) that a hitherto faithful husband claims to be giving an evening seminar on eighteenth-century French literature, when in fact he is becoming all too familiar with Olga Olavsen, the new Swedish instructor. "What did you discuss in class tonight?" his wife

[30] The example is taken from Paul Ziff, *Philosophic Turnings*, p. 138.
[31] Hirsch, *Validity in Interpretation*, p. 55.

asks. "*Les liaisons dangereuses*," he quickly replies. "Again? I thought you did that two weeks ago." The man blushes deeply and hesitates: "Oh, er—well, I hadn't quite finished —some final remarks I hadn't quite gotten to before—I mean . . ."; and this is broken off with a gesture of uncertainty.

If we took the man to mean 'really' (unconsciously) that he was not in fact giving a seminar on French literature, then we would clearly not be interpreting the man's meaning (that he was giving a seminar) in terms of some other symbolism, in which the *meaning* (or proposition) that a certain person was giving a seminar signifies (means) that he was not; rather, we would be taking the circumstances of the utterance (the man blushes deeply, hesitates, seems very embarrassed) as indications that he does not 'really' mean what he says, that his utterance does not 'really' mean that he was giving a seminar on French literature. The distinction here is between the words 'I was giving my French seminar' (or some synonymous expression) and what they represent (their meaning), namely, that he was giving his French seminar. It is the latter, the meaning or thought that the man was at his seminar, which I am denying we could reasonably be said to construe as meaning that the man was not giving a seminar. Clearly, what we would be interpreting are the *words* the man used (or, more precisely, his utterance of those words).

To summarize, Hirsch's distinction between meaning and significance does not help us explain interpretive disputes. For, in the first place, the distinction presupposes that the meaning of a work *is* what the author intended. But whether that is true is usually one of the crucial questions at issue in the kinds of cases which the meaning-significance distinction is supposed to explain, namely, cases in which, for example, one critic construes a work in accordance with the author's intention, while another interprets it according to a different criterion. Furthermore, the assumption that the meaning of a work is logically tied to the author's intention

The Theory of E. D. Hirsch

is inconsistent with one of Hirsch's basic premises. Secondly, even if we assume that there is such a connection between the meaning of a work and the author's intention, typical interpretive disagreements cannot be correctly described in terms of the distinction between meaning and significance.

None of this is to deny the value of Hirsch's distinction. It is merely to show what this distinction involves and, in particular, that it does not help us explain typical disputes about the meaning of a work. For a critic who in an interpretive controversy confuses meaning (what the author intended) with, say, "subject matter" is not relating the meaning of the work in question, or what the author intended, to something else; to put it differently, such a critic is not saying something about the relationship between the meaning of the work and a certain subject matter. Rather, he is quite simply saying what he thinks the work means, even if he is in fact misconstruing it because he is mistaken about the proper frame of reference or about what determines the meaning of a work.[32]

5. Meaning and Significance: The Understanding of Literary Works

We do, however, frequently comment on the relationship between the meaning of a work and something else, or on the relationship between a work and something else. And in these cases our comments do presuppose an interpretation of the work. The sort of statements I have in mind fall under the category of criticism (in a narrower sense) as opposed to interpretation. For example, a critic might point out "that Gibbon's comments on superstition reflect the common attitudes of his own time."[33] Or, to take another example of Hirsch's:

[32] This point holds even if the claim that the meaning of a work is determined by the author's intention is abandoned. See Hirsch, "Three Dimensions of Hermeneutics," in *The Aims of Interpretation*, pp. 79f.
[33] Hirsch, *Validity in Interpretation*, p. 62.

The Theory of E. D. Hirsch

Simone Weil's emphasis on the role of force in *The Iliad* brilliantly exploited the experiences she shared with her audience [the horrors of Nazism], and probably she did not overemphasize the role of force within Homer's imagination. The element of *criticism* in her commentary was her implication that Homer was right—human life is like that, and we, in this age, know it. The element of *interpretation* in her commentary was her laying out in an ordered way Homer's implications about the role of force in life.[34]

Both Simone Weil's statement about the *Iliad* ("that Homer was right . . .") and the observation about Gibbon's comments on superstition illuminate the respective works in some way; they enhance our understanding of those works. Of course, the fact that we can and do draw a distinction between the meaning and the significance of a work does not imply that the meaning of a work is logically determined by the author's intention. Consequently, if we are not to beg the question whether the meaning of a work is what the author intended, we must leave the precise definition of the meaning of a work open. And this is in fact what Hirsch has done in a more recent formulation of his distinction.[35]

Now the value of Hirsch's (modified) distinction lies in its throwing into relief the difference between the ways in which critical statements of the sort illustrated by the examples above and interpretative statements properly so called enhance, or purport to enhance, our understanding of literary works. Interpretation and criticism provide different kinds of understanding of a work.[36] When one speaks, in the abstract, of understanding literary works, it is easy to lose sight of this distinction, especially since, apart from

[34] *Ibid.*, p. 138.
[35] "Three Dimensions of Hermeneutics," in *The Aims of Interpretation*, p. 79.
[36] *Validity in Interpretation*, p. 142.

a particular context, an interpretive statement is not readily distinguishable from a critical remark.[37]

To appreciate the significance of Hirsch's (modified) distinction, consider the following argument which is often given to show that what a work means cannot be identified with what the author intended.

The meaning of a literary work, it is claimed, cannot be determined by the author's intention or by the (historical, social, and cultural) context in which the work was produced because a considerable number of older literary works continue to be of interest and value to modern readers and play an important part in contemporary life.[38] The crucial premise in this argument is this: If (1) a literary work continues (or could continue) to be of interest and value to a wide variety of readers of later generations and periods, then (2) its meaning cannot be determined by the author's intention or by the (historical, social, and cultural) context in which it was written. For if (2) follows from (1), then, since there are a large number of literary works which continue to be of interest and value to a wide variety of readers of later periods, it follows that the meaning of those works cannot be determined by the author's intention or by the context in which they were produced.

Now Hirsch's distinction between meaning and significance can help us see that (2) does not in fact follow from (1). Let us suppose, for example, that Swift's "A Modest Proposal" is merely about a certain unique historical situation. The question then is: How could the work, under this assumption, be of (more than merely historical) interest and value to a modern reader? The answer is this: A reader may perceive similarities between the situation which Swift satirized (or between the situation as satirized by Swift) and historical events of direct concern to him. He may be able to see his own historical situation (or aspects thereof) in much the same light as Swift saw his. And in that case Swift

[37] *Ibid.*, pp. 140f.
[38] See Ellis, *The Theory of Literary Criticism*, pp. 138f.

The Theory of E. D. Hirsch

certainly "has something to say"[39] to him. But this answer does not imply that Swift's work is, or that our reader must construe it as being, a satire on something other than an historical situation of Swift's time.

"A Modest Proposal" may indeed "make a great impact on a modern reader in the context of the war in Vietnam"[40]; but this need not be because it is a satire on (among other things) the war in Vietnam—as Ellis seems to suggest.[41] It may rather be because a modern reader can relate Swift's satire to his own life, because he can see the relevance or applicability of what Swift said about the contemporary Irish situation to historical events of his own time and possibly of immediate concern to him, such as the war in Vietnam. And that is a matter, not of construing what the work means, but of appreciating its significance, of relating the meaning of the work to a wider realm of human experience. Hence it does not follow that to find out what particular social and historical situation Swift was writing about is "to trivialize the meaning of the satire."[42] It is true, however, that to leave it at that would be to ignore the significance of the work, to ignore its relevance to social and political problems of later (and earlier) periods and therefore to ignore an important part of its value.

Thus the distinction between meaning and significance is extremely important because it shows that the assumption that the meaning of a literary work is determined by the intention of its author (or by the historical, social, and cultural context in which it was written) is perfectly consistent with the fact that many works survive their time and continue to be of wider interest to readers of subsequent ages. The distinction does not, of course, show that the assumption is correct. It may still very well be true that a literary work does not mean what its author intended and hence that

[39] *Ibid.*, p. 138.   [40] *Ibid.*, p. 139.
[41] *Ibid.*, pp. 138f.: "to identify actual historical personages in his texts is to ignore the fact that they are not uniquely the people known to Swift—they are still with us."
[42] *Ibid.*, p. 139.

The Theory of E. D. Hirsch

"A Modest Proposal," for instance, is about *inter alia* the Vietnam war. What the distinction shows is that this does not follow from the fact that a work survives it age.[43]

Hirsch's distinction can help clarify two other closely related claims which are sometimes adduced in support of the view that the meaning of a work cannot be limited to what its author intended.

It is often said that all great literary works are inexhaustible,[44] and that every age must understand the great literary works in its own way or in its own terms.[45] As for the first claim, this need not imply that meanings accrue to a work in the course of time[46] or that a work always means more than the author intended.[47] A work may be

---

[43] In the above discussion I have assumed that "A Modest Proposal" is merely about a particular, unique historical situation. This may not, of course, be true. I have made this assumption primarily to show that even an unduly restrictive view of what a literary work means is entirely consistent with the fact that a work may be of wider interest and of value to readers of later ages. Swift may very well have had other similar situations in mind and may have intended his satire to apply to them as well, or he may have intended to satirize a certain *kind* of situation. It is obviously not true that an author can only intend his work to be about the historical, social, cultural, or biographical context in which, or in response to which, he wrote it. He may certainly intend to convey something about a particular kind of problem, experience, situation, and so on. (It does not follow from this, however, that if an author *would* regard a particular situation, were it known to him, as an instance of the kind he had in mind, then he is writing about that situation as well.) Consequently, in order to show that, say, "A Modest Proposal" does not mean what Swift intended, it is not sufficient to show that it is a satire on the kind of situation in response to which Swift wrote it, for that is very likely what he intended; rather, it needs to be shown, in order for this sort of argument to be plausible, that the work is indeed about a situation which Swift could not have had in mind, such as the Vietnam war.

[44] See, e.g., Wellek and Warren, *Theory of Literature*, p. 152, and Gadamer, *Wahrheit und Methode*, p. 282 (*Truth and Method*, pp. 265-66).

[45] See Gadamer, *Wahrheit und Methode*, p. 280 (*Truth and Method*, p. 263).

[46] Cf. Wellek and Warren, *Theory of Literature*, pp. 42f.

[47] Cf. Gadamer, *Wahrheit und Methode*, p. 280 (*Truth and*

The Theory of E. D. Hirsch

inexhaustible in the sense that readers of different ages or even of the same age can always find something in the work which illuminates yet another aspect of the problems and experiences of their own time or of their own lives. Thus readers may be able to continue to relate the work or different parts of it, as construed in a certain way, to their own changing personal experiences as well as to changing historical, social, and cultural conditions of their age. Hence the fact that a particular literary work is inexhaustible does not imply that its meaning is not what the author intended. It is perfectly plausible to suppose that what is inexhaustible about a particular work is not its meaning, but rather its significance. The second claim, that every age must understand the great literary works in its own terms, is easily analyzable along the same lines,[48] and in particular as involving an 'ambiguity' of the term 'understand'.

None of the three claims I have considered implies, then, that the meaning of a literary work is not (or not just) what its author intended. That a literary work may survive its time, that it may be inexhaustible and understood differently in different ages, can be explained without relinquishing the assumption that the meaning of a literary work is determined by the author's intention. And it is the distinction between the meaning and significance of a work which, at least in principle, makes another explanation possible.

6. Hirsch's Claim That the Meaning of a Literary Work Cannot Change

Hirsch asserts that "a verbal meaning . . . is changeless."[49] This is not an uncontroversial claim.[50] Hirsch gives the fol-

---

Method, p. 264): "Nicht nur gelegentlich, sondern immer übertrifft der Sinn eines Textes seinen Autor." ("The meaning of a text transcends its author not just occasionally, but always.")

[48] See Hirsch's discussion, *Validity in Interpretation*, pp. 136-38.
[49] *Ibid.*, p. 46.
[50] See, e.g., Monroe C. Beardsley, *The Possibility of Criticism*, pp. 19f.; George Dickie, "Meaning and Intention," pp. 182-89; Oscar

lowing argument for it: If we allow that the meaning of a work may change, then there is no way of determining "the real meaning"[51] of the work. Again, Hirsch's argument seems to be purely pragmatic; he appears to assume that what is at issue is not a conceptual but merely a pragmatic question:

> Once it is admitted that a meaning can change its characteristics, then there is no way of finding the true Cinderella among all the contenders. . . . To the interpreter this lack of a stable normative principle is equivalent to the indeterminacy of meaning. As far as his interests go, the meaning could have been defined as indeterminate from the start and his predicament would have been precisely the same.[52]

It seems best, therefore, to construe Hirsch's claim that the meaning of a work cannot change in the same way as his definition of verbal meaning, namely, as a recommendation.

Yet shortly after the passage just quoted, Hirsch seems to be assuming that what he has established is that the meaning of a work *is* changeless. In other words, he seems to treat his statement no longer as a proposal as to how we ought (for pragmatic reasons) to conceive of the meaning of literary works, but rather as an analytic claim about our notion of "verbal meaning":

> But if a determinate word sequence does not in itself necessarily represent one, particular, self-identical, unchanging complex of meaning, then the determinacy of its verbal meaning must *be accounted for* by some other discriminating force. . . .[53]

Now it clearly does not make sense to "account for" the

Cargill, "Viable Meaning in Literary Art," pp. 111-13; and Roman Ingarden, *Das literarische Kunstwerk*, pp. 353-80, esp. pp. 377-80 (Engl. trans. by George G. Grabowicz, *The Literary Work of Art*, pp. 331-55, esp. pp. 352-55.)

[51] Hirsch, *Validity in Interpretation*, p. 46; see also pp. 249ff.
[52] *Ibid.*, p. 46.   [53] *Ibid.*, p. 47 (italics added).

The Theory of E. D. Hirsch

determinacy of verbal meaning unless we assume that it *is* determinate. Furthermore, Hirsch seems to be assuming that what a work means *is* what the author intended (or "willed"); for he continues:

> That discriminating force must involve an act of will, since unless one particular complex of meaning is *willed* (no matter how "rich" and "various" it might be), there would be no distinction between what an author does mean by a word sequence and what he could mean by it.[54]

Let us assume, then, that Hirsch's statement that the meaning of literary works cannot change is not a recommendation, but a claim about our concept of the meaning of a work. The question now arises: What reason do we have for supposing that there can be only one 'real' meaning of a work? Why should there be anything like 'the real (unchanging) meaning' of a work? As I have suggested already, it is not obvious that the meaning of a work cannot change. A particular word or expression, for example, may have one meaning in the seventeenth century and quite another in the twentieth. How do we determine what that word or expression 'really' means? Plainly there is no such thing. What reason do we have for supposing that the same is not true of literary works as well?[55]

Hirsch contends that if the meaning of a work can change, is "indeterminate," then its meaning is not "sharable."[56] But this is a *non sequitur*. For the meaning of a particular word in a given language may change and yet that meaning is certainly sharable. Hence from the assumption that the

---
[54] *Ibid.*
[55] See Beardsley, *The Possibility of Criticism*, p. 19. Beardsley argues that since the expression "'plastic arm' has acquired a new meaning in the twentieth century, . . . the line [of Mark Akenside's *The Pleasures of Imagination* (II, 313)] in which it occurs has also acquired a new meaning."
[56] Hirsch, *Validity in Interpretation*, pp. 44-46.

The Theory of E. D. Hirsch

meaning of a literary work may change, it does not follow that its meaning is not sharable. It is *prima facie* perfectly plausible to hold that the meaning of a literary work may change and hence is "determinate" only in the sense in which the meaning of a particular word in a language is determinate.

Let us suppose, for example, that a literary text of the seventeenth century was construed by its contemporary readers as meaning m_1, but now, in the twentieth century, a controversy arises as to whether the text means m_1 or m_2. Hirsch argues that if the meaning of a work can change, then we have no principle for determining what the text 'really' means. Readers "could not measure their interpretations against what the text had meant in the past, since it no longer means what it meant before. Apparently there is no way of determining what a text means at a given moment."[57] But suppose that what a text means "at a given moment" is determined by the rules of the language or conventional usage at that particular time. In that case readers could evaluate the adequacy of an interpretation on the basis of contemporary usage. It may very well be true that the latter does not constitute as restrictive a criterion as the author's intention; but Hirsch has given no reason to assume that our notion of the meaning of a literary work warrants a more restrictive criterion.[58]

Wellek and Warren have suggested that "the retention of the modern association in verses like Marvell's 'My vegetable love would grow/ Vaster than empires and more slow' [could] be defended as an enrichment of its meanings."[59] In commenting on their discussion, Hirsch argues that although

---

[57] *Ibid.*, p. 249; see also p. 46.

[58] Furthermore, it is arguable that the criterion of contemporary linguistic usage can be modified so as to provide as objective a standard as the author's intention. See Beardsley, *Aesthetics*, pp. 144-47, and *The Possibility of Criticism*, pp. 38-61.

[59] *Theory of Literature*, p. 177.

The Theory of E. D. Hirsch

the associated meaning *is* here desirable (since it supports the mood of the poem, . . . Wellek could not even make his point unless we could distinguish between what "vegetable" probably means as used in the text and what it commonly means to us. Simply to discuss the issue is to admit that Marvell's poem probably does not imply the modern connotation, for if we could not separate the sense of "vegetative" from the notion of an "erotic cabbage," we could not talk about the difficulty of making the separation.[60]

But from the fact that we can distinguish between what the word "vegetable" meant in the seventeenth century, or what Marvell probably meant by it, and what it means or suggests today, it does not follow that this is not now part of the meaning of the poem. Even though we can distinguish between what "vegetable" meant in the seventeenth century and what it means or suggests today, it would be incorrect to say that the word means no more and no less today than what it meant in the seventeenth century. To argue, in other words, that since we can distinguish between what "vegetable" meant in the seventeenth century, or what Marvell probably meant by the word, and what it means or suggests today, the "poem probably does not imply the modern connotation" is to beg the question whether the meaning of a text may change as a result of changes in the language and culture, or whether its meaning is indeed determined by the author's intention.

If we assume that the meaning of a speaker's utterance or speech act, unlike the meaning of a word in a language, cannot change,[61] then the question is this: Is our notion of the meaning of a literary work like our notion of the meaning of a word in a language, or is it like our notion of the meaning of a person's speech act?[62]

[60] Hirsch, "Objective Interpretation," in *Validity in Interpretation*, p. 215.
[61] See L. Jonathan Cohen, *The Diversity of Meaning*, pp. 3-5.
[62] Cf., e.g., Kenneth Burke's conception of a literary work as a

The Theory of E. D. Hirsch

As we have seen, Hirsch sometimes vacillates between two incompatible views: (i) that our concept of the meaning of a work is such that what a particular work means is determinate; and (ii) that while our concept of the meaning of a work is such that what a given work means depends (within the limits imposed by the rules of the language) on the reader's purpose, we *ought*, for pragmatic or epistemological reasons, to define the meaning of a work in such a way that it will be determinate and unable to change. His basic position, however, as I have tried to show in section 1, is (ii).[63] Consequently, it is not surprising that he does not present a sustained argument for (i).

7. Conclusion

I have tried to show:

(1) Hirsch's definition of verbal meaning in terms of the speaker's or author's intention is not an analytic claim about

---

"symbolic act," *The Philosophy of Literary Form*, pp. 8ff. *et passim*, and "Symbolic Action in a Poem by Keats," p. 259.

[63] But see also his earlier article, "Objective Interpretation" (1960), reprinted in *Validity in Interpretation*, pp. 209-44, in which the first view (i) predominates. In *The Aims of Interpretation* (1976) this thesis is explicitly rejected (p. 79) and replaced by a recommendation. But, as I mentioned earlier, instead of relying on pragmatic or epistemological considerations in support of his recommendation—as he does in *Validity in Interpretation* (pp. 26-27)—Hirsch now defends it on ethical grounds (*Aims*, pp. 7f., 90ff.).

Even in *The Aims of Interpretation*, however, Hirsch claims that the "important feature of meaning as distinct from significance is that meaning is the determinate representation of a text for an interpreter" (p. 79). The qualification "for an interpreter" is crucial here, since Hirsch no longer wants the meaning of a text to be "restricted . . . to those constructions where the interpreter is governed by his conception of the author's will" (*ibid.*). Hence a text may have different meanings for different interpreters, although for any given interpreter the meaning of a text will be "determinate." To take this position is, as Hirsch is clearly aware, to abandon the view that the meaning of a literary work is determinate in the sense of his earlier notion of "determinacy" (*Validity in Interpretation*, pp. 45-47).

The Theory of E. D. Hirsch

our concept of the meaning of an utterance or of a literary work, but rather a recommendation as to how we ought to conceive of it. For, as we have seen, one of Hirsch's basic assumptions is that the only constraint which our notion of the meaning of a literary work imposes on a 'correct' interpretation is that it must be linguistically possible. But if Hirsch's definition is a recommendation, then it does not assert anything. It follows that the question whether it is true or false does not arise.

(2) Hirsch's claim that only the author's intention provides "a genuinely discriminating norm" is false. But even if it were true, it would not by itself constitute an adequate reason for accepting Hirsch's recommendation. For if Hirsch's assumption about our concept of the meaning of a literary work is correct, then to adopt Hirsch's criterion would be to seriously distort the meaning of literary works for the sake of objectivity.

(3) Hirsch's distinction between meaning and significance does not help resolve or explain interpretive disagreements. For it presupposes that the meaning of a work *is* what the author intended. And that is usually one of the questions at issue in the kinds of cases which the distinction is supposed to explain. Furthermore, that assumption is inconsistent with Hirsch's basic premise about our concept of the meaning of a work. But even if what a work means *is* what the author intended, Hirsch's distinction does not correctly characterize typical interpretive disputes; for a critic who interprets a work as meaning something other than what the author intended is not as a rule relating the meaning which the author intended to something else; nor does his interpretation appear to presuppose any claim about what the author meant.

Hirsch's distinction does, however, shed considerable light on certain common claims often adduced in support of the thesis that the meaning of a literary work cannot be what the author intended to convey by it. It offers us a possible explanation of the survival of literary works, their inexhaustibility, and the fact that some works are reinterpreted in every age which is consistent with the assumption that the meaning of a work is logically tied to the author's intention.

(4) Hirsch's claim that the meaning of a literary work is "determinate," just like his definition of verbal meaning, seems to be offered as a recommendation, not as an analytic claim. Yet, contrary to his basic premise, Hirsch sometimes tacitly assumes that our concept of the meaning of a literary work is such that what a given work means *is* determinate. But since that view is incompatible with his basic position, he does not offer any substantial arguments for it.

III

Is Evidence of the Author's Intention Irrelevant?

1. Introduction

WHEN AN AUTHOR writes, say, a poem or a novel, he typically intends to convey or express something by it; he means something by the words he writes. We may ask, therefore, what the relation is between the meaning of a word sequence in a literary work and what the author meant by the word sequence in question; and similarly we may ask what the relation is between the meaning of a work as a whole and what the author intended to convey (what he meant) by it.

One possible answer is this: Although the meaning of a literary work is frequently, or at least sometimes, what the author meant, there is no logical connection between the meaning of a work and what the author meant. In other words, from the fact that a work means, say, m, it does not necessarily (logically) follow that the author intended to convey m; and, conversely, from the fact that the author intended to convey m, it does not necessarily follow that the work means m. I shall call this 'the anti-intentionalist thesis'. Although not always stated in quite this way, it is widely held both by professional critics and by philosophers who have dealt with this issue.[1] Perhaps the most forceful de-

[1] See, e.g., Wellek and Warren, *Theory of Literature*, pp. 42, 148f., 155f.; Lionel Trilling, *The Liberal Imagination*, pp. 48-49; Eliot, "The Frontiers of Criticism," pp. 113f.; Northrop Frye, *Anatomy of Criticism*, pp. 86ff.; Peter Jones, *Philosophy and the Novel*, pp. 197-201; Barbara Herrnstein Smith, *On the Margins of Discourse*, pp.

fense of this thesis is William K. Wimsatt and Monroe C. Beardsley's article "The Intentional Fallacy."[2] In subsequent publications both Wimsatt and Beardsley have clarified and elaborated their position.[3]

Many of those who have criticized Wimsatt and Beardsley's view that an author's intention is irrelevant to what his work means have insisted on the usefulness of knowledge of the author's intention.[4] They have claimed that what an author meant is likely to be a valuable clue to what the work means. Although this is undoubtedly true, it is entirely consistent with the anti-intentionalist thesis. For the latter does not deny that information about the author's intention may be useful in understanding a work or in discovering nuances of meaning which one might otherwise have overlooked. It

---

133-54; Gadamer, *Wahrheit und Methode*, pp. 372-73 (*Truth and Method*, pp. 356-57); John Kemp, "The Work of Art and the Artist's Intentions," pp. 146-54; Peter Szondi, "Über philologische Erkenntnis," *Hölderlin-Studien*, pp. 9-34; George Dickie, *Aesthetics*, pp. 110-21; Stevenson, "Interpretation and Evaluation in Aesthetics," in Kennick (ed.), *Art and Philosophy*, pp. 473ff.; Virgil Aldrich, *Philosophy of Art*, pp. 92f.; Redpath, "The Meaning of a Poem," in Weitz (ed.), *Problems in Aesthetics*, pp. 363f.; Ellis, *The Theory of Literary Criticism*, pp. 106-54; Erwin Leibfried, *Kritische Wissenschaft vom Text*, pp. 317-18; James Thorpe, "The Aesthetics of Textual Criticism," p. 467; Savile, "The Place of Intention in the Concept of Art," in Osborne (ed.), *Aesthetics*, pp. 158-76; Jonathan Culler, *Structuralist Poetics*, pp. 132-33; Paul Ricoeur, "The Model of the Text," pp. 95f., 100f., 105, 113-14, and "Writing as a Problem for Literary Criticism and Philosophical Hermeneutics," pp. 6-7; Palmer, *Hermeneutics*, pp. 246-47.

[2] *The Sewanee Review*, Vol. LIV (1946); reprinted in Wimsatt and Beardsley, *The Verbal Icon*, Ch. I, pp. 3-18.

[3] William K. Wimsatt, "Genesis"; Beardsley, *Aesthetics*, pp. 17-29, and *The Possibility of Criticism*, pp. 16-37.

[4] See Henry David Aiken, "The Aesthetic Relevance of Artists' Intentions," p. 750; M. M. Eaton, "Liars, Ranters, and Dramatic Speakers," p. 61; I. C. Hungerland, "The Interpretation of Poetry," in Beardsley and Schueller (eds.), *Aesthetic Inquiry*, pp. 126f.; John Hospers, "Implied Truths in Literature," in Kennick (ed.), *Art and Philosophy*, p. 317.

Is Evidence of the Author's Intention Irrelevant?

denies rather that the meaning of a literary work is necessarily—in virtue of our concept of the meaning of a work—what the author meant by it.[5]

In the following four chapters I shall argue that the anti-intentionalist thesis is incorrect. I shall attempt to show that there is a logical connection between the meaning of a literary work and the author's intention or, to put it differently, that to understand a literary work *is*, in virtue of our concept of the meaning of a literary work, to understand what the author intended to convey or express. My general strategy in trying to establish this counter thesis will be as follows. I shall consider texts (or utterances) which, under the rules of the language, have at least two possible interpretations. I will argue that the author's intention logically determines which of the linguistically possible interpretations of a text is correct. It follows that a claim about the meaning of the text is at least in part a claim about the author's use of the words in question.

I shall suggest first that a speaker's or author's statement as to what he meant ordinarily suffices to disambiguate an utterance. I will then examine two specific types of claim about the meaning of a work, namely, (a) that it contains an allusion and (b) that it is ironic. I shall argue that both claims logically depend on what we take the author to have meant.

Since any analysis of our concept of the meaning of a work must be able to account for the kinds of facts and the criteria to which critics commonly appeal in support of an interpretation, the next step in my argument will be to take a close look at those facts and criteria. I shall argue that the appeal to the text, to coherence or complexity, or to the nonlinguistic context *is* an appeal to the author's intention. That is, a feature of the text or of the nonlinguistic context will constitute evidence for the meaning of a work if and

---

[5] As Wimsatt has remarked in reply to Aiken: "If he [the author] says there is red in his poem, we will look carefully in the expectation of *finding* it" ("Genesis," p. 211).

only if it is evidence of what the author intended to convey. Similarly, that a work is more coherent, or more complex, on one interpretation than on another will not make the former more likely to be correct than the latter unless this fact makes it more likely that the author intended to convey the meaning corresponding to the former rather than the latter. I shall also argue that statements as to what the narrator or a character in a work means by an utterance are properly analyzed as statements about what the author intends the speaker to mean.

Part of my argument will be based on what it would and what it would not make sense to say about the meaning of a text produced by chance. Thus I shall try to show that our concept of the meaning of a literary work created by a person differs from our concept of the meaning of a text produced by chance, such as by a monkey or a computer. That is, our concept of the meaning of a literary work appears to involve the notion of an author's intentional activity, of his actual use of the words in question to express or convey something.

So far I shall have confined my discussion to claims about the meaning of a text which *in abstracto* has at least two possible interpretations. The question then arises whether an author's intention is irrelevant to the meaning of a text which has only one linguistically possible interpretation. Stated another way, the question is whether a claim about the meaning of a text which has only one linguistically possible interpretation is *different in kind* from a corresponding claim about the meaning of a text which has more than one linguistically possible interpretation. I shall try to show that there is no such difference by arguing that even an appeal to the rules of the language is an implicit appeal to the author's likely use of the words in question.

Finally, I shall attempt to account for several other aspects of critical discourse which might appear to pose serious problems for an analysis of the meaning of a work in terms of the author's intention: (1) that critics sometimes cite aesthetic considerations in support of an interpretation; (2) that an author is unlikely to have been thinking about the various meanings and implications of the details of his work; and (3) that we occasionally reject an author's statement about his intention in writing a particular work.

2. THE ANTI-INTENTIONALIST THESIS

Wimsatt and Beardsley have maintained that the author's intention does not determine what a literary work means. One may ask, therefore, what does on their view determine its meaning. In addressing this question, they distinguish between "internal" and "external" evidence of what a work means. And they continue:

> [T]he paradox is only verbal and superficial that what is (1) internal is also public: it is discovered through the semantics and syntax of a poem, through our habitual knowledge of the language, through grammars, dictionaries, and all the literature which is the source of dictionaries, in general through all that makes a language and culture; while what is (2) external is private or idiosyncratic; not a part of the work as a linguistic fact: it consists of revelations (in journals, for example, or letters or reported conversations) about how or why the poet wrote the poem—to what lady, while sitting on what lawn, or at the death of what friend or brother. There is (3) an intermediate kind of evidence about the character of the author or about private or semi-private meanings attached to words or topics by an author or by a coterie of which he is a member. The meaning of words is the history of words, and the biography of an author, his use of a word, and the associations which the word had for *him*, are part of the word's history and meaning.[6]

[6] Wimsatt and Beardsley, *The Verbal Icon*, p. 10.

Is Evidence of the Author's Intention Irrelevant?

If Wimsatt and Beardsley are prepared to admit (1) and (3) as evidence for the meaning of a literary work, then it is not clear what they wish to exclude. For if "the biography of an author, his use of a word, and the associations which the word had for *him*" can legitimately be adduced in support of an interpretation, then it would seem to be difficult to exclude the kind of evidence referred to under (2). In a later essay Wimsatt has characterized their thesis as asserting that while poems can "contribute their own kind of meaning, and a very rich and subtle kind, to the writing of biography," "biographical evidence does not establish meaning *in* poems."[7] Beardsley has similar remarks in his *Aesthetics*.[8]

What they want to say, as becomes clear from their examples,[9] is this: The meaning of the words and sentences of a literary work, and hence the meaning of the work as a whole, is determined by the rules of the language in which the work is written or, in Beardsley's words, by the "public conventions of usage."[10] It is the latter, not the author's intention or statements by the author about his intention, which determine what a literary work means.

Hence even if the rules of the language allow two or more interpretations of a particular work, the author's intention is irrelevant, since in such a case the work would simply have two or more equally correct interpretations.[11] An author's intention does not even in part (logically) determine what a work means. Consequently, no amount of evidence

[7] Wimsatt, "Genesis," p. 199.

[8] Pp. 24-26. See also Beardsley, *The Possibility of Criticism*, pp. 16-37.

[9] Wimsatt and Beardsley, *The Verbal Icon*, pp. 12-14, 17-18.

[10] *Aesthetics*, p. 25.

[11] See Beardsley, *Aesthetics*, p. 145, and *The Possibility of Criticism*, p. 29. It must be added here that Beardsley also admits coherence and complexity (his "Congruence" and "Plenitude") as supplementary criteria of what a work means; hence even if the rules of the language allow several different readings of a text, it would be possible, on his view, that only one of them is correct. See *Aesthetics*, pp. 144-47.

Is Evidence of the Author's Intention Irrelevant?

about what the author meant could in principle ever establish that a work does or does not have a particular meaning. As far as its status as evidence for the meaning of a word in, say, a poem is concerned, an author's statement as to what he meant by the word is logically on a par with any critic's statement about the meaning of the word in question.[12] Similarly, as Wimsatt's discussion of Blake's "London" makes plain, an author's beliefs are also irrelevant to the meaning of a literary work.[13] Furthermore, an author's particular use of words and the associations they have for him would seem, according to Wimsatt and Beardsley's thesis, to be no more relevant to the meaning of his work than the usage and associations of any other author whose work belongs to "all the literature which is the source of dictionaries," to "all that makes a language and culture."

It is important to notice that if we allow an author's particular usage and associations a privileged status in regard to the meaning of a literary work, then the whole anti-intentionalist thesis is in danger of breaking down, since an author's beliefs, feelings, and intentions are obviously closely connected with his use of words and especially with the associations and connotations that certain words have for him. One of Wimsatt's comments on the last stanza of Blake's "London" leaves no doubt about his position on this score. Against the interpretation by E. D. Hirsch, who construes the stanza, and in particular the "Marriage hearse," in accord with Blake's views, Wimsatt argues *inter alia* as follows:

> The tough fact was that the word "marriage" in the history of English usage and culture was not the name of an evil. . . . It was the name of a sacred institution and a first principle of stability for nearly every important value in a whole religiously and ethically oriented civilization and culture.[14]

[12] See Wimsatt, "Genesis," p. 211.
[13] *Ibid.*, p. 218. [14] *Ibid.*

Hence the associations which the word "marriage" had for Blake or what he may have thought about marriage are, according to Wimsatt, irrelevant to the meaning of the poem.

3. Can a Speaker's Statement about His Intention Disambiguate His Utterance?

In order to dispose of the notion that a poem means what its author intended to convey, Beardsley draws a distinction between what a speaker who utters a particular sentence means (what he intends to express or convey) and what the sentence means.[15] Beardsley points out that what the speaker means may not always coincide with what the sentence means. Someone might say, for example, 'Fred is bald' and tell us he meant that eating is fun. Clearly, what he meant (or said he meant) is not what the sentence means. Elaborating on his distinction, Beardsley continues:

> For what the sentence means depends not on the whim of the individual, and his mental vagaries, but upon public conventions of usage that are tied up with habit patterns in the whole speaking community. It is perhaps easy to see this in the case of an ambiguous sentence. A man says, "I like my secretary better than my wife"; we raise our eyebrows, and inquire: "Do you mean that you like her better than you like your wife?" And he replies, "No, you misunderstand me; I mean I like her better than my wife does." Now, in one sense he has cleared up the misunderstanding, he has told us what he meant. Since what he meant is still not what the first sentence succeeded in meaning, he hasn't made the original sentence any less ambiguous than it was; he has merely substituted for it a better, because unambiguous, one.[16]

[15] *Aesthetics*, p. 25.   [16] *Ibid.*

Is Evidence of the Author's Intention Irrelevant?

Beardsley claims that the speaker "hasn't made the original sentence any less ambiguous than it was" because "what he meant is still not what the first sentence succeeded in meaning." But how could the speaker now, (presumably) after having given his explanation, influence what the sentence *succeeded* in meaning? Clearly, the speaker cannot possibly influence what the sentence succeeded in meaning, since that lies in the past; the most he could achieve by giving his explanation is that the sentence now, after the explanation, succeeds in expressing what the speaker intended. Hence I do not see the force of Beardsley's objection that "what he meant is still not what the first sentence succeeded in meaning."

Perhaps Beardsley means that even after the explanation the first sentence does not succeed in meaning what the speaker meant. If he does, I think he is mistaken; for after the explanation the (first) sentence would surely succeed in conveying to a hearer (unless he wants to misunderstand) what the speaker means. If a speaker *could not*, by offering an explanation, affect the way his utterance is taken, then it would be odd that he should even attempt to do so. And the speaker need not substitute another sentence for the ambiguous one. He might, for example, in reply to the question 'Do you mean that you like her better than you like your wife?' say: 'Didn't I tell you how much more I like my wife in spite of her unwarranted jealousy?'. Can there be any doubt that this kind of information about the speaker, concerning his beliefs, feelings, and so on, affects the way we would take the sentence?[17]

Since the sentence in Beardsley's example is, by hypothesis, ambiguous, the "public conventions of usage" provide at least two readings for it. Hence, on Beardsley's view, we should have to say that the speaker's utterance means, and consequently that the speaker is saying, *both* that he likes his secretary better than he likes his wife *and* that he likes

[17] See on this point Paul Ziff, "What is Said," pp. 713, 715.

his secretary better than his wife does.[18] But it would be odd to take the speaker to be saying both of these things at once. And surely the reason is that it would be odd to suppose that *he means* both. (There are, of course, cases in which it would be natural to take a speaker to be saying several things at once; but to do so would be natural only because in those cases it would be natural to suppose that the speaker meant all of them.)

It seems that it is in order to avoid this consequence, having to allow that the speaker is saying *both* that he likes his secretary better than he likes his wife *and* that he likes his secretary better than his wife does, that Beardsley tacitly identifies the meaning of the speaker's utterance with what it "succeeded in meaning." But this won't do; for if the meaning of an utterance were what it succeeded in meaning, then it would be impossible to misunderstand an utterance as long as it succeeds in conveying anything.[19]

4. Sentence-Meaning and Utterance-Meaning

What lends some plausibility to Beardsley's claim that the speaker's intention is irrelevant is that even after the speaker's explanation we might be unsure about what the utterance means. But is this so because we are unsure about what the *sentence* means? Any competent speaker of English knows that the sentence is ambiguous and what its linguistically possible readings are.[20] Hence if after the explanation we are still unsure what the speaker's utterance means, it cannot be because we are unsure about what the *sentence* means. I suggest that it is because we are unsure about what the speaker means.

To see that this is so, consider a different example. Sup-

---

[18] I am indebted for this point to Robert Howell.

[19] See Hospers, "Implied Truths in Literature," in Kennick (ed.), *Art and Philosophy*, p. 314.

[20] He may not, however, always be readily able to recognize its ambiguity; see Chomsky, *Aspects of the Theory of Syntax*, p. 21.

pose that in an essay on marriage the sentence (1) 'Everyone likes his wife' occurs and the context does not disambiguate it. The author might in the second edition of his essays add a note to the effect that he meant 'Everyone likes his own wife'. Now clearly the note suffices to disambiguate the sentence; we will interpret the sentence in just the way indicated. No one would think of asking, 'Does the sentence really mean that?' Or take the sentences (2) 'They are visiting professors' and (3) 'He killed the man with the gun'. Sentence (2) would no doubt succeed in meaning what the speaker or author intended if he added, 'I meant they are visiting various professors'. Similarly, (3) would succeed in conveying what the speaker intended if he explained, 'I meant that he killed the man who had the gun'. We would think it very odd if someone were to ask, 'Does the sentence really mean that?'; or if someone were to say, 'That may be what the speaker meant, but that is not what the sentence means'. In the latter case, one would be inclined to think that the skeptic was making a distinction between the sentence in isolation—taken in abstraction from its use on a particular occasion—and the particular *use* (or utterance) of the sentence by someone in order to convey a certain meaning.

Thus although the *sentence* a speaker uses may be ambiguous, it does not follow that his *utterance* of that sentence is ambiguous. Furthermore, as the examples show, a speaker's statement about his intention seems ordinarily to be sufficient to disambiguate his utterance (of an ambiguous sentence). And the speaker's statement seems to be able to disambiguate his utterance because, ordinarily, it is sufficient evidence of his intention. Consequently, if we do not interpret the utterance mentioned by Beardsley in the way the speaker's explanation indicates, it would appear to be because we do not believe that that is what the speaker means.

The following considerations confirm this point. The qualms one might have about taking the sentence in the way indicated by the speaker are, I think, due to the relatively low probability (except in a special context) that someone would use that sentence to convey what the speaker says he means. (One would say, 'I like my secretary better than my wife does.') And this is clearly evidence of what the speaker is likely to mean (but it is not evidence that the utterance does not mean what the speaker means). In other words, after the speaker's statement about his intention, we might wonder why he uttered a sentence which so obviously suggests a different interpretation. We might feel that he really means something else which he does not want to admit (or of which he is not aware). Moreover, if a man prefers his secretary to his wife, he would probably not want to admit this in public. Hence his statement about what he means might not entirely convince us.

If even after the speaker's explanation we thought that the utterance means 'I like my secretary better than I like my wife', we would not simply say "The utterance means 'I like my secretary better than I like my wife'". Rather, we would say something like "The utterance *really* means 'I like my secretary better than I like my wife'". And this brings out the difference in the way we view the utterance after the speaker's statement about what he meant. In the absence of the speaker's statement about what he meant, it would be odd for someone who took the utterance to mean 'I like my secretary better than I like my wife' to say "The utterance *really* means 'I like my secretary better than I like my wife'" rather than simply "The utterance means 'I like my secretary better than I like my wife'". After the speaker's statement we seem to feel constrained to take the utterance in the way he indicates, unless we have a better explanation of his linguistic behavior—that is, unless it would be more plausible to suppose that he (really) means something else.[21]

[21] Wimsatt has given an example—to show that an author is not necessarily the best critic or interpreter of his work—which bears on this point. When asked whether he meant "tardiness of locomotion"

Is Evidence of the Author's Intention Irrelevant?

Beardsley's claim that a speaker's intention is irrelevant to what his utterance means, then, seems to be false. For, as I have tried to show, (a) a speaker's statement about what he meant does ordinarily affect the way we construe his utterance of an ambiguous sentence; and (b) in cases in which we reject the speaker's statement about his intention, it appears that we do so because we are not convinced that that is what he meant.

In claiming that a speaker's intention does not, even in part, (logically) determine the meaning of an utterance, Beardsley is in effect assimilating *utterances* to *sentences*—speech acts to word sequences considered in abstraction from their use on a particular occasion. For it is only if we take the words a man utters in abstraction from their use on a particular occasion that only the "public conventions of usage" are relevant to determining their meaning. But to know what a sentence means is not the same as to understand an utterance of that sentence.[22] To know what a sentence means is, very roughly, to know how it can be used. Questions about the meaning of a particular utterance of a sentence, however, are not about how the sentence *can* be

---

by the word "slow" in the first line ("Remote, unfriended, melancholy, slow") of "The Traveller," Goldsmith answered in the affirmative; whereupon Samuel Johnson cut in and said, "No, Sir; you do not mean tardiness of locomotion; you mean, that sluggishness of mind which comes upon a man in solitude." (Boswell's *Life of Johnson*, 9 April 1778, pp. 917f.) Wimsatt concludes that the grounds of our judgment "must lie in the observable force and relevance of the word 'slow' in the *context* of the first line of Goldsmith's pensive travelogue" ("Genesis," p. 214). It is worth noting, however, that Johnson did not simply deny that in the context of the line the word means what Goldsmith meant by it. Rather, he is denying that *Goldsmith* meant "tardiness of locomotion," that Goldsmith in fact meant what he *said* he meant by the word. The point is this: When we interpret a work contrary to the author's statement about what he meant, we are not necessarily taking the work to have a meaning other than what (we believe) the author meant.

[22] See Ludwig Wittgenstein, *Philosophical Investigations*, § 525.

used but about how it *is* used. If this is so, then we can see why the speaker's intention should be relevant; for the speaker's use of certain words appears to depend, at least where there is more than one possible interpretation, on his intention.

In the following sections and the next three chapters I shall develop the view that the meaning of an utterance and, in particular, the meaning of a literary work depends on the speaker's or author's intention. I shall try to show that a fairly wide range of facts are difficult, if not impossible, to account for unless we assume that what a literary work means is determined by what the author meant.

5. ALLUSION

The relevance of an author's intention to what his text means is perhaps most obvious in the case of allusion. In discussing the possibility that the line "I have heard the mermaids singing, each to each," in T. S. Eliot's "Love Song of J. Alfred Prufrock" is an allusion to a line in a poem by Donne, Wimsatt and Beardsley say:

> Is Eliot's line an allusion to Donne's? Is Prufrock thinking about Donne? Is Eliot thinking about Donne? . . . [T]he way of poetic analysis and exegesis . . . inquires whether it makes any sense if Eliot-Prufrock *is* thinking about Donne. In an earlier part of the poem, when Prufrock asks, "Would it have been worth while, . . . To have squeezed the universe into a ball," his words take half their sadness and irony from certain energetic and passionate lines of Marvell "To His Coy Mistress."[23]

But suppose that Eliot did not know, had not read, nor was in any other way acquainted with Marvell or the poem "To His Coy Mistress." The lines from "Prufrock" might still for some readers take "half their sadness and irony" from that

---

[23] Wimsatt and Beardsley, *The Verbal Icon*, p. 18.

poem; but could we still maintain that the lines from "Prufrock" are an allusion to Marvell? Could we still draw inferences from the latter to the former? Does it make no difference whether Eliot knew Marvell and the poem in question? Suppose we find a striking similarity between some lines of Eliot's "Prufrock" and a poem written in 1980. Is Eliot-Prufrock alluding to this poem also? And can this question be settled by inquiring merely "whether it makes any sense" if Eliot-Prufrock is thinking about this poem?

The difficulty with this sort of question is that when we find a striking similarity between two lines from different authors, which enhances the value of the poem written later, we are inclined to think that the resemblance is not accidental but intended. I am supposing, however, that Eliot was in no way whatever familiar with the lines to which we might at first think he was alluding. In this case, Eliot *could not* have alluded to those lines. Are we still to say that the only criterion of whether Eliot-Prufrock is or is not alluding to them is whether or not the similarity enhances the value of the lines from "Prufrock"? Clearly, the question whether or not Eliot-Prufrock is alluding to certain lines makes sense *only if* Eliot *could have* alluded to them. Thus if we interpret the lines in "Prufrock" as an allusion to, say, a poem written in 1980, we must assume that it does not make any difference who wrote them, and we must assume that we are free to posit any author (and speaker) necessary for our interpretation; for the particular author in question could not have made the allusion.[24]

[24] This conclusion is supported by the following remarks of Beardsley's ". . . Wimsatt and I once argued that the question whether *Eliot* is alluding to Marvell in certain lines is irrelevant to the question whether the *speaker* is alluding to Marvell. Cioffi says that if our interpretation of the lines as allusive is *not* based on the assumption that Eliot intended the allusion, then he doubts that our appreciation of the lines, insofar as it depends on recognizing the allusion, would survive the discovery that Eliot did not have that intention. In this way, 'biographical remarks . . . can serve the eliminative function of showing that certain interpretations of a work are based on mistaken

Is Evidence of the Author's Intention Irrelevant?

To invoke the distinction between speaker and author and to say that the only relevant question is whether the *speaker*, not whether the author, is alluding to certain lines from a poem is clearly of little help here. For (1) no speaker of a literary work can know what the author does not know, in the sense of being familiar with a certain event, a certain piece of information, a literary work or individual passages or lines from a work. Furthermore, (2) no word or word sequence can be an allusion unless some person uses it to allude to something. (3) It is not possible for a speaker in a work to allude to certain lines in another work unless he knows the lines in question. It follows that a given line or lines cannot be an allusion to certain other lines unless the author of the former knows the latter.

One might raise the following objection to (1): Suppose a character in a play is modelled exactly after a certain historical figure. The author reproduces verbatim one of the speeches of the latter but does not know that it contains an allusion. Has the speaker not made an allusion? The answer depends on whether we consider the speaker a character in the play or an historical person. Insofar as we regard the speaker as a character in the play—and within the confines of the drama we cannot regard him as an historical person— he has not made an allusion. It is instructive to compare in this respect playwright and historian. If a historian quotes the speech, it contains the allusion whether he is aware of it or not. The reason is that we do not consider the historian, in contrast to the dramatist, as (in some sense) the 'author' of the speech. The historian merely records, whereas the dramatist *uses* the speech for his own purpose in the play.

---

beliefs about the author's state of knowledge.' Notice the shift of ground. *If* the interpretation was based on the biographical assumption about Eliot, then of course the negative biographical discovery will sink it; but if the original interpretation was *not* based on any assumption about Eliot's intentions, then how can any biographical discovery take away its basis?" (Beardsley, review of C. Barrett, S.J. [ed.], *Collected Papers on Aesthetics*, p. 146.)

Is Evidence of the Author's Intention Irrelevant?

Hence it may have a very different significance in a play than in the actual historical circumstances in which it occurred.

I have argued that certain lines (l_1) in a literary work cannot be an allusion to certain other lines (l_2) unless the author of l_1 knows the latter.[25] Why should this be so?

---

[25] John M. Ellis has objected to an earlier version of this argument (Juhl, "Intention and Literary Interpretation," pp. 21-22) on the grounds that it is "self-destructive; to demonstrate a negative of the order 'Y never read nor heard of X' is virtually impossible. Since the most that could be shown is that there is no known evidence that Y read or heard of X, it must always be possible that the author could have alluded to the work in question; and so, Juhl's test creates no means of distinguishing one case from another." (Ellis, *The Theory of Literary Criticism*, p. 141.)

Ellis appears to have overlooked, however, that the claim to which he objects is not (and was not) intended to provide a practical test for determining whether or not a certain passage contains an allusion. The point of the argument was (and is) rather to show that the anti-intentionalist thesis implies that it does not matter who wrote a particular work, and hence that we can properly treat a work by, say, Milton, as though it had been written by T. S. Eliot, for example.

Furthermore, Ellis' claim that "it must always be possible that the author could have alluded to the work in question" is manifestly false. To see that it is, one need only consider works written (or events which have occurred) after the death of the particular author with whose work we are dealing.

Obviously, it is plausible to assume that an author is familiar with those works which are part of the general knowledge of the community in which he lives. But it may be considerably less plausible to assume that he is familiar with certain extremely obscure works. Consequently, at least in some cases, it may certainly be necessary to produce specific evidence that the author was familiar with the work or works in question.

On Ellis' view, it would appear that a literary work can contain an allusion only to those works or (historical, social, political, etc.) events which are "part of the shared experience of a given community" (p. 141). But this is clearly false. It may be true that "biblical allusions can be a meaningful part of a literary text only because the Bible is part of the shared experience of a given community, not because the author of that text in particular has read it" (*ibid.*) That is, it may be true that if the Bible were not "part of the shared experience

Is Evidence of the Author's Intention Irrelevant?

Clearly, it is so because otherwise the author could not intend to allude to l_2. The author's knowledge of lines l_2 is a necessary condition of his intention to allude to l_2. And his intention to allude (by means of l_1) to l_2 is—given that l_1 can be used to allude to l_2—a necessary and sufficient condition for l_1 to be an allusion to l_2.

6. IRONY

The relevance of an author's intention is also evident in the case of questions about irony. Consider, for example, an utterance of the sentence 'Palmer gave Nicklaus quite a beating'.[26] If both the speaker and the person to whom the utterance is addressed have just watched Nicklaus beat Palmer, the utterance is likely to be ironic. But suppose that, owing to a misunderstanding of the rules of the game, the speaker mistakenly thinks that Palmer defeated Nicklaus. The utterance would then very likely not be ironic. Clearly, we would misunderstand it if we took it to mean 'Nicklaus gave Palmer quite a beating'. The reason is that, under the present assumption, the speaker is not likely to have meant the utterance ironically.

To see that the force of the example is not restricted to ordinary discourse, suppose that the narrator in a novel describes the match in such a way that, according to the rules of golf, it would be Nicklaus who defeated Palmer. In that case, the narrator's remark 'Palmer gave Nicklaus quite a beating' would very likely be ironic. But now suppose that

---

of a given community," then what is intended as, and can linguistically be, an allusion to the Bible might not be *understood* as such. But it obviously does not follow that the words in question are not an allusion to a certain passage of the Bible. To suppose that it does would be to rule out by fiat the possibility of an allusion to an obscure work, event, fact, and so on.

[26] Borrowed from H. P. Grice, "Utterer's Meaning, Sentence-Meaning, and Word-Meaning," in Searle (ed.), *The Philosophy of Language*, p. 56.

Is Evidence of the Author's Intention Irrelevant?

the author is under a similar misapprehension as our above speaker and thus mistakenly thinks that it is Palmer who defeated Nicklaus. In this case, as in the analogous situation above, we would surely misconstrue the narrator's comment if we took it to be ironic.[27] What this example shows is that our interpretation of the narrator's remark rests on an implicit assumption about the author's intention (via an assumption about his knowledge of golf). Hence whether an utterance in ordinary discourse or in a literary work is ironic would appear to depend on the speaker's or the author's intention.[28]

One is inclined to suppose, nevertheless, that even if an author means a particular passage ironically, it may not be. Consider the following case:

> ... the author did not want to be taken seriously, and he used a number of literary signals to make this clear, and he believed that he had succeeded. But he was wrong. The signals he used were too subtle, the audience too unsophisticated, or the circumstances of publication and reading unhappy. Thus the work was intended to be ironical, but it was not understood in this way.[29]

This description does not entitle us to conclude, however, that the work is not ironic. From the fact that the work is not understood ironically, it does not follow that it is not ironic. Critics are sometimes mistaken. They also occasion-

---

[27] There are, of course, possible complications; for example, the narrator might nonetheless believe and thus mean that Nicklaus defeated Palmer. But, as I shall argue in the next chapter, what the narrator or a speaker in a literary work means is analyzable in terms of what the author *has* him mean—that is, in terms of what the author intends him to mean.

[28] See also Wayne C. Booth, *A Rhetoric of Irony*, pp. 11f., 120f., 242, *et passim*.

[29] Göran Hermerén, "Intention and Interpretation in Literary Criticism," p. 73.

Is Evidence of the Author's Intention Irrelevant?

ally change their mind about whether a work is ironic. Wayne Booth has noted:

> Purged of the author's explicit judgment, the resulting work [*Portrait of the Artist*] was so brilliant and compelling, its hero's vision so scintillating, that almost all readers overlooked the satiric and ironic content—except, of course, as the satire operated against *other* characters. So far as I know, no one said anything about irony against Stephen until after *Ulysses* was published in 1922, with its opening in which Icarus-Stephen is shown with his wings clipped. Ironic readings did not become popular, in fact, until after the fragment of *Stephen Hero* was published in 1944.[30]

Furthermore, it is not at all clear that critics would not interpret the hypothetical work in the above example ironically once they became aware how it was meant. As Booth has remarked about *A Portrait of the Artist*: "It is true that, once we have been alerted, signs of ironic intention come rushing to our view." And he adds, "Those of us who now believe that Joyce is not entirely serious in the passages on aesthetics must wonder, for example, how we ever read them 'straight'."[31] How are we to account for this change on the assumption that whether a certain passage is or is not ironic depends on objective signals? The example suggests that whether we construe a certain passage as ironic or not depends on what we take the author to have meant. Surely, it is not a coincidence that *A Portrait of the Artist* was interpreted ironically only *after* critics came to think that Joyce intended it so.

The considerations I have advanced in this chapter do not, of course, provide conclusive evidence that there is a logical connection between the meaning of a work and the

[30] Wayne C. Booth, *The Rhetoric of Fiction*, p. 333.
[31] *Ibid.*, p. 334n.

author's intention. They do, however, make the idea that there is such a connection a little less implausible than it might seem by showing that one cannot categorically dismiss evidence of the author's intention as irrelevant to the meaning of a literary work.

IV

The Appeal to the Text:
What Are We Appealing to?

1. INTRODUCTION

IN SUPPORTING an interpretation of a literary work, we commonly appeal to facts such as the following: that a certain image or metaphor recurs throughout the text, that the hero's actions belie his professed beliefs, that the hero does not achieve any self-recognition, that a certain character commits suicide, that such-and-such an event occurs in the final scene, that a word is qualified in a certain way, that certain words stand in a particular syntactic or semantic relation to other words (parallelism or antithesis, for example), that a particular word or phrase is in an emphatic position, that it occurs only in such-and-such a context, and so on. Of course, we do not generally set out the evidence for our interpretation in any detailed or systematic way. But unless the idea that the text can justify or fail to justify an interpretation of a work is an illusion, the claim that a work means one thing rather than another depends on facts such as these.

In the following I want to examine the relation between such facts and an interpretation of a work. If textual features constitute evidence of what a literary work means, then there must be some connection between the two which makes it possible for such features to be evidence for an interpretation. The question is: what connection? Furthermore, we require an interpretation to be able to account in some plausible way for the various textual features of a

The Appeal to the Text

work. What kind of explanation are we asking for? And what must we be saying in claiming that a work means so-and-so in order for that claim to be able to provide an explanation of this kind?

2. Internal and External Evidence

None of the various ways in which critics commonly support their interpretation of a literary work enjoys more widespread approval in theory and acceptance in practice than the appeal to the text. It is often favorably contrasted with the appeal to facts about an author's life, his beliefs, values, concerns, and so on, as revealed in diaries, notebooks, letters, or conversations. Textual features are part of the 'internal' evidence, whereas biographical facts of the kind mentioned fall under 'external' evidence.[1] According to the anti-intentionalist thesis, to say that a work means so-and-so

---

[1] 'Internal' evidence is usually taken to include also a competent speaker's knowledge of the language or, in Beardsley's words, the "public conventions of usage," whereas 'external' evidence consists of "evidence from the psychological and social background of the object" (*Aesthetics*, pp. 25 and 20).

For the view that only 'internal' evidence can confirm or disconfirm an interpretation, see e.g. Wimsatt and Beardsley, "The Intentional Fallacy," in *The Verbal Icon*, pp. 10f.; Beardsley, *Aesthetics*, pp. 20f., and *The Possibility of Criticism*, pp. 22ff.; Wimsatt, "Genesis," pp. 210ff., 222ff.; Ellis, *The Theory of Literary Criticism*, pp. 123ff., 127f., 134ff.; Robert J. Matthews, "Describing and Interpreting a Work of Art," pp. 12-13; and Christine Brooke-Rose, "The Squirm of the True," pp. 517, 530.

For a critical examination of the distinction and the claim that 'external' evidence is irrelevant, see Cioffi, "Intention and Interpretation in Criticism," in Barrett (ed.), *Collected Papers on Aesthetics*, esp. pp. 168-75; Skinner, "Hermeneutics and the Role of History," pp. 221-28; Leslie Fiedler, "Archetype and Signature," pp. 253-73, esp. 265; S. J. Kahn, "What does a Critic Analyze?," pp. 241-43; Walter Kaufmann, "Literature and Reality," pp. 250-61, esp. 252-56; Emilio Roma, "The Scope of the Intentional Fallacy," in Newton-de Molina (ed.), *On Literary Intention*, pp. 77-80, 83-86.

does not logically imply that the author meant this. If the thesis is true, then biographical facts and textual features are evidence for two different *kinds* of claim.

Consider typical examples of biographical evidence: that an author expressed a certain belief in a letter or conversation, that he indicated in a notebook that he meant so-and-so by a particular passage in a work of his, that in his diary or in essays he revealed certain concerns and values. Facts such as these are evidence, although of course not conclusive evidence, of what the author intended to convey by a work. But if the meaning of a work is not necessarily what the author intended to convey by it, then such facts will constitute at best "*indirect* evidence"[2] of what the work means. No matter how much evidence of this kind we may possess, the most that it can establish is what the author (in all probability) intended. If the anti-intentionalist thesis is correct, this is not to establish what the work means.

Contrast biographical facts with textual features of the sort indicated above—that, for example a certain image recurs throughout the text or that a certain event occurs in the final scene. Such facts are direct evidence of what a work means or does not mean. On the anti-intentionalist thesis, textual features, unlike biographical facts, are not evidence for a statement about the meaning of a work only *by way* of being evidence for another statement (about the author's intention) which is at best related probabilistically to the interpretive claim. To rely on biographical evidence in support of an interpretation is thus—or so the argument goes—a little like ascertaining the dominant color of, say, Picasso's *Mother and Child* (1905) by asking the artist about his intention rather than by looking at the painting.

Though oversimplified, the analogy makes clear why on this view evidence of an author's intention is held to be inadmissible. Either the textual evidence allows only one interpretation or it supports several interpretations more or

[2] Beardsley, *Aesthetics*, pp. 19f.

The Appeal to the Text

less equally well. In the first case, any evidence that the author intended the interpretation in question will be superfluous, since we already possess all the evidence which, in the nature of the case, we could have. On the other hand, evidence that the author intended something else will be no less irrelevant, since by hypothesis the textual features do not allow that interpretation. In the second case, biographical facts are again irrelevant; for regardless of what the biographical facts are, we would have to say that the work is ambiguous in the sense that it has several equally correct interpretations.[3]

This picture of the relation between various kinds of facts and an interpretation is no doubt attractive, notably because it draws a sharp line between textual and biographical or, more generally, between 'internal' and 'external' evidence for a claim about the meaning of a work. I shall argue, however, that its basic assumption—namely, that there is no logical connection between the meaning of a work and the author's intention—is false. In doing so, I shall present an alternative picture of the logic of interpretation which, I hope to show, accounts more adequately for the relevant facts about the function of textual features in confirming or disconfirming an interpretation.

3. INTERPRETATION AND THE EXPLANATION OF TEXTUAL FEATURES

When we appeal to the text in support of an interpretation, we also invoke some general criterion such as, most commonly, coherence or, less frequently, complexity. We say that the text, or a certain part of the text, supports this interpretation rather than that because under the former the text is more coherent, or more complex, than under the latter.

[3] See *ibid.*, pp. 25, 145f., and Beardsley, *The Possibility of Criticism*, p. 29f.

The Appeal to the Text

Consider an example based on the following poem by Wordsworth.

> A slumber did my spirit seal;
>   I had no human fears:
> She seemed a thing that could not feel
>   The touch of earthly years.
>
> No motion has she now, no force;
>   She neither hears nor sees;
> Rolled round in earth's diurnal course,
>   With rocks, and stones, and trees.

One might argue that the words "in earth's diurnal course" which qualify "rolled round" suggest that the woman's motion is relatively "slow and gentle . . . since one revolution takes twenty-four hours" and that it is "an orderly motion, since it follows a simple circular path."[4] One might claim, therefore, that on the assumption that "rolled round" connotes slow and gentle motion, the line is more coherent than on the assumption that the woman is "being whirled about"[5]—that is, that the words "rolled round" connote "violent motion."[6] I shall not argue for or against this claim; rather, I shall try to show what it involves.

Let us call the interpretation according to which the words "rolled round" suggest slow and gentle motion I_1 and the interpretation according to which they connote violent motion I_2. The question then is: What could it mean to say that on I_1 the line is more coherent than on I_2? Someone defending I_1 might say: 'On the assumption that I_2 is correct, it would be odd that the phrase "rolled round" should be qualified by words which suggest slow and gentle motion rather than by words suggesting violent motion.' In other words, what is being claimed is that I_1, but not I_2, *can account for* the fact that "rolled round" is qualified by words connoting gentle motion rather than by words which would

---

[4] Beardsley, *The Possibility of Criticism*, p. 46.
[5] Cleanth Brooks, "Irony as a Principle of Structure," p. 736.
[6] *Ibid.*

The Appeal to the Text

suggest that the woman is being violently whirled about.[7] As Beardsley has put it: "A proposed explication may be regarded as a hypothesis that is tested by its capacity to account for the greatest quantity of data in the words of the poem...."[8]

What, then, is the explanation which I_1 provides for the fact—let us call it f—that "rolled round" is qualified by the words "in earth's diurnal course"? It is this: On the assumption that "rolled round" connotes slow and gentle motion, it would be natural or plausible to suppose that the phrase is qualified by the words "in earth's diurnal course" *because* they are an appropriate means to suggest a slow and gentle motion. The explanation in question here is a functional explanation; that is, I_1 explains f by specifying a function or purpose (namely, to suggest gentle motion) for which the words "in earth's diurnal course" are an appropriate means. If there is no purpose specified by, or in accord with, I_2 such that the words "in earth's diurnal course" would be at least an equally appropriate means for it, then the line is more coherent on I_1 than on I_2. Hence to say that (with respect to f) the line is more coherent on I_1 than on I_2 is to say (roughly) that the words "in earth's diurnal course" are a more appropriate means for a purpose in accord with I_1 than for a purpose in accord with I_2; and from this we infer that the function of "rolled round" is more likely to be that specified by I_1 than the function specified by I_2.

Now suppose that the poem I have quoted above is not in fact by Wordsworth but has been accidentally typed out by a monkey randomly depressing keys on a typewriter. (Or

[7] I am deliberately dealing here only with very basic explanations in the interpretation of a text. For it is clear, I think, that higher level explanations (answering questions such as 'Why does character X do y?') presuppose or involve answers to the more basic questions discussed in this chapter. See Beardsley, *Aesthetics*, pp. 242ff., and Morris Weitz, *Hamlet and the Philosophy of Literary Criticism*, pp. 245-68.

[8] Beardsley, *Aesthetics*, p. 145. See also Culler, *Structuralist Poetics*, p. 171, and Shlomith Rimmon, *The Concept of Ambiguity*, pp. 9-10.

The Appeal to the Text

suppose that we found the lines as marks—on, say, a large rock—produced by water erosion.)[9] It is immediately obvious that we can no longer say that the words "in earth's diurnal course"—rather than some other words which suggest violent motion—qualify "rolled round" *because* they are an appropriate means to suggest gentle motion (or because they suggest gentle motion). We can no longer explain *f* in functional terms at all, in terms of some purpose for which the words "in earth's diurnal course" are an appropriate linguistic means. All we can now say is: The words "in earth's diurnal course," rather than some other words, qualify "rolled round" because the monkey just happened to hit that series of keys there (or because the water just happened to erode the rock in such a way that those marks, rather than some others, were produced there).

Consequently, given any interpretation (*I*), it would not be possible for *I* to account for *f* more adequately than any other interpretation; that is, on no interpretation of the words "rolled round" could we understand any more or any less than on any other interpretation of those words why they should be qualified by "in earth's diurnal course" rather than by some other words. No matter what interpretation we choose, *there could be nothing odd*, on that interpretation, about the fact that "in earth's diurnal course" qualifies "rolled round"[10]; for, regardless of which interpretation we assume, it would simply be an 'accident' that

[9] A reader who finds these examples too improbable is invited to substitute his own. The only requirement is that the text have been produced by chance. Computer poetry is a more realistic example. The reason I have decided to use the example of a text produced by a monkey (or by water erosion) is that it is less easily associated with a person's intentions.

[10] It is, of course, odd that the monkey should have typed out a word sequence which yields sense at all—and not just a nonsense jumble of words or letters—or that water erosion should have produced a sequence of marks resembling such a word sequence; but this obviously calls for a different *kind* of explanation than that which an interpretation of a poem could provide.

The Appeal to the Text

"rolled round" is qualified by the words "in earth's diurnal course" rather than being followed by a meaningless jumble of letters.[11]

What is odd (when there *is* something odd) on the assumption that I_2 is correct—that "rolled round" connotes violent motion—is not that the words "in earth's diurnal course" qualify the phrase "rolled round," but that *the author* should have *used them to qualify* (or in qualifying) the phrase "rolled round"; for that is the only relevant difference between the 'poem' produced by the monkey or by water erosion and the poem written by Wordsworth. Thus only if the words "in earth's diurnal course" have been used to qualify "rolled round," only if the qualification is the result of a person's (intentional) action, could it be odd on I_2 that the latter words are qualified by the former. Hence it is logically possible for I_1 to account more adequately than I_2 for f only if f is the result of a person's action, only if what is to be accounted for is the fact that *the author used* the words "in earth's diurnal course" to qualify "rolled

[11] It is perhaps worth noting that Christine Brooke-Rose in her structuralist reading of *The Turn of the Screw* remarks that "in view of the extraordinary repetition of the figure four and other parallels *it can hardly be a coincidence* that the governess finds a job ten years later with a young girl who has a brother of university age (Miles/ Flora/, Douglas/ sister; also, on the level of the fictional cause for the narrative: governess/sister; Douglas/Miles = Douglas as a boy in the story she tells him)" ("The Squirm of the True," pp. 530-31, my italics). What could it mean to say that "it can hardly be a coincidence that the governess finds a job ten years later with a young girl who has a brother of university age" except that James surely intended this to form part of the pattern? It clearly does not mean simply that this fits into, or forms a part of, the pattern; for as the sentence indicates, it is *because* this element of the story fits into the pattern that we infer that James very likely intended it as such. Furthermore, this interpretation of the remark is confirmed by similar comments (see pp. 517, 519, 523, 532). That such remarks occur in a rigorously structuralist interpretation by a critic who denies any relevance of the author's intention shows how deeply the notion of what an author intended is embedded in our concept of the meaning of a work.

round." Therefore, in saying that on I_2 it would be odd that the words "in earth's diurnal course" qualify "rolled round," what we are saying is: 'On I_2 it would be odd that the author should have used the words "in earth's diurnal course" to qualify "rolled round."'

4. The Role of an Author's Intention in the Explanation of Textual Features

These considerations shed light on what it is to say that "rolled round" connotes gentle motion. For the only kind of explanation appropriate to the fact to be accounted for (a person's use of certain words rather than others) is an explanation referring to the agent's (the author's) motive, reason, purpose, or intention. Furthermore, the only kind of explanation which an hypothesis about the meaning (here connotations) of "rolled round" could provide for f would be a functional explanation, one couched in terms of a purpose or function for which the words "in earth's diurnal course" are an appropriate means.

Hence the fact that the words "in earth's diurnal course" connote, or are an appropriate means to suggest, gentle motion could in principle explain f (that the author used them to qualify "rolled round") only under the assumption that *the author had a certain purpose or intention.* Thus if it is logically possible for an interpretation of "rolled round' to provide this kind of explanation of f, an explanation in terms of the function for which the words "in earth's diurnal course" are appropriate, then that interpretation must be, or logically imply, a statement about the author's intention.

It follows that unless I_1 is, or logically implies, a statement about what the author meant, f could not have any bearing on the truth or falsity of I_1. In other words, if in assuming that I_1 is correct, we were *not* assuming that the author intended the words "rolled round" to suggest gentle motion, then the assumption (I_1) that "rolled round" (here) connotes gentle motion *could not in principle* explain what we

The Appeal to the Text

would require any interpretation of those words to explain, namely, the fact that the words "in earth's diurnal course," rather than some other words, are used to qualify "rolled round." It would not be possible for an interpretation (I) of the words "rolled round" to explain f if, for example, the assumption that I is correct only made it likely (did not logically imply) that the author intended to convey the corresponding meaning (m). For if I only makes this likely, then it is always possible that I is correct while the claim that the author intended m is false (no matter how great the probability that it is true, given that I is correct). Hence the fact (or the assumption) that the interpretation (I) is correct could not explain f.

Furthermore, it cannot plausibly be argued that what we are concerned with is only what the *speaker*, not the author, means. For the question 'Why, if I_2 is correct and "rolled round" connotes violent motion, is that phrase qualified by "in earth's diurnal course," rather than by words suggesting violent motion?' is clearly a request for an explanation, not (or not just) of the speaker's action, but of the author's. Moreover, would it make sense to suppose that a 'poem' (that is, the corresponding physical marks) produced by water erosion has a speaker?

In claiming, therefore, that, with respect to f, the line "rolled round in earth's diurnal course" is more coherent on I_1 than on I_2 and in inferring from this that I_1 is more likely to be correct than I_2, we are implicitly saying (roughly): 'Since the words "in earth's diurnal course" are a more appropriate means to suggest gentle motion than to suggest violent motion, the author is more likely to have used them, and hence the phrase "rolled round," to suggest the former than the latter.'

I have argued that unless an interpretation is a statement about the author's intention, it cannot in principle account for f. To what extent can we generalize from this example? It is clear, I think, that what I have shown for f holds for any textual feature which can be described in terms of what the author has done. This is fairly obvious for facts about the use of language in a work—that, for example, a certain event is described in terms of such-and-such imagery, that a certain sentence is in the passive, or that it is in the subjunctive, that this word, rather than such-and-such a word, occurs here, or that a certain word is in a curious position, and so on. For by the same argument I have given above one can easily show that an interpretation can account for such facts only if it is a statement about the author's intention.

This is somewhat less obvious for facts about the actions of characters; but we need not go through the whole argument once more to see that its conclusion holds for such facts as well. I have already suggested that it does not make sense to talk of a speaker or narrator of a 'text' produced by a monkey or by water erosion. Consequently, it would be unintelligible to say of such a 'text' that its speaker or narrator 'told' of the exploits of so-and-so. Moreover, it would make no sense here to speak, for example, of a character or the hero, the protagonist or the antagonist of the 'work'. Thus the only way we can make sense of statements about what the narrator in a work says or what the hero or a character does is by construing them as statements about what the author has the narrator say or what he has his hero or a character do. It follows that an interpretation can in principle account for such facts only if it is a statement about the author's intention.

5. Can't We Dispense with the Explanation of Textual Features?

I shall now consider an objection to the account I have given. One might wonder whether it is not possible to dispense altogether with the idea that an interpretation is an explanation of an author's use of the words which constitute the text; if it is, then we can avoid the conclusion that an interpretation is a statement about the author's intention.

The Appeal to the Text

For it would be possible to hold that the line "rolled round in earth's diurnal course" is more coherent on I_1 than on I_2 even if it had been produced, not by Wordsworth, but by a monkey. That is, the claim that the words "in earth's diurnal course" are a more appropriate means to suggest gentle motion than to suggest violent motion would still be intelligible. Couldn't we therefore simply say:

(1) 'With respect to f, the line is more coherent on I_1 than on I_2'

and hence

(2) 'f makes I_1 more likely to be correct than I_2'?

One problem with this objection is that it entails that an interpretation cannot in principle account for any textual feature of the kind to which critics commonly appeal in support of their interpretations. But wouldn't we require any interpretation to be able to account in some way for facts such as f?

Furthermore, proposition (2) above follows from (1) only if an interpretation can in principle account for facts such as f. That is to say, the claim that with respect to the words "in earth's diurnal course" the line is more coherent on I_1 than on I_2 will be relevant to the truth or falsity of I_1 and I_2 only if those interpretations are at least in principle capable of accounting for the fact (f) that the words "in earth's diurnal course" qualify "rolled round." Hence (2) follows from (1) only if the interpretations in question are, or logically imply, corresponding statements about the author's intention.

To see that this is so, assume once more that the poem has been produced by chance, say, by a monkey or by water erosion, and hence is not the record of someone's *use* of the words in order to convey or express something. In that case, the fact (f) that the words "in earth's diurnal course" qualify "rolled round" *could not be evidence* for the claim (I_1) that "rolled round" here connotes gentle motion or for

The Appeal to the Text

any other interpretation of those words. To put it differently, if the line had been produced by a monkey or by water erosion, then the fact that the words "in earth's diurnal course" are a more appropriate means to suggest gentle motion than to suggest violent motion *could not make it more likely* that "rolled round" here connotes gentle rather than violent motion.

Thus the fact that the words "in earth's diurnal course" are a more appropriate means to suggest gentle motion than violent motion can make I_1 more likely to be correct than I_2 only if a person (the author) *used* the words "in earth's diurnal course" (rather than others suggesting violent motion) *to qualify* "rolled round." In other words, only if the line represents a person's speech act can the fact that, with respect to f, the line is more coherent on I_1 than on I_2 make I_1 more likely to be correct than I_2. Hence what constitutes evidence that I_1 is correct and I_2 incorrect is the fact that the author used the words "in earth's diurnal course" (rather than others suggesting violent motion) to qualify "rolled round." And now the implicit appeal to intention becomes transparent; for the latter fact is obviously evidence of the author's intention, and whatever else it may be evidence of cannot plausibly be said to have any bearing on the question what the line means. Consequently, f can be evidence for or against an interpretation of "rolled round" only if f is evidence of what the author intended to convey by the phrase.

It follows that an interpretation (I) of "rolled round" is, or logically implies, a statement about the author's intention; for otherwise f could not be evidence for or against I. To summarize, f is evidence for or against an interpretation of "rolled round" in virtue of the fact that it is evidence of the author's intention. And f is evidence for I_1 and against I_2 in virtue of the fact that, with respect to f, the line is more coherent on I_1 than on I_2—that is, in virtue of the fact that f can be more adequately or plausibly explained on the assumption that the author intended to suggest gentle motion than on the assumption that he intended to suggest violent motion.

Hence in saying

(1) 'With respect to f, the line is more coherent on I_1 than on I_2.'

and therefore

(2) 'f makes I_1 more likely to be correct than I_2',

we are saying roughly:

(1a) 'If the author (or a person similar in relevant respects to the author) used the phrase "in earth's diurnal course" to qualify "rolled round," it would be more likely that he intended to suggest gentle motion by the latter than violent motion, since the words "in earth's diurnal course" are a more appropriate means to suggest gentle motion than to suggest violent motion';

and hence

(2a) 'The fact that the author used "in earth's diurnal course" to qualify "rolled round" makes it more likely that he intended to suggest gentle motion than violent motion'.

For, as we have seen, (2) follows from (1) only if (2a) follows from (1); and (2a) follows from (1) only if (1) is roughly equivalent to (1a), that is, to some conditional statement relating an author's use of a word or phrase to his likely intention.

It may be that the analysis of the inference from (1) to (2) is somewhat more complicated than I have allowed. One might want to say that (1) is equivalent, not to (1a), but only to the claim:

(1a′) 'The words "in earth's diurnal course" are more functional on I_1 than on I_2'.

The Appeal to the Text

But even if we construe (1) as equivalent to (1a′), this does not significantly affect the analysis since, as I have shown, f will be evidence for or against an interpretation of the words "rolled round" only if it is evidence of the author's intention. Hence in analyzing the argument from (1) to (2) we can simply substitute (1a′) for (1a) and add the further premise:

>(1b) 'If the author (or a person similar in relevant respects to the author) used the phrase "in earth's diurnal course" to qualify "rolled round," then in view of (1a′) it would be more likely that he intended to suggest gentle motion by the latter rather than violent motion'.

In other words, if we take (1) to be equivalent to (1a′), instead of to (1a), then we must assume that the inference from (1) to (2) contains a further (tacit) premise, namely, (1b); for, as we have seen, f will make I_1 more likely to be correct than I_2 only if f makes it more likely that the author intended to convey I_1 rather than I_2. It follows that if we treat (1) as equivalent to (1a′), we need (1b) in order to be able to infer (2).

We can now see why it is not possible to dispense with the idea that an interpretation is an explanation of the author's use of the words which constitute the text. For only if an interpretation (I) of the words "rolled round" can in principle explain the fact (f) that the author used the words "in earth's diurnal course" to qualify "rolled round" can f be evidence for or against I. And only if I in fact provides a more adequate explanation of f than another interpretation (J) does f make I more likely to be correct than J.

What I have shown, then, is that in appealing to the fact that a text is more coherent on one interpretation than on another, or to the fact that certain features of a text can be more adequately explained on one interpretation than on another, we are implicitly appealing to the author's likely intention. For if it is *possible* for textual features to constitute evidence for an interpretation of a literary work, or if an interpretation *can in principle* account for textual features, then an interpretation must be a claim about what the author intended.

6. THE COMPLEXITY CRITERION

I can now deal more briefly with the complexity criterion, since the logical structure of arguments involving the latter is the same as that of arguments involving an appeal to coherence.

One might say that the word "trees" in the last line of the poem quoted above (section 3) could very well—since trees, unlike rocks and stones, are animate—suggest the idea of animation or of being alive; that is, it would be a suitable means to intimate this. Furthermore, the position of the word (occurring as it does at the end of a series and as the last word of the poem) is very appropriate for emphasis.

Hence a defender of the pantheistic interpretation (I_1), according to which the poem suggests that the woman referred to has (after her death) become part of the grander "life of Nature,"[12] might argue that on his reading the last line is more complex, or richer in meaning, than on the interpretation (I_2) according to which the woman is "wholly assimilated to inorganic things."[13] He might point out that on his interpretation (I_1) "trees" is more functional, in both its meaning and its position, than on I_2. For—or so the proponent of the pantheistic reading might argue—on I_2 "trees" must be taken as a synonym for "rocks" and "stones" and cannot be taken as emphatic.[14]

[12] F. W. Bateson, *English Poetry*, p. 59.
[13] Melvin Rader, *Wordsworth*, p. 172.
[14] This is, of course, a problematical claim; for on I_2 one might with equal justification take "trees" to suggest, not the idea of life, but that of being "chained . . . to one particular spot" (Brooks, "Irony as a Principle of Structure," p. 736). There are further arguments which might be given to show that the line is not in fact more

The Appeal to the Text

What is being claimed, then, is that I_1 can more adequately explain or account for certain features of the text, namely, that the word "trees" (which, unlike "rocks" and "stones," is very appropriate to intimate the idea of life) rather than some more obvious synonym of "rocks" and "stones" occurs in the series of the last line, and that the word "trees" is in a position very appropriate for emphasis.

This is sufficient to show that the structure of the argument involving the criterion of complexity is the same as that of an argument based on coherence. By the same reasoning I have used above, it can easily be shown that to invoke complexity in support of an interpretation is to appeal to what the author is likely to have meant.

7. On Interpreting a Text Produced by Chance: Can It Constitute a Whole?

Implicit assumptions as to what an author intended are much more pervasive than might appear at first sight. The interpretation of even the simplest text involves such assumptions.

Consider the following little poem:[15]

(1) The cat is on the mat.
(2) The cat is very fat.

Ordinarily we would take "The cat" in (1) and (2) to refer[16] to the same animal (or person, if we construe "cat" in

---

complex or richer in meaning on I_1 than on I_2. But since I am concerned with the structure of the argument, not with the truth or falsity of the premises, this can be ignored for present purposes.

[15] Taken from Dickie, *Aesthetics*, p. 112.

[16] One might object that the question what "The cat" refers to is not, strictly speaking, a question about its meaning. This is true; but in the sense in which critics commonly speak of "the meaning" of a poem, the question whether "The cat" in lines (1) and (2) refers to the same animal may be of some importance to the meaning of the lines. The fact that this is not a genuine but rather a pretended

The Appeal to the Text

the sense in which it is often used in a certain dialect) and hence infer that it is the cat on the mat which is very fat. What justifies this inference is the fact that the text is more coherent on the assumption that the referent of "The cat" is the same in (1) and (2) than on the assumption that it is not. In particular, since (2) follows immediately upon (1) and since the second occurrence of "The cat" is not qualified in any way so as to distinguish its referent from that of "The cat" in (1), it is more likely than not that the referent is the same.

Now suppose that the poem was typed out accidentally by our monkey who randomly depresses keys on a typewriter. Can we still say 'Since (2) follows immediately upon (1) and since the second occurrence of "The cat" is not qualified in any way so as to distinguish its referent from that of "The cat" in (1), it is more likely than not that the referent is the same'? Clearly not, for surely there is no longer any connection between the facts in question (that (2) immediately follows (1), etc.) and the probability that the referent of "The cat" in (1) and (2) is the same. If, for example, the monkey had typed out (1) and (2) on separate pages (amid a jumble of meaningless combinations of letters and words), then we would certainly not assume that the referent of "The cat" in (1) and (2) is the same. Is it then because the monkey, by pure chance, happened to type out (2) immediately after (1), because the lines stand in physical proximity, that we are justified in assuming that the referent of "The cat" in (1) and (2) is the same? Indeed, does it make any sense to suppose that in such a case the words "The cat" could have a referent?

What the example brings out is that we cannot even take

---

reference or that, though it could be a genuine reference, the phrase in fact fails to refer is irrelevant for our purposes. See John R. Searle, "The Logical Status of Fictional Discourse," pp. 329-31, and Richard Gale, "The Fictive Use of Language," pp. 325-35. See also Charles Crittenden, "Fictional Existence," pp. 318ff., and A. G. Pleydell-Pearce, "Sense, Reference and Fiction," pp. 225-36, esp. 228-32.

The Appeal to the Text

the various parts of a text (its lines, sentences, and so on) as constituting a whole, as forming a unit or as (here) belonging together, in the sense which our concept of a literary work requires, without assuming that the text represents a person's (intentional) action. To call something a poem or even a text is to say among other things that the words, phrases, lines, or sentences of which it consists have not been arranged in this way by chance but have been produced by a person and with certain kinds of intentions.[17] In particular, the example shows that only if the text has been produced by a person and with certain kinds of intentions can the facts in question make it more likely that the referent of "The cat" in (1) and (2) is the same—that is, only if those facts are evidence of what the author intended to express or convey. Thus to say 'The referent of "The cat" is (probably) the same in (1) and (2)' *is* to say 'The author (probably) intended "The cat" to refer to the same animal in (1) as in (2)'.

There is clearly something odd about *interpreting* a 'text' produced by chance. Would it be possible to interpret a series of marks on a rock which closely resemble the words of an English sentence if we knew that they had been produced by water erosion? Could one even call them "words"?[18] Could one say of an appropriate 'word' or 'words' that they *refer* to so-and-so? That they are an *allusion* to such-and-such? That they are *ironic*? What could it mean to say of such marks that they *mean* so-and-so? It might be possible to construe this in terms of Grice's natural sense or

---

[17] See also Colin Lyas, "Personal Qualities and the Intentional Fallacy," p. 197, and George Dickie, *Art and the Aesthetic*, pp. 21-27. This is, of course, not a sufficient condition for something to be a poem.

[18] Construing a text even on this most basic level appears to involve the assumption that it has been produced by a being capable of using language. See John R. Searle, "What is a Speech Act?" in Searle (ed.), *The Philosophy of Language*, p. 40, and *Speech Acts*, pp. 16f.; Karl Aschenbrenner, "Intention and Understanding," pp. 237-38.

The Appeal to the Text

senses of "mean"—in the sense, for example, in which we say of certain spots that they mean measles.[19] But that is obviously not the sense in which we say of a literary work or of an utterance in ordinary discourse that it means so-and-so.

A statement about the meaning of the marks on the rock or about the meaning of a computer 'poem' cannot be a statement about the meaning of a particular utterance of the corresponding words, or about their meaning on a particular occasion of utterance,[20] since of course there is no such utterance. It could only be a statement about what Grice has called the "timeless meaning(s)"[21] of the words in question—a statement, for example, about the meaning of the word "man" in English, as opposed to a statement about the meaning of a particular *utterance* of the word, or about the meaning of the word on a particular occasion on which it is used. Thus what we would be interpreting (one or more *possible* speech acts)[22] is quite independent of the existence of the marks on the rock or the production of the 'poem' by the computer. That is, the computer 'poem' exists even before the computer produces it or even if it never

---

[19] See H. P. Grice, "Meaning," in Olshewsky (ed.), *Problems in the Philosophy of Language*, pp. 251ff.

[20] The latter is Grice's *"applied timeless meaning* of a complete utterance type (on a particular occasion of utterance)." ("Utterer's Meaning and Intentions," pp. 148ff., and "Utterer's Meaning, Sentence-Meaning, and Word-Meaning," in Searle [ed.], *The Philosophy of Language*, p. 56.)

[21] Grice, "Utterer's Meaning and Intentions," pp. 147, 149, and "Utterer's Meaning, Sentence-Meaning, and Word-Meaning," in Searle (ed.), *The Philosophy of Language*, p. 55.

[22] See John R. Searle, "Reiterating the Differences," p. 202.

Peter Jones has maintained that although understanding "a novel involves assuming that the work is purposive, is the product of human agency (with all that that involves) . . . this assumption . . . does not commit us to a search for the *actual* purposes that informed the work." *Philosophy and the Novel*, p. 197. But if the main argument of this chapter is valid, then the meaning of a work is indeed logically tied to the author's actual purpose or intention.

does—something one would surely not want to say of a poem.

In other words, it would be possible to 'interpret' a 'text' produced by chance in the sense in which we might be said to 'interpret' a sentence when we explain its meaning to a foreigner, by explaining to him what the individual words mean, how they function in the sentence, and thus how the sentence *could* be used or what it *could* be used to express or convey. It would be an 'interpretation', so to speak, of a "piece of language."[23] But although that is the only possible way to 'interpret' a 'poem' produced by chance, it is not, as I have tried to show, to interpret a poem.[24]

8. Conclusion

We typically support our interpretation of a literary work by adducing textual features as evidence for it. Indeed, if we are to justify our reading by an appeal to the text at all, we must appeal to such facts as I have discussed. Now we do not just appeal to these facts; we also invoke some criterion which specifies a general condition or conditions under which a fact is evidence for an interpretation. This

[23] William Empson, *Seven Types of Ambiguity*, p. 1. See also Beardsley, *The Possibility of Criticism*, p. 17.

[24] For a related point, see Jeremy M. Hawthorn, *Identity and Relationship*, p. 91.

Homer Hogan in "Hermeneutics and Folk Songs" (pp. 223-29) has maintained that an intentionalist theory cannot adequately deal with folk songs, since it is "in the great majority of cases a real possibility, if not probability" that they have not been "composed by one discoverable author, but rather evolved through a historical process" (p. 225). Even though this is no doubt true, it does not present any problems essentially different from those which arise in interpreting a work (by an individual author) which has undergone a number of substantial revisions. In such cases, a critic must evidently decide which version he is going to interpret. Furthermore, Hogan's own comments on Cleanth Brooks' interpretations of three folk ballads indicate that knowledge of the original author's (or authors') intention is crucial to an interpretation of folk songs (pp. 226-28).

The Appeal to the Text

criterion appears in a (further) premise of an interpretive argument—that, for example, with respect to some fact or facts (f), the text is more coherent on I_1 than on I_2. If this premise is true, then f makes I_1 more likely to be correct than I_2; or, stated differently, given the truth of this premise, then on the basis of f—not necessarily on the basis of all the relevant facts—I_1 is more likely to be correct than I_2.

I have argued that an appeal to coherence or complexity in support of an interpretation of a literary work *is* an appeal to the author's likely intention. More explicitly, coherence and complexity are criteria of what a text means *only insofar as* they are criteria of the author's intention. Hence in cases (such as texts produced by chance) in which coherence and complexity are not criteria of what the author intended, they will not be criteria of what the text means. Assume, for example, that a certain text is more coherent (or complex) under one interpretation (I_1) than under another (I_2). Now if this does not make it more likely that the author intended the meaning corresponding to I_1 than the meaning corresponding to I_2, then the fact that the text is more coherent on I_1 than on I_2 does not make I_1 more likely to be correct than I_2.

I have tried to establish this as follows. An interpretation is expected to provide an explanation of the features of the text. The kind of explanation in question, as we have seen, is an explanation referring to some purpose or function for which those features are an appropriate means. Thus one of the interpretations considered explains the fact (f) that the words "in earth's diurnal course" qualify "rolled round" by specifying a purpose or function for the qualifying phrase, namely, to suggest slow and gentle motion. And it is of some importance to the assessment of the interpretation whether or not the words "in earth's diurnal course" are in fact an appropriate means for the purpose which the interpretation specifies.

Now an interpretation, I have argued, cannot in principle account for f unless f represents a human action—unless, that is, what is to be accounted for is the fact that the author used the phrase "in earth's diurnal course" to qualify "rolled round." But the only kind of explanation appropriate to the fact to be explained (a human action) is an explanation in terms of the agent's motive, reason, purpose, or intention. And the only kind of explanation which an interpretation can, and is expected to, provide is a functional explanation—that is, an explanation of f in terms of some purpose or function for which the words "in earth's diurnal course" are an appropriate means. Consequently, the only kind of explanation which is both appropriate to the fact to be explained and which an interpretation can, and is expected to, provide is an explanation in terms of the author's purpose or intention. But an interpretation can provide such an explanation only if it is a statement about the author's intention.

I have argued also—and this is just the other side of the coin—that a textual feature (f) will constitute evidence for an interpretation if and only if f is evidence of what the author intended. It follows that to appeal to the text (to textual features) as evidence for an interpretation *is* to appeal to the author's (likely) intention. It follows further that no matter what criterion (whether coherence, complexity, or any other standard) we might invoke to justify our claim that certain textual features are evidence for our interpretation, the criterion will have no bearing on the question whether our interpretation is correct or incorrect unless it is a criterion of what the author intended.

And now we can return briefly to the view I outlined in section 2. I have argued that textual features are evidence for a claim about the meaning of a work *in virtue of* the fact that they are evidence of the author's intention; it follows that insofar as facts about the author's beliefs, values, concerns, and so on are evidence of his intention—irrespective of where they are revealed, whether in his diaries, notebooks, letters, conversations, or in other literary works—they will be no less relevant than textual features. No doubt, biographical evidence by itself does not have the same

The Appeal to the Text

weight as textual evidence. An author may change his mind about what he wants to convey, he may forget what he meant, or he may intend one thing before he begins to write and then, possibly without being fully aware of it, come to do something else.[25]

Nevertheless, biographical facts may always be decisive by showing, for example, that an interpretation is based on mistaken assumptions about the author's knowledge.[26] Furthermore, textual features may, no less than biographical facts, impose only weak constraints on an interpretation, in cases in which they can be explained in a number of plausible ways. At any rate, whether the biographical facts about a certain author constitute strong or weak evidence, are or are not decisive, depends on the particulars of the case. It has no bearing whatever on the question whether such facts are in principle relevant to the meaning of a literary work.

[25] Henry James is a good example; see Booth, *The Rhetoric of Fiction*, pp. 347ff. Thus I think that Skinner is quite right in claiming that "the contextual approach recently advocated by Close, Iser, and others" exaggerates "the extent to which [background information] is genuinely useful, in the case of strongly autonomous texts." ("Hermeneutics and the Role of History," p. 227) But as Skinner (p. 228) and Cioffi have pointed out, we cannot know what 'external' facts will illuminate the meaning of a work until we have read it in the light of those facts. (Cioffi, "Intention and Interpretation in Criticism," in Barrett (ed.), *Collected Papers on Aesthetics*, p. 172.)

[26] See Chapter III, sections 5 and 6; Chapter V, sections 2 and 4; and Cioffi, "Intention and Interpretation in Criticism," in Barrett (ed.), *Collected Papers on Aesthetics*, pp. 167-69.

V

Context and the Rules of the Language

Perhaps the most common argument for (or against) an interpretation of an utterance or a passage from a literary work is that the interpretation is (or is not) supported by the context. I want to consider what it is about a context that allows it to disambiguate or to clarify the meaning of an utterance. I shall try to show that in adducing features of the context in support of an interpretation, we are implicitly appealing to the author's intention. I shall then argue that the same is true when we invoke the rules of the language to exclude an interpretation or to show that a certain passage can only mean so-and-so.

1. What Makes the Context of an Utterance Relevant to Its Meaning?

George Dickie has said:

> I cannot make "I saw her duck" mean that I saw a duck which was a bird *simply* by uttering "I saw her duck" or by uttering "I saw her duck" and *intending* the bird interpretation. An act of intending will get me nowhere. What I have to do is utter "I saw her duck" and then do something else—point my finger, utter other sentences, or the like—or see that certain conditions obtain.[1]

This is true in the sense that unless I "do something else" a hearer is likely to be puzzled or might misunderstand the

[1] Dickie, *Aesthetics*, p. 114.

Context and the Rules of the Language

utterance. But what Dickie seems to be overlooking is that the "something else" that I might do to disambiguate the utterance will disambiguate it only in virtue of the fact that it is evidence of my intention.

Consider Dickie's example:

> Suppose I suddenly realize that what I said to you yesterday was ambiguous. I phone you and straighten things out. Still, what I said yesterday, taken by itself, remains ambiguous; what is no longer ambiguous after the phone conversation is what I *meant* (or intended to say) yesterday. With yesterday's conversation plus today's phone conversation, I have now succeeded in saying what I meant to say. When the sentences uttered yesterday and the sentences uttered today are taken as constituting a single disclosure, they mean what I meant all along.[2]

What Dickie wants to say, I think, is roughly this: The original uterance (call it u_1) is and remains ambiguous no matter what the speaker meant. That is, even after we know what the speaker meant, the original utterance (u_1) "taken by itself"—without the later utterance on the phone (call it u_2)—remains ambiguous. It is only if we consider u_2 together with u_1 "as constituting a single disclosure" that u_1 is no longer ambiguous. Thus it is not in virtue of what u_2 indicates about the speaker's intention, but in virtue of the meaning of u_2 and u_1 when taken together, that after the phone call the earlier utterance (u_1) is no longer ambiguous. It follows that u_1 has a different meaning before the phone call than afterwards, that is, when taken together with u_2. This is what Dickie seems to have in mind when he says "When the sentences uttered yesterday and the sentences uttered today are taken as constituting a single disclosure, they mean what I meant all along."[3]

[2] *Ibid.*
[3] See also *ibid.*, p. 119, and Beardsley, *Aesthetics*, p. 25.

Context and the Rules of the Language

One problem with Dickie's view is that it is not possible to take the later utterance (u_2) as belonging to the former (u_1) without taking them to have been intended to belong together. It follows from what I have argued in the last chapter that u_2 will not disambiguate u_1 unless u_2 is evidence of what the speaker meant by u_1. In other words, it would appear that u_2 disambiguates u_1 because it is evidence of what the speaker meant. The following consideration confirms this.

Since the original utterance (u_1) is ambiguous (by hypothesis), we may assume that it could mean m_1 or m_2 or possibly both. Suppose that the speaker meant m_1. Now if after the phone call we interpret u_1 in the way the speaker intended (namely, as m_1), then we would say that m_1 is the meaning of u_1 even if the speaker had not called—although in that case we may never have *known* what the utterance means. In other words, if before the phone call we construed u_1 to mean m_2, and if in the light of the phone conversation we change our interpretation and now take u_1 to mean m_1, then we would certainly say that before the phone call we had *misunderstood* the utterance or what the speaker said (unless we believe that the speaker meant something else before). But we would not say that before the phone call the utterance (u_1) had a different meaning from the one it has now, even if we understood it differently then; that is, we would not say that u_1 means what the speaker intended to convey only *after* the phone call, even though, if he had not called, u_1 might have *failed to convey* to us what the speaker meant. This consideration implies that u_1 meant m_1 even before the phone call; the latter only allows us to *tell* that u_1 means m_1. In other words, after the phone call we construe the original utterance (u_1) in the light of what u_2 indicates about the speaker's intention in uttering u_1.

This discussion brings out that what determines the meaning of u_1 is the fact that the speaker meant m_1; for otherwise the phone call could not, so to speak, retroactively disambiguate u_1. That u_1 means m_1 even before the phone call shows that u_2 is relevant to the meaning of u_1 *because* (or insofar as) u_2 is evidence of what the speaker meant by u_1.

Hence Dickie is mistaken in thinking that before the phone call the original utterance (u_1) has a different meaning than afterwards, when taken together with u_2. For as we have seen, the meaning of u_1 is the same (namely, m_1) before and after the phone call. The only difference is that after the phone call we can tell what it means. Thus the original utterance (u_1) is not ambiguous in the sense that its meaning is the set of its linguistically possible readings, that is, m_1, m_2, and perhaps $m_1 m_2$ (nor in the sense that each of the latter readings would be equally correct).[4] Rather, to call the utterance ambiguous is to say that without further information or context we cannot *tell* what it means. The above consideration shows that in order for the context to be able to disambiguate an utterance or for the context to be evidence of what an utterance means, it is sufficient for it to be evidence of what the speaker meant by the utterance.

To see that this condition is not only sufficient but also necessary, consider the following example. Suppose a parrot utters the words 'I saw her duck' in the presence of a group of people among whom is a woman who has just ducked her head. Let us assume that no duck is or has been present. (This is Dickie's example of the sort of context that might disambiguate an utterance of the words in question.)[5] Does the context now disambiguate the utterance? Does it now mean 'I saw the woman duck her head'? Surely not. One might even imagine the parrot 'pointing' with a small wooden stick in his claws at the woman in question.

Or suppose that, in the situation just described, a blind old man daydreaming about his late wife's pet duck says

[4] Of course, in certain cases the existing evidence may provide more or less equal support for each of two or more incompatible interpretations. This is the sort of case Shlomith Rimmon is concerned with (*The Concept of Ambiguity*, pp. 9-16, 27, 52).

[5] Dickie, *Aesthetics*, p. 113.

'I saw her duck'. Does the context (the fact that a particular woman has just ducked her head) now disambiguate the utterance? Does the utterance mean 'I saw the woman (in the group) duck her head'?

Clearly, the fact that the woman just ducked her head does not in this case disambiguate the man's utterance; and it fails to do so (it is irrelevant to the meaning of the utterance) surely because it is (in this case) not evidence of what the speaker meant. We would probably not even regard the fact that the woman just ducked her head as part of the context of the utterance, since the man (who is daydreaming) is not likely to have been aware of what the woman did and (since he is blind) obviously could not have seen her duck her head.

What the relevant context of the utterance is, in other words, is not somehow 'objectively' given, irrespective of the speaker, but depends on how the speaker views the situation. Otherwise it would be difficult to see why it should be irrelevant (in this case) to the meaning of the utterance that the woman ducked her head. Surely, the reason is that the man did not see the woman duck her head, and hence her action is not likely to be one of the elements of the situation in response to which he uttered the words 'I saw her duck'.

To put the point differently, the fact (a) that the speaker was not aware of what the woman was doing and the fact (b) that he was daydreaming about his late wife's pet duck are relevant to the meaning of the utterance because they are indications of what he meant. Given (a) and (b), it is unlikely that the man meant 'I saw that woman duck her head', whereas it is very likely that he meant 'I saw my late wife's pet duck'. Clearly, under the circumstances, we would in fact interpret the man's utterance in this way.[6] To take the man's utterance to mean 'I saw that woman duck her head' would certainly be to misconstrue it.

[6] For a similar example, see Ziff, "What is Said," p. 716.

Context and the Rules of the Language

2. The Speaker's Beliefs, Personality, and Knowledge of the Language

Consider another example:

> . . . [S]uppose you ask me who is the President of France, and I say Debré. You address the man, and he says he is not Debré. You reproach me with having misled you. It would be of no help for me to say that I had actually referred to Pompidou, since I had had him in mind.[7]

But surely the reason is that in the situation in question—assuming I know who Debré and Pompidou are and that 'Debré' is not the name of Pompidou—it is highly unlikely that I should not have intended to refer to Debré. It is, in particular, not true that "[o]nly if I habitually use "Debré is the President of France," and in a Pickwickian way does my intention decide what is identified."[8] For suppose that just before the exchange mentioned, someone had pointed out to me the President of France and, as a result of a misunderstanding, I thought his name was 'Debré'. If I then (not knowing who Debré is or anything about him) say 'Debré', to someone who asks me who the President of France is, then surely I am not referring to Debré. Rather (provided Pompidou is the President of France at the time of the utterance), I am referring to Pompidou under the wrong name.[9] If I were then reproached by the person who

---

[7] F.X.J. Coleman, "A Few Observations on Fictional Discourse," p. 37.

[8] *Ibid.* See also Gale, "The Fictive Use of Language," pp. 329-30.

[9] For a detailed discussion of reference, see Searle, *Speech Acts*, pp. 72-96; P. F. Strawson, "On Referring," in Olshewsky (ed.), *Problems in the Philosophy of Language*, esp. pp. 316ff.; and Leonard Linsky, "Reference and Referents," in Olshewsky (ed.), *Problems in the Philosophy of Language*, pp. 339ff. For more recent views, see e.g. the papers in Stephen P. Schwartz (ed.), *Naming, Necessity, and Natural Kinds*, and Richard Rorty's lucid and helpful discussion in "Realism and Reference," pp. 321-40.

asked me for having misled him, it is surely not true that "it would be of no help for me to point out that I had actually referred to Pompidou," to point out, that is, the circumstances under which I was led to say 'Debré' instead of 'Pompidou'.

Let us consider a case in which understanding an utterance involves understanding its implications.

> If on being asked to play tennis a person replies 'I have work to do', what has he said by implication? That depends on him: no general answer is possible here. If the speaker is an ordinary sort then perhaps he was saying by implication that he couldn't play. But he needn't be an ordinary sort. Perhaps he's a queer sort who plays and is delighted to play only when he has work to do.[10]

In that case, the utterance most likely means that he is delighted to play. Of course, I need to know that he likes to play only when he has work to do in order to understand the utterance. (But this is just to say that I need to recognize his intention in order to understand what is said.) And he needs to know or believe that I know this fact about him in order for it to be likely that he should intend to convey to me by the utterance in question that he is glad to play. But even if I do not know this, the utterance would certainly succeed in conveying that he is glad to play if after his reply he explained that he only likes to play when he has work to do.

If before the explanation I took the utterance to mean that he cannot play, then clearly I *mis*understood it. Although I may understand the utterance differently after the explanation than before, its meaning does not change. It would be irrelevant to object here that it is, strictly speaking, not the *utterance* which implies that he is glad to play, but *the person* who does so *by* his utterance, for someone who thought that the utterance means *only* that he has work

[10] Ziff, "What is Said," p. 713.

Context and the Rules of the Language

to do (and nothing more) would clearly have misunderstood it.

As Ziff has pointed out:

> To understand what is said by implication it is not enough to understand what is said in the statement sense. One may have to have some knowledge of the speaker's beliefs, attitudes, convictions, opinions and so forth.[11]

Such knowledge is necessary to determining what an utterance means (or implies) because the speaker's beliefs, attitudes, and so on indicate what he is likely to mean.

That the context will be able to disambiguate an utterance if and only if it constitutes evidence of the speaker's intention is brought out also by cases in which our ordinary assumptions about a speaker's knowledge of the language do not hold. If, for example, a speaker is not familiar with the use of 'to lick' for 'to beat', then his utterance of the sentence 'My cat licked your cat'[12] is not likely to mean 'My cat beat your cat'. (I am ignoring here the ambiguity of 'beat', since it is irrelevant to the point of the example.)

It is important to notice that in a case in which the context makes this reading very likely to be correct, the context would provide evidence that that is what the speaker means (and *a fortiori* that he is familiar with the use of 'lick' for 'beat'). Suppose a boy says: 'My dog licked his dog. So I thought: "Would my cat also beat his cat?" Well, we've just seen it: My cat licked his.' Here the context (the speaker's apparent use of 'beat' as a synonym for 'lick') provides strong evidence that the speaker means 'My cat beat his cat'.

To see that if the context does not provide such evidence, it will not make this reading probable, consider the following: Suppose the speaker knows what 'lick' means in 'to lick a lollypop', for example, but does not know that it can also mean 'beat'; he also does not know what 'to beat' means.

---

[11] *Ibid.*, pp. 712-13.   [12] From Ziff, *ibid.*, p. 715.

Context and the Rules of the Language

Suppose further that he is told that 'to beat' means the same as 'to lick'; and thus he thinks that 'to beat' means 'to lick' in the sense of 'to lick a lollypop'. Under these circumstances, the fact that 'beat' occurs as a synonym of 'lick' in 'So I thought: "Would my cat also beat his cat?"' Well, we've just seen it: My cat licked his' clearly would *not* be evidence that the speaker's utterance 'My cat licked his' means 'My cat beat his cat'.

The reason surely is that in this case the speaker's use of 'beat' (as a synonym for 'lick') does not make it likely that he means 'My cat beat his cat'. Ordinarily, of course, we would take the utterance 'My cat licked his cat', in the linguistic context given above, to mean 'My cat beat his cat'. But we would do so, not because the context *per se* (regardless of whether it is evidence of the speaker's intention) determines what the utterance means, but because ordinarily we would assume that the speaker knows what 'to beat' means and in what ways 'to lick' is ambiguous.

In order to understand an utterance of some sentence, it is not sufficient to know what the sentence means; it is necessary to know in what context the utterance occurred.[13] In order, for example, to understand an utterance of the sentence 'Tigers growl', we may need to know whether the words are being used to assert, inform, warn, mock, to practice pronunciation, to imply or suggest something and, if so, what, and so on. Thus in order to know whether an utterance of the sentence 'Two plus two is four' means, say, 'Of course what you just said is true' or 'That adds up to what we need', it is necessary to know something about the context in which the sentence was uttered.

---

[13] Beardsley's view (*The Possibility of Criticism*, p. 25) that it is "a considerable exaggeration" to say that almost any word sequence can, under the rules of the language, be used to convey different things—can have more than one meaning—seems to be false; see Jerry A. Fodor and Jerrold J. Katz, "The Structure of a Semantic Theory," p. 489, and L. Jonathan Cohen and Avishai Margalit, "The Role of Inductive Reasoning in the Interpretation of Metaphor," p. 736.

Context and the Rules of the Language

Now to know the context of an utterance is, I have argued, a matter of understanding how the speaker views the situation in which his utterance occurs.[14] Suppose "someone hunted out all the green books in his house and spread them out carefully on the roof"[15] and, in reply to the question why he was doing this, said 'No particular reason' or 'I just thought I would'. Even though the words he uttered are perfectly intelligible, his utterance is not. As Miss Anscombe has put it,

> his words would be unintelligible unless as joking and mystification. They would be unintelligible, not because one did not know what *they* meant, but because one could not make out what the man meant by saying them here.[16]

In other words, the utterance is unintelligible because we cannot understand how the man is viewing the situation such that it would make sense to say those words here.[17]

If it is frequently obvious what the context of an utterance is, this is so, I have suggested, not because the context of an utterance is somehow objectively given, independently of the speaker, but because in most cases we can simply assume what features of the situation the speaker is aware of and that he views them in the same way we do. It is only cases in which there is a discrepancy between what we initially take to be the context of an utterance and what turns out to be in fact its context which bring out the point that it is the speaker's view of the situation which is decisive. What makes it possible, then, for the context to clarify the meaning of an utterance is the fact that it is evidence of what the speaker intended to express or convey.

---

[14] See Peter Winch's analogous point about the understanding of social events, *The Idea of a Social Science*, pp. 108ff.
[15] G.E.M. Anscombe, *Intention*, p. 26.
[16] *Ibid.*, pp. 26-27.
[17] See also A. I. Melden, *Free Action*, pp. 103f.

3. SPEAKER AND AUTHOR

In the preceding sections I have argued that in appealing to the context of an utterance in support of the claim that the utterance means (or does not mean) so-and-so, we are in fact appealing to the speaker's (likely) intention. One might ask what bearing this has on the question whether the *author*'s intention is relevant to the meaning of a literary work. After all, we cannot simply assume that the narrator of a novel (or the speaker of a poem) is identifiable with the author.[18] Hence it might seem that the meaning of a literary work depends only on the speaker's (or narrator's), not the author's, intention.[19] A little reflection will show, however, that this view is unfounded.

Consider, for example, stage directions in a play. These may be statements about the setting of the play, about the background of a character, his personal history, his social status, his idiosyncracies, what he looks like, and so on. Stage directions further typically include statements about the way—in what tone of voice, for example—a character speaks certain words, whether he is pleading, commanding, warning, mocking or whatever. They may describe a character's gestures or facial expressions that accompany his utterance and underline or reveal his reaction to what is said (delight, shock, amusement, embarrassment, quiet satisfaction, and the like). In addition to specifying the speaker of an utterance, they may also indicate to whom a charac-

---

[18] Beardsley, *Aesthetics*, pp. 238ff., and *The Possibility of Criticism*, pp. 36, 45, 58ff.; Dickie, *Aesthetics*, p. 116. See also e.g. Victor Lange, "Erzählformen im Roman des achtzehnten Jahrhunderts," in Klotz (ed.), *Zur Poetik des Romans*, pp. 32-47.

[19] Even to admit that what the *speaker* means is relevant to what the text means is to attenuate the anti-intentionalist thesis; for if Beardsley is right in holding that what a man intends to convey by his utterance has no (logical) bearing on the question what his utterance means, then the intention of a speaker in a literary work could be no more relevant than the intention of its author. See Beardsley, *The Possibility of Criticism*, pp. 45f., 58ff.

ter's utterance is addressed and what happens in the background.

It is clear even from this cursory glance at the functions of stage directions that they determine in considerable measure what the actual utterances of a play (and the play as a whole) mean—that is, what is being said, expressed, conveyed, or implied. Furthermore, an interpretation which ignores, for example, the way in which according to the stage directions a certain line is to be spoken, say, mockingly, and instead takes it as spoken, say, imploringly, is clearly incorrect. The same is true of an interpretation which posits a context or background different from that specified by the stage directions and thus construes certain utterances (or the whole play) in a manner significantly different from what the stage directions indicate.[20]

[20] See on this point B. R. Tilghman, "The Literary Work of Art," pp. 148-51. Tilghman maintains that in "the case of many works of literature, poems, plays and novels, the context requisite for full understanding is as a matter of fact not always there. In a great many cases it was never there. Furthermore, there is no a priori guarantee that the author himself could supply all the answers; and if he offers answers there is no guarantee that we would be satisfied with them: we might be able to make better sense of the thing than he can. If a context must be supplied, there is always the possibility of supplying alternative contexts that will produce alternative interpretations" (p. 151). The problem is that if, as Tilghman appears to admit (pp. 149-50), stage directions and explanatory comments by the author provide the proper context for interpreting a work, in the sense that an interpretation that simply dismissed them would be wrong, then we cannot reject the context which an author would have provided (if, for example, he had not thought that it could be taken for granted) on the grounds that "we might be able to make better sense of the thing than he can." In interpreting a play, the question of "being satisfied" with stage directions does not arise unless there is some reason to think that they are incomplete or that the author made a mistake, by 'assigning' certain lines to one character which he intended to be spoken by another, for example. In other words, if the context in which the author 'sees' the work is the proper context (in the sense indicated) for interpreting it, then it does not matter whether the author has actually supplied it for us (in notes and the

Context and the Rules of the Language

Now since it is not any speaker or character but rather the author who provides the stage directions, their relevance is difficult to explain unless we assume that the *author's* intentions are relevant to what a character in the play means. More precisely, the way in which stage directions constrain our interpretation of a play shows that an interpretation of a character's utterance is at least in part a statement about what the author intended the character to mean.

Or consider explanatory comments or notes to literary works. They serve a function similar to that of stage directions. They might indicate the way certain words are used, what the author associates with a certain word, what connotations it has for him; they might identify allusions or literary or other sources of certain ideas, of details of the plot, and so on. Thus they provide or supplement the context in terms of which the work is intended to be understood. It is true, of course, that "the notes may look like unassimilated material lying loose beside the poem, necessary for the meaning of the verbal symbol, but not integrated, so that the symbol stands incomplete."[21] This may be important for an *evaluation* of the work, but as Wimsatt and Beardsley themselves indirectly acknowledge here, it has

---

like) as long as he does in fact 'see' the work in a certain way. Hence the fact that often we have to fill in the context of a work, since the author has not supplied it, has no bearing on the question whether there is one and only one correct interpretation. (The author may very well, for example, have been able to take it for granted that the audience of his time would understand the work in the context he intended.) For although it is always possible to provide "alternative contexts that will produce alternative interpretations," it does not follow that it would be *in principle* impossible to decide between such alternative interpretations on the basis of the context in which the author is likely to have 'seen' the work. The actual evidence for assuming one context rather than another may in many cases *in fact* be slim, but that does not imply that there *could not* in principle be any evidence that would decide the issue.

[21] Wimsatt and Beardsley, *The Verbal Icon*, p. 16. See also Wimsatt, "Genesis," pp. 211f.

Context and the Rules of the Language

no bearing on the relevance of such notes to what the work *means*.

In view of the relevance of stage directions, it would be very odd if an author's explanatory comments or notes were not relevant in the same way. For if stage directions are relevant because they tell us how the author wants his work to be performed and hence construed—and it would be difficult to account for their relevance otherwise—then it is hard to see that explanatory notes and comments should not be relevant as well and for the same reason. In any case, it would be very odd if an author's comments about how his work is to be construed would be relevant only in a play and only if they happened to be printed in a certain way and on the same pages or in the same volume as the text in question. The claim that an author's comments about his work in a diary or letter, for example, are in principle irrelevant rests on a distinction between 'internal' and 'external' evidence which, I have tried to show in the last chapter, is untenable.

Furthermore, regardless of whether we take an author's notes as part of the work, it is clear that we cannot construe them as spoken (or provided) by the *speaker* (or a character of the work). We can only take them as evidence of what the *author* intended the speaker to mean. Consider, for example, Yeats' note to his poem "Among School Children" to the effect that he has taken the phrase "honey of generation" from an essay of Porphyry's to refer to "the 'drug' that destroys the 'recollection' of pre-natal freedom."[22] This is evidence of what Yeats intended the speaker to mean; it may or may not conflict with what the speaker tells us in the poem, in much the same way as a note to an essay may or may not conflict with what the author has told us in the text. That is, the fact that an author's comments are relevant (insofar as they are evidence of his intention) does not mean, of course, that they are *conclusive* evidence

[22] Quoted by John Wain, "W. B. Yeats: 'Among School Children'," p. 198.

Context and the Rules of the Language

of what the passage in question or the speaker means. (This point and its implications will be taken up more fully in section 3 of the next chapter.)

One might argue that notes or comments by an author are relevant, not because they are evidence of the author's intention, but because they are likely to suggest the most coherent (or plausible) interpretation of a work (the interpretation which makes functional the greatest number of elements of the text).[23] Wimsatt and Beardsley's "true and objective way of criticism"[24] seems to be based on an assumption such as this. But, as I have tried to show in the last chapter, in appealing to coherence, or to the fact that under a certain interpretation we can account more adequately for the features of the text, we are implicitly appealing to the author's intention.

In cases in which the immediate linguistic context does not make clear what a certain word in, say, a poem means, critics commonly adduce parallel passages from similar works by the same author in support of their reading. Even Beardsley appears to admit that it is not a matter of indifference whether the parallel passages are by the same author.[25] Why should this matter? Clearly, passages parallel to a given passage p are relevant to determining what a cer-

[23] This may be the point of Wimsatt and Beardsley's statement that "whereas notes tend to seem to justify themselves as external indexes to the author's *intention*, yet they ought to be judged like any other parts of a composition (verbal arrangement special to a particular context), and when so judged their reality as parts of the poem, or their imaginative integration with the rest of the poem, may come into question" (*The Verbal Icon*, p. 16). See also Joseph Margolis, *The Language of Art and Art Criticism*, pp. 100ff., but cf. p. 97; Aiken, "The Aesthetic Relevance of Artists' Intentions," p. 751; Eaton, "Liars, Ranters, and Dramatic Speakers," pp. 60f.; Hungerland, "The Interpretation of Poetry," in Beardsley and Schueller (eds.), *Aesthetic Inquiry*, pp. 126f.; and Hospers, "Implied Truths in Literature," in Kennick (ed.), *Art and Philosophy*, p. 317.

[24] Wimsatt and Beardsley, *The Verbal Icon*, p. 18. "[T]he way of poetic analysis and exegesis . . . inquires whether it makes any sense if Eliot-Prufrock *is* thinking about Donne" (*ibid.*).

[25] *Aesthetics*, p. 158.

tain word (w) means in p because what the author meant (or had a speaker mean) by w in a passage similar in specified respects to p is evidence of what the author is likely to have meant, or intended the speaker to mean, by w in p.[26]

In the last chapter I argued among other things that statements about what the narrator or a character in a literary work means are statements about what the author intends the narrator or character to mean. Our brief survey here of typical kinds of evidence about what the narrator or a character in a work means has confirmed that conclusion. The distinction between speaker and author is important, however, for the following reason. Since we cannot assume that the speaker represents the author's beliefs (feelings, attitudes, concerns, and so on), we cannot attribute the speaker's beliefs to the author. Consequently, in contrast to the case in which we are dealing with an utterance of the author's in ordinary discourse, we cannot appeal to the author's beliefs in determining what the *speaker*'s beliefs (attitudes, feelings, concerns, and so on) are. But this does not imply that what the speaker means is not what the author has him mean and hence that evidence of the author's intention vis-à-vis a speaker is irrelevant to what he means.

---

[26] One might object here that the relevance of parallel passages can be explained without assuming that they are relevant *because* they are evidence of what the author meant. It could be argued that parallel passages are relevant, not because they are evidence of what the author meant, but because they are evidence of what the words in question mean in the language or culture. (See Wimsatt and Beardsley, *The Verbal Icon*, p. 11.) The problem with this objection is that it fails to account for the fact that a passage parallel to p in a work by the same author will always have considerably greater weight in determining what a word in p means than a parallel passage in a work by a different author. On the view that there is a logical connection between the meaning of a work and the author's intention (or between what the speaker means and what the author intends him to mean), it is easy to see why this should be so; but on the assumption that the author's intention is irrelevant to what his work or the speaker means, it is difficult to account for this. (See also the discussion of parallel passages below, Chapter VIII, section 5.)

4. CAN WE EXCLUDE AN INTERPRETATION ON THE BASIS OF THE RULES OF THE LANGUAGE?

I have been arguing that in interpreting an utterance in a literary work to mean m_1, we are implicitly saying that the author intended to convey m_1 (or intended the speaker to convey m_1). I have tried to support this claim by considering the kinds of arguments commonly given for construing a certain utterance of a sentence s to mean m_1, where s could, under the rules of the language, mean m_1 or m_2.

One is inclined to suppose that if the syntactic or semantic rules of a language do not allow a certain reading of some sentence in that language, then the sentence cannot have that meaning, regardless of the context in which it occurs or the intention of the speaker. (I am ignoring here symbolic or figurative interpretations, irony, parody, and cases of saying something by implication.) Thus one is inclined to suppose, for example, that the first sentence of Joyce's "The Boarding House"—"Mrs. Mooney was a butcher's daughter"—could not properly be construed as 'Mrs. Mooney butchered her daughter'. In the following I shall offer a few arguments in support of the claim that in excluding an interpretation ostensibly on the basis of the rules of the language, we are implicitly appealing to the author's likely intention, given his knowledge of the rules of the language.[27]

If a sentence could mean m_1, or m_2, then the claim that an utterance of the sentence in a particular context means m_1 is, I have argued, a claim about the author's intention. Hence the assumption that in the case of an utterance of an

[27] On the general program of explaining linguistic meaning in terms of speakers' intentions, see P. F. Strawson, "Meaning and Truth," pp. 170-89. For detailed accounts along those lines, see Grice, "Meaning," "Utterer's Meaning, Sentence-Meaning, and Word-Meaning," and "Utterer's Meaning and Intentions"; Searle, *Speech Acts*; Stephen Schiffer, *Meaning*; and Jonathan Bennett, *Linguistic Behavior*. But see also Noam Chomsky's critical discussion, *Reflections on Language*, pp. 55-77.

unambiguous sentence the author's intention is irrelevant to its meaning would appear to entail that there is a conceptual difference between the meaning of an utterance of an unambiguous sentence and the meaning of an utterance of an ambiguous sentence. We can state this point more explicitly as follows: Let s_1 be the sentence 'My cat licked your cat'; let s_2 be the sentence 'My cat won in the race against your cat'; and let m_1 be the proposition 'My cat beat (defeated) your cat'. Then the above assumption entails that in saying of a particular utterance of s_1 that it means m_1 and in saying of a particular utterance of s_2 that it means m_1, we are making a claim about the utterance of s_1 that is *different in kind* from the claim about the utterance of s_2. And this seems implausible. In any case, it would be more desirable, other things being equal, to have an account on which the two statements do not differ in kind.

Furthermore, the fact that in the case of an utterance of a sentence which has only one linguistically possible reading (m) the author (provided he is competent in the language) is very likely to have intended to convey m should further caution us against assuming that in such a case his intention is irrelevant. For it is possible that we will interpret the utterance of the sentence to mean m, not because the rules of the language allow only this reading, but because on the basis of the author's knowledge of those rules it is highly likely that he meant m.

Arnold Isenberg has related the following incident. A foreign colleague of his would sometimes come into their office and say " 'Please don't make trouble' " which he (Isenberg) "could easily interpret" as " 'Please, do not trouble yourself on my account.' "[28] The example illustrates the fact that ordinarily we do not, so to speak, strictly enforce the rules of the language. That is, we do not ordinarily take a man to have *said*, or his utterance to mean, what we know or believe he did not mean (on the basis of our knowledge

[28] Arnold Isenberg, "Some Problems of Interpretation," in Callaghan et al. (eds.), *Aesthetics and the Theory of Criticism*, p. 208.

about the speaker, his facial expressions, gestures, what else he says, and so on), even if the rules of the language do not allow the sentence he uttered to mean what he intended to convey.[29] Nor do we do so in the interpretation of literature.[30]

Our interpretation of a literary work frequently depends on our knowledge that the author associated certain beliefs, emotions, doctrines, and so forth with certain words. Many authors in fact write in a distinct idiolect, and this is certainly relevant to determining what their works mean.[31] It is a commonplace that literary and especially poetic texts frequently violate the syntactic and semantic rules of the language in which they are written. If we construed those works in terms of the standard linguistic rules (or if we did not take into consideration the beliefs, feelings, doctrines, and such which a particular author associates with certain words), many of them would make little sense and some none at all.

If, for example, a sentence in Joyce's *Finnegans Wake* does not make sense given the syntactic and semantic rules of English, then we would not simply dismiss it as nonsense. We would try to find an interpretation that does make sense,

[29] But see also the examples given by Paul Ziff to show that the meaning of an utterance cannot be defined in terms of the speaker's intentions ("On H. P. Grice's Account of Meaning," *Understanding Understanding*, pp. 78-89. For arguments against Ziff's claims, see T. E. Patton and D. W. Stampe, "The Rudiments of Meaning," pp. 2-16. Games, as Strawson and Cavell have pointed out, are an area where a man's intentions are largely irrelevant (P. F. Strawson, "Intention and Convention in Speech Acts," in Searle (ed.), *The Philosophy of Language*, p. 36; Stanley Cavell, "A Matter of Meaning It," p. 236.)

[30] See Michael Hancher's helpful discussion in "Three Kinds of Intention," pp. 844-46.

[31] See e.g. T. M. Gang's comments on Blake; "Intention," in Levich (ed.), *Aesthetics and the Philosophy of Criticism*, p. 390; see also Helen Gardner, *The Business of Criticism*, p. 52, and Manfred Bierwisch, "Poetik und Linguistik," in Žmegač (ed.), *Methoden der deutschen Literaturwissenschaft*, p. 298.

even though we have to assume that the sentence is constructed according to very unorthodox syntactic and semantic rules—that is, even though the interpretation which does make sense of the sentence is such that it is not, according to the linguistic rules of English, a possible reading of that sentence. What this consideration suggests is that in cases in which we rule out an interpretation on linguistic grounds, what we are really claiming is not simply that the rules of the language do not allow this interpretation, but rather that, given his knowledge of those rules, the author is not likely to have used the relevant words in the way the interpretation in question would require.

For unless we regard the text of a literary work as the record of someone's use of the words in question to say something, it would make no sense to attempt seriously to interpret it. If, for example, a parrot utters a syntactically or semantically deviant sentence, then the question of interpreting it, of making sense of the parrot's 'utterance', clearly could not arise.[32] And surely the reason is that the parrot cannot (properly speaking) be said to have *said* anything. Suppose the parrot utters the words 'Water is pouring down from the sky'; we could say that the words mean 'It is raining'. But could we say 'The parrot *said* that it is raining' or 'The parrot *said* that water is pouring down from the sky'?

It is difficult to escape the conclusion that we try to make sense of a syntactically or semantically deviant utterance in a literary work *because* we assume that someone meant something by it; and we choose an interpretation which makes sense of the passage in question over one which does not (or one which makes more sense over one which makes less sense) *because* the fact that a certain reading makes sense is evidence that that is what is meant. For if it were irrelevant that a reading which makes (optimum) sense of a passage is likely to correspond to what was meant—if, that is, it did not matter what someone meant

[32] See Searle, "What is a Speech Act?" in Searle (ed.), *The Philosophy of Language*, p. 40.

but only what his words mean—then it would be difficult to explain why the question of making sense of, say, a parrot's 'utterance' of a semantically or syntactically deviant sentence (or the question of interpreting physical marks produced on a rock by water erosion) *could not* arise.

One might object that this argument shows only that what matters is *whether* someone meant something by a word sequence he has produced, not *what* the person meant by it. But it is hard to see why it should matter *that* someone meant something by the words if it does not matter *what* he meant. If an interpretation of a work is not a statement about what someone meant, then why should it matter whether anyone meant anything by it? In other words, the reason why it matters whether someone meant something by his utterance of a word sequence appears to be that understanding that utterance involves recognizing what the speaker meant.

To see that in ruling out an interpretation of a work or passage on the basis of the rules of the language, we are implicitly appealing to the fact that the author is not likely to have intended the coresponding meaning, consider the following example.[33]

Suppose that in a novel we encounter the sentence

(s_1)   He barked his shin

Suppose further that in the context (c_1) in which the sentence occurs, it would make equally good sense if instead of s_1 the sentence

(s_2)   He made his shin bark

[33] It is adapted from an example of Ziff's ("What is Said," p. 717). By constructing a suitable context (see the passage quoted below), Ziff shows that the sentence 'He barked his shin' can, the linguistic rules of English notwithstanding, mean 'He made his shin bark'. The reason why Ziff's example as it stands is not quite sufficient for my purposes is that an appeal to the context of an utterance is not as obviously an appeal to the author's intention as an appeal to a parallel passage. For a similar (actual) case in music, see Kendall Walton, "Categories of Art," pp. 360-61.

Context and the Rules of the Language

(that is, 'He made it seem as though his shin barked') occurred. Now if a critic construed s_1 to mean the same as s_2 and not as 'He skinned his shin', one would be inclined to rule out that interpretation on syntactic grounds; that is, in s_1 'bark' is used transitively, and as such it would seem that it can only mean something like 'skin'.[34]

But suppose that in the same work, or in another work by the same author, the critic finds the following passage:

> He was a remarkable ventriloquist. First, he made it seem that the cat was barking. Then he made the parrot bark. Then he barked a monkey, and then a shoe, then his hand, and then he barked his shin.[35]

In this context (c_2) 'He barked his shin' (s_1) clearly means the same as (s_2) 'He made his shin bark' ('He made it seem as though his shin barked'). Surely, this would considerably weaken the force of the argument against the interpretation of s_1 (in c_1) as equivalent to s_2. That is, it would considerably weaken the claim that since the rules of the language do not allow s_2 as a possible reading of s_1, s_1 (in c_1) cannot mean the same as s_2. Surely, the fact that s_1 in c_2 means the same as s_2 would be evidence that s_1, in c_1, might very well mean the same as s_2.

The parallel may, of course, not be wholly persuasive; the original reading of s_1 may still be more plausible because in c_1 it might be more 'natural' to take s_1 as meaning 'He skinned his shin'. On the other hand, we could strengthen the case for the unorthodox reading by assuming, for example, that in the author's dialect 'bark' does not mean 'skin' and that he was in fact unfamiliar with this use of the word. We might make this assumption plausible by supposing that though 'bark' occurs fairly often elsewhere in his works, it is never used to mean 'skin' but frequently has the

---

[34] One might object that 'bark' can be used transitively in the sense of 'yap' as in 'He barked (out) the command'. But one could still, on semantic grounds, rule ous s_2 as an interpretation of s_1 because 'shin' is not an appropriate object of 'bark' used in the sense of 'yap'.

[35] From Ziff, "What is Said," p. 717.

sense of 'yap'. We might assume further that there are a number of passages in his work in which 'bark' is used in the same deviant way as in the passage quoted above and that in referring in his diary to a passage from an admired contemporary, in which 'bark' occurs in the sense of 'skin', he mistakenly takes it to be used in a different sense. Such assumptions would make it difficult, I think, to insist that s_1 in c_1 does not, let alone cannot, mean the same as s_2.

In any case, one cannot deny that the parallel passage would be *relevant*. And that is sufficient to show that in ostensibly appealing to the rules of the language in dismissing an interpretation, we are in fact appealing to *the author's likely use* of the words in question, given his knowledge of the rules of the language. For the fact that in another part of the work the words are clearly used in an unorthodox sense or stand in an unorthodox syntactic relation to one another but can nonetheless be quite 'naturally' construed in that way is not evidence that such use is in fact not linguistically deviant.[36] Futhermore, the fact that in the work of some *other* author the word sequence is used in a similar deviant way (as s_1 would be on the view that it means the same as s_2) would be considerably weaker evidence than a parallel passage in the same work or in another work by the same author.[37]

5. Conclusion

I have argued that the context of an utterance constitutes evidence of what the utterance means only insofar as it is evidence of what the author intended. Since the speaker or narrator of a literary work cannot be assumed to be identifiable with its author, the question arose what constraints the author's intention imposes on utterances of the speaker or narrator. The function of stage directions in a play, of

[36] See Noam Chomsky, "Degrees of Grammaticalness," p. 385.
[37] I should like to thank Quentin Skinner for helpful comments on an earlier version of this section.

Context and the Rules of the Language

explanatory comments or notes, and the use of parallel passages in support of claims about the meaning of a work confirm the view proposed (on independent grounds) in Chapter IV, namely, that what a speaker or the narrator in a literary work means is what the author intends him to mean. Finally, I have tried to show that even an appeal to the rules of the language in suport of a claim about the meaning of a work is an implicit appeal to the author's intention.

VI

Aesthetic Arguments and Other Aspects of Critical Practice

IN ADDITION to the appeal to the rules of the language, there are certain other aspects of critical discourse which may appear to be obviously resistant to an account of the meaning of a work in terms of the author's intention: that critics sometimes offer aesthetic considerations in support of an interpretation, that meanings and implications of which an author was not thinking can properly be attributed to a work, and that we sometimes reject an author's statement of what he meant by a particular work. In this chapter I should like to show that the intentionalist thesis can adequately account for these facts.

1. AESTHETIC ARGUMENTS

Critics sometimes adduce aesthetic considerations in support of an interpretation.[1] The form of such arguments is usually something like this. It is claimed that a particular interpretation is more likely to be correct than another interpretation of a given passage because on the former the passage is better, richer, more profound, and so on than on the latter. Inasmuch as a text's being better, richer, or more profound on one interpretation than on another does not make it more likely that the author intended the former rather than the latter, such arguments present a problem for my account. For it appears that we have here evidence

---

[1] I want to thank Professor Hans Eichner for his comments on an earlier version of Chapter IV which suggested the need for a discussion of aesthetic arguments in literary interpretation.

for a claim about the meaning of a work which is not evidence of what the author intended.[2]

There are at least two ways in which one could try to accommodate this without abandoning the essentials of the intentionalist thesis. (1) We might assume that the meaning of a literary work depends not only on the author's intention but also on aesthetic considerations. In order for a given interpretation to be correct, it might be sufficient (a) that the interpretation accord with the author's intention or (b) that (of all possible interpretations) it maximize the aesthetic value of the work. Hence where the two conditions do not coincide, such that what the author intended does not, of all possible readings, make the best work, we would have at least two equally 'correct' readings. (2) Or we might suppose that while the meaning of a work depends both on the author's intention and on aesthetic considerations, the two criteria are operative at different levels of interpretation. For instance, we might distinguish between statements about the meaning of the work as a whole and statements about the meaning of a particular passage or detail. We could then assume that while at higher levels of interpretation statements are more firmly tied to the author's intention, at lower levels, where the interpretation of the work as a whole is not significantly affected, aesthetic criteria are decisive.[3]

---

[2] For some discussion about the relevance of aesthetic arguments to an interpretation, see Eike von Savigny, *Argumentation in der Literaturwissenschaft*, pp. 42, 89; Skinner, "Hermeneutics and the Role of History," pp. 211, 223f., 226f.; Günther Grewendorf, *Argumentation und Interpretation*, pp. 75, 77ff.; Stevenson, "On the Reasons That Can Be Given for the Interpretation of a Poem," pp. 124, 125, 132; Hancher, "Three Kinds of Intention," p. 851; Marcia M. Eaton, "Good and Correct Interpretations of Literature," pp. 227-33; Graham Hough, "An Eighth Type of Ambiguity," in Newton-de Molina (ed.), *On Literary Intention*, pp. 232-33; Walton, "Categories of Art," pp. 357-63; Daniel O. Nathan, "Categories and Intentions," pp. 539-41; and Walter A. Davis, *The Act of Interpretation*, pp. 138, 145.

[3] This alternative is similar to the view proposed by Hough, "An

Aesthetic Arguments

Although both of these proposals are plausible, it may be worthwhile considering whether we can adequately account for the relevant facts without complicating the analysis by adding a separate condition involving aesthetic considerations. I shall suggest that we can. I shall argue that many, if not most, aesthetic arguments given in support of an interpretation depend on implicit assumptions about the author's intention, that those aesthetic arguments which run counter to the evidence of the author's intention will be unacceptable, and that aesthetic arguments which do not constitute an implicit appeal to intention are not decisive even in cases in which the evidence of the author's intention supports two or more readings to roughly the same degree.

1.1 Aesthetic Considerations as Evidence of Intention

Aesthetic arguments for an interpretation of a work are a diverse lot; they have little more in common than the name. To say that a particular work is aesthetically better on one reading than on another may be to say, for example, that the work is more coherent on this reading, that it accounts more adequately for the relevant features of the text. It may be to say that the favored reading makes the work richer or more complex, more profoundly human, more subtle, more balanced, or that on this reading the work has greater relevance for us. Similarly, to say that a work is aesthetically inferior under a certain interpretation may mean, for instance, that the interpretation in question makes the text incoherent, superficial, or trivial, sentimental, grotesque, too pessimistic, or mere propaganda; that under the reading in question the work lacks unity, balance, complexity, or humanity.

Now it would seem on the face of it that aesthetic arguments have no bearing on the question what the author is

---

Eighth Type of Ambiguity," in Newton-de Molina (ed.), *On Literary Intention*, pp. 228ff., 233ff.

likely to have meant. Hence they pose a problem for an intentionalist analysis of literary interpretation. If we examine aesthetic arguments a little more closely, however, it appears that many, if not most of them, do in fact depend on tacit assumptions about the author's beliefs and intentions. I have argued already, in Chapter IV, that appeals to coherence or complexity in support of an interpretation are implicit appeals to intention. Furthermore, if we look at the contexts in which other aesthetic arguments are advanced, we will see that they often rest on assumptions about the author as well.

Eike von Savigny has claimed that in view of the use of aesthetic arguments in interpretation, it is questionable whether the meaning of a passage depends on what the author meant by it.[4] Here is an example of an aesthetic argument Savigny cites in a different context: "(302, an aesthetic argument) If the third 'zum' of stanza 9 had a grammatical function different from that of the two preceding 'zum', then that would not be one of the bold syntactic constructions common in the late Hölderlin, but simply bad German."[5] As the argument stands, one evidently cannot tell whether or not its force depends on assumptions about the author. The context, however, leaves no doubt. The passage quoted continues: "(303, PB) but we cannot attribute bad German to Hölderlin; consequently one cannot say that (237, V) the passage 'denn darum rief ich . . . dich zum Fürsten des Festes' is to be understood as. . . ."[6] This

---

[4] Savigny, *Argumentation in der Literaturwissenschaft*, p. 42.

[5] "(302, ein ästhetisches Argument) Wenn das dritte 'zum' der Strophe 9 eine andere grammatische Funktion besäße als die beiden vorausgegangenen 'zum', so würde das keine der beim späten Hölderlin häufigen syntaktischen Kühnheiten, sondern einfach schlechtes Deutsch bedeuten. . . ." *Ibid.*, p. 54. See also p. 89.

[6] "(303, PB) schlechtes Deutsch aber kann man Hölderlin nicht zumuten; daher kann man nicht sagen, daß (237, V) die Stelle 'denn darum rief ich . . . dich zum Fürsten des Festes' so zu verstehen sei: ich rief dich zum Fürsten des Festes aus, ich rief dich als Fürsten des Festes." *Ibid.*, p. 54.

Aesthetic Arguments

makes clear that the aesthetic argument is not independent of facts about the author; provided the aesthetic claim is correct, its force rests wholly on the assumption that Hölderlin is not likely to have written bad German. This point is important not only for an assessment of the significance of aesthetic arguments for the logic of interpretation, but also for the conclusions that one might draw from an evaluation of the relative strength of such arguments as compared with psychological or biographical arguments,[7] for example.

E. D. Hirsch has interpreted the last stanza of William Blake's "London,"

> But most, thro' midnight streets I hear
> How the youthful Harlot's curse
> Blasts the new-born Infant's tear,
> And blights with plagues the Marriage hearse.

as follows:

> It is the marriage hearse that breeds youthful (and thus potentially innocent) harlots, by creating the necessity for prostitution. If there were no marriage, there would be no ungratified desires, and therefore no harlots. Thus it is ultimately the marriage hearse itself and not the youthful harlot which breeds the pestilence that blights the marriage hearse.[8]

W. K. Wimsatt contests Hirsch's interpretation on what appear to be aesthetic grounds:

> Mr. Hirsch gives us a good and learned instance of the new cryptography in Blake reading. "If there were no marriage, there would be no ungratified desires, and therefore no harlots." One thing, however, which perhaps he does not notice, or perhaps does not worry about, is that these ideas are silly. (Why wouldn't there

---

[7] See *ibid.*, pp. 61f., 89, and also Grewendorf, *Argumentation und Interpretation*, p. 75.

[8] E. D. Hirsch, *Innocence and Experience*, p. 265.

Aesthetic Arguments

be *many* ungratified desires, as many at least as there were losers in stag combats, or wooers rejected, or pursuers eluded, or matings frustrated? and *many* harlots? and *many* whoremasters?[9]

Again, when the argument is presented in this way, it appears to depend, not on assumptions about the author, but simply on the question whether or not the ideas which on Hirsch's interpretation the stanza expresses are indeed "silly," as Wimsatt maintains. That Wimsatt's argument does depend on the assumption that the poet did not share the beliefs in question comes out quite clearly if we look at the context of the argument. Thus Wimsatt adds:

> An admirer of *Blake the poet* might well be content to leave these ideas, if he could, on a back shelf *in the doctrinaire part of Blake's mind.*

And a little further he suggests:

> It will be worthwhile to look closely at the difference between the last stanza of the engraved poem "London" and the crude second line ["Remove away that marriage hearse"] of "An Ancient Proverb," *which stayed in the sketchbook.* Blake's struggle with "London" was in part a struggle *to make the last line of the last stanza viable....* Here, the angry conscience of William Blake the doctrinaire prophet and activist clashed violently with the more tactful and skillful conscience of William Blake the poet, master and servant of the English language. The latter conscience, apparently after a hard struggle, won and (perhaps without Blake's being fully aware of what happened—who knows?) saved him from engraving a poem with a lame, perhaps even silly and ruinous last line.[10]

It is significant that Wimsatt should find it necessary to sup-

[9] Wimsatt, "Genesis," pp. 217-18.
[10] *Ibid.*, p. 218 (italics added).

Aesthetic Arguments

port his interpretation by adducing biographical facts about Blake, by introducing, that is, "the more tactful and skillful conscience of William Blake the poet, master and servant of the English language" as opposed to "the angry conscience of William Blake the doctrinaire prophet and activist." What Wimsatt is in effect doing here is suggesting that while one part of Blake, "the doctrinaire prophet and activist," may have held the "silly" revolutionary beliefs about marriage, another part of him rejected them. It is also worth noting that Wimsatt quotes with approval this passage from Wicksteed:

> I do not doubt that he [Blake] *continued to accept* marriage at its face value even after his mind had learnt to entertain the revolutionary suggestions of the rationalistic and antinomian circles he came to mingle in.[11]

Furthermore, Wimsatt refers twice to the fact that "An Ancient Proverb" and, in particular, the second line ("Remove away that marriage hearse"), unlike the last stanza of "London," "remained in the sketchbook, where [it] deserved to remain."[12] Surely, the force of this repeated reminder, together with Wimsatt's contention that "Blake's struggle with 'London' was in part a struggle to make the last line of the last stanza viable," is to suggest that in the last line of "London" Blake did not mean what he meant in the second line of "An Ancient Proverb." That Wimsatt's interpretation of the last stanza (to the effect that prostitution, not the institution of marriage itself, is responsible for the "Marriage hearse") is tied to the claim that this is what Blake meant is confirmed further by his remark that "the more tactful and skillful conscience of William Blake the poet . . . won."

According to Wimsatt's explicit assumption (on page

[11] J. H. Wicksteed, *Blake's Innocence and Experience*, p. 215 (italics added). Quoted by Wimsatt, "Genesis," p. 219n.
[12] "Genesis," p. 216.

Aesthetic Arguments

215), this is a case in which the meaning of a poem does not coincide with the author's intention. Consequently, it is difficult to see why Wimsatt should attribute what he takes to be the beliefs which the poem expresses to another side of Blake, rather than say that in this case, at any rate, the beliefs expressed by the poem are simply not beliefs which Blake held or intended to convey.

Wimsatt has remarked in a note that he has introduced the evidence of the Rossetti manuscript (that the poet Blake won over the doctrinaire activist apparently only "after a hard struggle") "for the sake of dialogue with the biographically minded."[13] Hence it might be objected that I have distorted his argument. But, on my view, nothing of importance to Wimsatt's argument depends on the apparent struggle between the activist and the poet. What is important to his interpretation, however, is that there should have been another side of Blake which did not share the convictions of "the doctrinaire prophet and activist"; for if indeed there is no evidence for such an assumption, then, I think, his interpretation is implausible.

1.2 Aesthetic Considerations versus Evidence of Intention

Let us consider now two cases in which aesthetic arguments do not rest on assumptions about the author and in fact run counter to the evidence of his intention.

The following lines, entitled "Auszug der Schmarotzer" ("Exodus of the Parasites"), were written by the Nazi poet Heinrich Anacker and published in 1934:

> Nun werden sie über die Grenze gehn,
> die Schmarotzer, die sattsam bekannten,
> und werden im Ausland um Mitleid flehn,
> als die völlig schuldlos Verbannten . . .
>
> Wir aber raten den Völkern gut:
> Bleibt taub! Lasst sie winseln und hadern!

[13] *Ibid.*, p. 218n.

Aesthetic Arguments

Sie sogen uns vierzehn Jahr lang das Blut
verbrecherisch aus den Adern!

Und Glaubt unsern ehrlichen Worten ihr nicht,
und nehmt ihr sie auf in Scharen—
ihr werdet dies Motten- und Wanzengezücht
am eigenen Leibe erfahren!

Wir haben genug von der Peinigung—
Wir wollen endlich genesen!
Drum her mit der Frühjahrsreinigung,
und her mit dem eisernen Besen!

(Now they will cross the border,
the parasites whom we know all too well,
and abroad they'll be begging for pity,
saying they are innocent exiles. . .

But we offer (other) nations a piece of good
    advice:
Remain deaf! Let them whimper and squabble!
For fourteen long years they sucked at our blood
    like criminals.

And if you don't believe our honest words,
and you accept them in flocks,
then you will experience this breed of vermin on
    your own body!

We have been tormented enough—
We intend at last to restore our health!
So let's have a spring-cleaning,
bring the iron broom!)[14]

No very refined aesthetic sensibility is required to recognize that this is a very bad poem, though needless to say its aesthetic shortcomings are not its worst fault. Now from a purely linguistic point of view it would be possible to take the

---

[14] Quoted and translated by Foulkes, *The Search for Literary Meaning*, pp. 108-9. (The text of the poem can also be found in Helmut Lamprecht [ed.], *Deutschland, Deutschland: Politische Gedichte vom Vormärz bis zur Gegenwart*, p. 388.)

Aesthetic Arguments

lines, not as advocating mass extermination, the "final solution," but rather as an ironic attack on the attitude of the speaker and its consequences. Certainly, the poem would be much better construed in this way. If we can bracket out for a moment certain facts about the author, it would be easy enough to take phrases like "die Schmarotzer" ("the parasites"), "Laßt sie winseln..." ("let them whimper..."), "sie sogen uns ... das Blut verbrecherisch aus den Adern" ("they sucked at our blood like criminals"), "unsern ehrlichen Worten" ("our honest words"), "dies Motten- und Wanzengezücht" ("this breed of vermin"), "Wir haben genug..." ("We have been tormented enough...") as ironic comments on the speaker's revolting attitudes and beliefs or on the kind of man who could write such a poem. Suppose these lines were written by Brecht and published in a collection of his poems about the Third Reich. What more obvious 'internal' "signals" than these could one demand to warrant an ironic reading?[15]

Nevertheless, I take it that such a reading (given that the poem is in fact by Anacker) would be clearly incorrect and the corresponding aesthetic argument preposterous. Surely, it is facts about the author, what we take to be his intention, which prevent us from accepting an ironic interpretation of

---

[15] What this example shows among other things is that we cannot always tell on the basis of the text alone whether a certain passage is ironic or whether certain textual features constitute "signals" of irony. It brings out further that whether certain textual features constitute "signals" of irony is logically tied to what we take the author to mean. If in many cases it seems clear on the basis of textual features alone that certain lines are ironic, this is so only because in those cases the relevant textual features (in the context of various tacit assumptions about the author) constitute strong evidence that the lines are meant ironically.

For the view that it is not the author's intention, but objective "signals" which are decisive for irony, see Monroe Beardsley's remarks in a letter to Göran Hermerén, quoted in Hermerén, "Intention and Interpretation in Literary Criticism," p. 72; Michael Riffaterre, "Describing Poetic Structures," in Ehrmann (ed.), *Structuralism*, p. 211; and Hospers, "Implied Truths in Literature," in Kennick (ed.), *Art and Philosophy*, p. 320.

the poem. Consequently, in a conflict between an aesthetic argument and the author's probable intention, it appears to be the latter which is decisive.

Another example which could more plausibly be given to show that the intentionalist thesis requires qualification concerns the interpretation of the "dark Satanic mills" in the poem ("And did those feet in ancient time") which opens Blake's short epic *Milton*. John Wain has suggested that the phrase be construed as referring to the textile factories of the nineteenth century—even though Blake could not have been referring to them—on the grounds that this reading "is manifestly superior . . . to the hotch-potch of altars, legends and repression-symbols that Blake 'really meant.' "[16] Is this reading any more acceptable than an interpretation of Swift's "Modest Proposal" as a satire on the Vietnam war? Indeed, is it any more acceptable than an ironic reading of Anacker's "Exodus of the Parasites"? Could one defend such an interpretation in a critical study of *Milton*?

It is perhaps significant that this proposal is not made in the context of such a study but rather in a theoretical debate about the relevance of intention. It may be worth noting, too, that Northrop Frye—who, if we may trust his metacritical discussion of the matter, has no scruples about intention—[17] is apparently not tempted by an argument such as Wain's and construes the "dark Satanic mills" in accord with what Blake is likely to have meant.[18] In fact, Wain himself seems to be somewhat uneasy about his proposal; he never asserts quite unequivocally that since the interpretation of "dark Satanic mills" as referring to steam-driven textile factories is so much better than what Blake meant, that is how the phrase is properly construed. Rather, he claims

---

[16] John Wain, F. W. Bateson, W. W. Robson, " 'Intention' and Blake's *Jerusalem*," in Levich (ed.), *Aesthetics and the Philosophy of Criticism*, pp. 376-77.

[17] See Northrop Frye, *Fearful Symmetry*, pp. 427-28, and *Anatomy of Criticism*, pp. 86ff.

[18] Frye, *Fearful Symmetry*, p. 290.

Aesthetic Arguments

that the critic's task is "to create and maintain a balance between the 'original' and the 'developed' significances [of a work],"[19] though he does not say just what creating and maintaining such a balance involves.

Furthermore, instead of just saying that since the popular interpretation of the lines ("And did those feet in ancient time...") "is manifestly superior" to what Blake meant, the former is the (or a) proper reading of the poem, Wain suggests that we should *abstract* the poem from *Milton*:

> But does the "intentionalist" assert that no lyric can ever be abstracted from a longer work? If it is self-sufficient (that is, if it yields a paraphrasable meaning answering the normal demands of logic and syntax) and if—as here—it is manifestly superior to the rest of the work, what hinders?[20]

The passage brings out that in order to be able to construe the poem in the way proposed by Wain, we need to divorce it from its literary and historical context. What we get when we interpret the poem thus severed from its context is akin to an adaptation—or perhaps, depending on how far one is prepared to go, the creation of a new work, like Pierre Menard's *Don Quixote*. Wain's argument thus implicitly attests to the logical connection between the meaning of the poem and the author's intention; for if we construe it in the way he suggests, we will in effect, as Barbara Herrnstein Smith has called it, have "reauthored"[21] the text. Conse-

[19] Wain, "'Intention' and Blake's *Jerusalem*," in Levich (ed.), *Aesthetics and the Philosophy of Criticism*, p. 380.

[20] *Ibid.*, p. 376. On the question why we ought not to treat a work in this way, see George Watson's good discussion in "The Literary Past," in Newton-de Molina (ed.), *On Literary Intention*, pp. 158-73.

[21] *On the Margins of Discourse*, p. 150. See also pp. 49-50, 58, 64-69. Bateson makes the same point: "To substitute for the Old Testament hand-mills (a civic institution) the steam-driven mills of the nineteenth century (the children of the capitalist *entrepreneur*) is, in fact, to re-write Blake's poem." ("'Intention' and Blake's *Jerusalem*," in Levich [ed.], *Aesthetics and the Philosophy of Criticism*, pp. 377-78).

Aesthetic Arguments

quently, we would no longer be interpreting the poem written by Blake.[22]

1.3 *Are Aesthetic Considerations Ever Decisive?*

If aesthetic arguments are unacceptable when they conflict with the evidence of the author's intention, perhaps they are decisive when they do not—when, that is, such evidence supports the reading on which the work is aesthetically better to roughly the same degree as the reading or readings on which it is aesthetically inferior.

Graham Hough has given an example which bears on this question. He quotes these lines from Shelley:

> Out of the day and night
> A joy has taken flight;
> Fresh spring, and summer, and winter hoar,
> Move my faint heart with grief, but with delight
> No more—O, never more.

And he comments:

> In the third line there is both a logical and a metrical gap. There ought to be a fourth season and there ought to be a fifth foot. The manuscript is in such a mess (or so I am told, for I have not seen it) that there is no knowing whether Shelley did not finally intend to insert the missing member, and write 'Fresh spring, and summer, *autumn* and winter hoar'. The line as it stands, with autumn missing, has been praised again and again

---

[22] This provides support for Cioffi's explanation of the fact that the popular reading of the poem has not been affected by the knowledge that it does not correspond to what Blake meant: "I suggest that what we have in this case is something in the nature of a spontaneous adaptation of Blake's poem. It is unlike what we ordinarily consider an adaptation in not being conscious (initially at any rate) and not involving any physical change in the work adapted. . . . The combination of resolution and exaltation which characterises Blake's poem carries over into its adaptation; it functions like a melody." "Intention and Interpretation in Criticism," in Barrett [ed.], *Collected Papers on Aesthetics*, p. 169.)

for its rhythmical and suggestive beauty. And we can see why, or partly see why. The whole poem is about loss and absence; and in a key line something that is expected is absent and lost. And the question of intention is left entirely in abeyance. We simply do not know whether Shelley intended it or not.

After alluding to three other textual cruces,[23] Hough concludes:

> In all these cases scrupulous editors labour to recover the intention of the author, and readers of poetry remain steadfastly indifferent, and simply prefer what they believe to be the best reading. . . . [W]hat stands out from these textual confusions is how completely in the minds of most readers the question of authorial intention tends to disappear.[24]

It should be observed, however, that the evidence of intention does not in this case support both readings in equal measure. There may be evidence (based on the state of the manuscript) that Shelley was quite uncertain whether he should add "autumn" in line 3; but since he did not, and apparently did not feel compelled to change the line later, it would seem to be more likely that he intended the line as it stands. In addition, the claim that the poem is better if line 3 is taken the way it is, rather than being read as including "autumn," is an appeal to coherence: "The whole poem is about loss and absence; and in a key line something that is expected is absent and lost." The aesthetic argument is thus an implicit appeal to intention. Hence one cannot say that "the question of intention is left entirely in abeyance." Nor does this example show "how completely in the minds of most readers the question of authorial intention tends to disappear" or that regardless of what the author intended,

---

[23] For a discussion of two of these, see Cioffi, *ibid.*, pp. 176-77.
[24] Hough, "An Eighth Type of Ambiguity," in Newton-de Molina (ed.), *On Literary Intention*, pp. 232-33.

readers "simply prefer what they believe to be the best reading." That this is not true is confirmed by the examples I have given above, as well as by the following: although the reading "soiled fish of the sea" may, as some have claimed, be better than "coiled fish of the sea," the former, as Alastair Fowler has pointed out, "lost ground very quickly when the authenticity of the *White Jacket* retaining Melville's 'coiled fish of the sea' became obvious."[25]

Let us change Hough's example slightly so that it approximates more closely the case in which an aesthetically better reading is more or less equally likely to correspond to what the author intended as an aesthetically inferior reading. Suppose that Shelley had inserted the word "autumn" in line 3, but that it is not clear, because of the state of the manuscript, whether he had later crossed it out or whether there was just a stray mark partly through the word. Suppose further that as a result the poem is usually printed with both readings indicated. No doubt, some critics would still prefer Hough's reading; some would opt for the version which includes "autumn"; and yet others would want to leave the question undecided. Surely, one cannot say here that the aesthetic considerations are decisive, that they would rule out the other alternatives.

2. Intention and Awareness: Or How Much Can the Author Have Meant?

Critics frequently analyze texts in considerable detail. Empson's search for ambiguities is only one instance among many. Now in general it is unlikely that in the process of composition the author of a given work was thinking about all the meanings and implications which a critic might properly attribute to various textual details. This raises the following problem for the intentionalist thesis: How can

[25] Alastair Fowler, "Intention Floreat," p. 255. See also James Thorpe, "The Aesthetics of Textual Criticism," p. 465.

an author have intended to convey all these meanings or implications if he was not thinking about them while writing the work? I shall try to show that the intentionalist thesis can adequately account for the meanings or implications of the details of a work by arguing that appearances to the contrary rest on a mistaken view of what is involved in intending to convey something. As a concrete point of reference, I shall take specific interpretations by a critic who holds that the intentionalist thesis cannot account for the meanings and implications of textual details.

2.1 *Are the Meanings of Textual Details Unintended?*

In an important paper Graham Hough has made a number of acute observations concerning the difference between the main illocutionary act which an author performs in writing a poem and "the achieved meaning" which is far more complex and derives from the meanings, implications, and associations of the details.[26] Hough's position is roughly this. In order to understand a work, we must correctly identify the basic illocutionary act the author is performing and hence must ascertain what he intended to convey. But this is only the beginning of an interpretation. It tells us very little about the work. Its life lies in the details; their cumulative effect constitutes "the achieved meaning." Now many of the meanings, implications, and associations of the details which make up this "achieved meaning" are, according to Hough, typically unintended; therefore, understanding these details is not a matter of recognizing illocutionary acts.[27]

In support of these claims, Hough offers a reading of the following lines from a poem by Donne:

[26] Hough, "An Eighth Type of Ambiguity," in Newton-de Molina (ed.), *On Literary Intention*, pp. 222-41. The quoted phrase is from p. 228.
[27] *Ibid.*, pp. 229-30.

Aesthetic Arguments

> Goe, and catche a falling star
> Get with child a mandrake roote,
> Tell me, where all past yeares are,
> Or who cleft the Divels foot,
> Teach me to heare Mermaides singing,
> Or to keep off envies stinging,
>   And finde
>   What winde
> Serves to advance an honest minde.

Here is Hough's interpretation:

> We have a catalogue of impossibilities. The first is, 'Goe, and catche a falling star'—do something impossible, catch and possess an object of haunting beauty that is by nature evanescent and unseizable. The second 'Get with child a mandrake root'—an equally impossible enterprise, but now one that is sinister and dubious. A mandrake root looks like a human being but is not; to copulate with it would be against nature. It is soporific, aphrodisiac and a fertility charm. It is also perilous, for it is supposed to shriek on being pulled from the ground, and whoever hears the shriek will die. We are in the region of perverse and dangerous sexuality. 'Tell me where all past yeares are'— i.e. find out the secrets of time, memory and survival, satisfy the insatiate metaphysical curiosity. 'Or who cleft the Divels foot'—a trivial impossibility derived from popular superstition, and casting a backward gleam of contempt on the more serious and emotionally charged impossibilities that have preceded it. Yet not all magical and mythical beliefs are contemptible—'Teach me to heare Mermaides singing'; there are no mermaids, or they don't sing, but it would be delightful if there were. It would be delightful if there were, but the world as we know it is full of vain wishes, so teach me 'to keep off envies stinging'—equally impossible, for in such a

world we must long for what we have not. And then, if you can perform all these impossible feats you can perhaps perform the most impossible of all—'finde / What winde / Serves to advance an honest minde'. But you cannot do any of these things, so you cannot do that either. There is no way to advance an honest mind, just as there is no mermaid's song; and if there were it would only be a 'winde', which notoriously bloweth where it listeth, ungraspable and uncontrollable.[28]

Hough is clearly right in pointing out that Donne was probably not thinking of all the implications or associations in these lines or of their connections. It is very unlikely that Donne should have considered all of these before or while writing the stanza and then chosen these words and images because they suited his purpose. Poems are not usually written that way.

Does it follow, however, that understanding the details does not involve recognizing illocutionary acts, as Hough contends? He claims that his reading goes "beyond the identification of illocutionary acts."[29] But isn't Hough here identifying and elucidating illocutionary acts? Isn't Donne, on Hough's interpretation, "casting a backward gleam of contempt on the more serious and emotionally charged impossibilities that have preceded it [line 4]"? Isn't Donne, on Hough's interpretation, suggesting (in line 2) that "we are in the region of perverse and dangerous sexuality"? That "there are no mermaids, or they don't sing, but it would be delightful if there were" (in line 5)? That there "is no way to advance an honest mind, just as there is no mermaids' song; and if there were it would only be a 'winde', which notoriously bloweth where it listeth, ungraspable and uncontrollable" (lines 7-9)? Surely, these are all illocutionary acts which Donne is performing here.

Hough's whole interpretation is a series of comments

[28] *Ibid.*, pp. 228-29. [29] *Ibid.*, p. 228.

identifying and differentiating the speech acts Donne is performing in these lines. Consider, for example, the following sentences: "A mandrake root looks like a human being but is not; to copulate with it would be against nature. It is soporific, aphrodisiac and a fertility charm. It is also perilous, for it is supposed to shriek on being pulled from the ground, and whoever hears the shriek will die." What is the function of these remarks? How do they contribute to clarifying the meaning of line 2? They tell us something of what "mandrake root" meant, what associations it had for Donne and his contemporaries. They clarify the speech act Donne is performing here by giving us pertinent information about what Donne is suggesting by the line; thus Hough summarizes his discussion of line 2 with the comment "We are in the region of perverse and dangerous sexuality."

But if Donne is suggesting in line 2 that "we are in the region of perverse and dangerous sexuality", is it plausible to suppose that he did not *intend* to suggest this? No doubt, Donne was not thinking of all the associations Hough mentions, but surely they are the sort of thing Donne meant.[30] Hough's comments draw out, make explicit, what was in the back of Donne's mind, so to speak. The same is true of Hough's remarks about the other speech acts he identifies in the stanza.

It may be that "the achieved meaning" is "partly a matter of temperament—Donne's own diffused but everpresent energy and spirit" and "partly the ethos of a class and an age."[31] But it does not follow that in elucidating that achieved meaning we are not identifying and elaborating on specific illocutionary acts. Nor does it follow that the "achieved effect . . . of energy, curiosity, intellectual and emotional life, even if enclosed within a recognition of limits and frustrations,"[32] is not intentional.

[30] See Cavell, "A Matter of Meaning It," p. 236.
[31] Hough, "An Eighth Type of Ambiguity," in Newton-de Molina (ed.), *On Literary Intention*, p. 229.
[32] *Ibid.*

2.2 *Planning and Intending*

The problem with Hough's argument is that it is based on an erroneous conception of intention. Hough assimilates 'intending to convey something' or 'doing something intentionally' to such notions as 'planning to convey something', 'acting with due forethought', or 'carrying out a premeditated act'. Thus he rejects the view that Donne intended to suggest, for example, that "there are no mermaids, or they don't sing, but it would be delightful if there were" on the grounds that such considerations never "reached the level of conscious intention."[33] Hough believes that if the interpretation of poetry were a matter of recovering the author's intentions, we would have to assume that writing poetry is like working out "chess problems—moving a certain number of pieces that have fixed powers, *with due forethought.*" Instead, Hough compares it to "playing tennis—reacting to unpredictable situations with *unpremeditated* moves, which may be abortive but may achieve an aptness and accomplishment that is absolutely *unforseeable* until it happens."[34]

There are two related difficulties here. One is the idea that in order to have intended to do so-and-so (suggest that there are no mermaids, for example), the author must have been aware of doing so-and-so, must have been thinking about it, as or before he wrote the corresponding words; the second is the assumption that an intention is a separate event which precedes (or accompanies) the performance of a speech act. To see that 'intending to do so-and-so' or 'doing such-and-such intentionally' does not entail being aware of doing such-and-such or planning to do so-and-so, consider some ordinary actions. In order to walk, for example, I need to move my legs and raise my feet in certain ways. We rarely think of this when we walk; nor do we plan to do it, when we decide to go somewhere on foot. Yet

[33] *Ibid.*, p. 230.
[34] *Ibid.* (italics added in both quotes).

we do not on that account say that these actions are unintentional; we fully intend to do them when we walk.[35] The same is true of any number of other actions: shifting gears while driving, raising one's arm in signaling, chewing one's food while eating, and so on.

Furthermore, when we decide to speak to someone or to write something, we usually do not plan in advance precisely what we will say; rather, our specific intentions are formed in the process of formulating the sentences we use.[36] There is often no specific "forethought" at all. Moreover, just as Donne probably did not ponder the associations of "mandrake root" before he wrote the line and then choose the words because the associations suited him, so he may not have planned, before he wrote the poem, to satirize "the falsity and corruption of the world."[37] He may simply have sat down to write a poem about honesty and jotted down lines as they occurred to him. If they turned out to be the lines quoted above, it would be a mistake to say that Donne unintentionally satirized "the falsity and corruption of the world," since he did not have this aim in mind before he wrote the poem, though it would be correct to say that he did not *plan* to do this. As Searle has put it: "rather few of one's intentions are ever brought to consciousness as intentions. Speaking and writing are indeed conscious intentional activities, but the intentional aspect of illocutionary acts does not imply that there is a separate set of conscious states apart from simply writing and speaking."[38]

[35] See Cavell, "A Matter of Meaning It," pp. 234-35, and Alasdair C. MacIntyre, *The Unconscious*, pp. 52-53.

[36] See Searle, "Reiterating the Differences," p. 202.

[37] Hough, "An Eighth Type of Ambiguity," in Newton-de Molina (ed.), *On Literary Intention*, p. 227. See also in this connection Watson, "The Literary Past," *ibid.*, p. 170.

[38] Searle, "Reiterating the Differences," p. 202. See also Wittgenstein's example of a cat stalking a bird (*Philosophical Investigations*, § 647); and Close' lucid discussion of the identification of intentions with mental events, "*Don Quixote* and the 'Intentionalist Fallacy'," in Newton-de Molina (ed.), *On Literary Intention*, pp. 176-80. On the

Aesthetic Arguments

Hence although a poet usually does not plan out in advance the details of a poem, nor in writing it think about the various associations of a word or phrase, it does not follow that such details are unintentional or that he did not intend to suggest various things associated with the words or phrases in question. That the associations which can properly be regarded as part of the meaning of a certain phrase or image in a poem are linked to the author's intention is confirmed by the fact that what these associations are depends on what associations the word or image had for the poet's contemporaries and in other contemporaneous or earlier texts only insofar as the author can be expected to have shared those associations. Thus, in a dispute about the associations of a word in a particular poem, facts about the associations which the word has for the author are always stronger evidence than facts about the associations of the word in works by other authors of the same period. In addition, 'external' evidence of the author's knowledge and beliefs also imposes constraints on what associations of certain words or images can be admitted as part of the meaning of the text.

2.3 The Author's Attitudes and the Associations of the Text

Hough's comments on Pope's "Elegy to the Memory of an Unfortunate Lady" illustrate this point:

> How loved, how honoured once, avails thee not,
> To whom related, or by whom begot;
> A heap of dust is all remains of thee;
> 'Tis all thou art, and all the proud shall be.

Hough quotes Empson's remarks about this poem to the effect that if the suggested antithesis in line 2 is to be taken seriously, it must mean something like this:

---

relation between the meaning of a text and what the author planned to convey, see also Hancher, "Three Kinds of Intention," pp. 830-33, 835-38.

Aesthetic Arguments

... '[O]ne of her relations was grand but her father was humble', or the other way about; thus one could take *how* to mean 'whether much or little' (it could mean 'though you were so greatly'), and the last line to contrast her with the *proud* so as to imply that she is humble (it could unite her with the *proud*, and deduce the death of all of them from the death of one). This obscurity is part of the 'Gothic' atmosphere that Pope wanted....

Empson goes on to say that the obscure antithesis is used here in another way, however, namely,

... to convey the attitude of Pope to the subject. 'How simple, how irrelevant to the merits of the unfortunate lady, are such relationships; everybody has had both a relation and a father; how little can I admire the arrogance of great families on this point; how little, too, the snobbery of the reader, who is unlikely to belong to a great family; to how many people this subject would be extremely fruitful of antitheses; how little fruitful of antitheses it seems to an independent soul like mine.'[39]

Commenting on Empson's reading, Hough suggests that the implications which Empson mentions are probably there but are unintentional. Again, Hough's claim that the implications were not intended seems to be based on the assumption that when he wrote the poem Pope did not plan them or did not think them through, in the way Empson has laid them out. But as I have suggested, that is no reason to suppose that they are unintentional. Also, Hough's argument that it would be "incompatible with any view of poetry possible to Pope to admit these multiple and partly conflicting implications in a single passage"[40] is unconvinc-

[39] William Empson, *Seven Types of Ambiguity*, pp. 22-23; quoted by Hough, "An Eighth Type of Ambiguity," in Newton-de Molina (ed.), *On Literary Intention*, p. 234.
[40] Hough, *ibid.*, p. 235.

Aesthetic Arguments

ing if for no other reason than that poets' views about poetry are notoriously at variance with their actual practice. Empson, at any rate, seems to take Pope to have intended the ambiguity he sees in the poem: "This obscurity is part of the 'Gothic' atmosphere that Pope wanted." Empson also identifies the implications of "the false antithesis" in line 2 with speech acts which Pope is performing here ("'How simple, how irrelevant . . .'"). Is it possible to say, as Empson does, that here the false antithesis "is finding another use," however—namely, "to convey the attitude of Pope to the subject"—if Pope did not intend to convey this attitude?

Hough concedes that if these implications were "incompatible with Pope's known social and personal attitudes we should perhaps be asked to believe too much in admitting them."[41] It is significant that Hough should be reluctant to admit Empson's ambiguities if the implications were in conflict with Pope's known attitudes or beliefs; for then it would be unlikely that Pope intended to convey them. Thus Hough's reaction is just what one would expect on the view that to accept the ambiguities Empson detects is to assume, as he does, that they are intentional, that Pope meant to suggest the attitudes Empson attributes to him. It is difficult to see why it should matter that the implications of line 2 correspond, as Hough notes, "very accurately"[42] to Pope's attitudes if it were irrelevant whether or not Pope intended to convey them. If, as far as the details of a poem are concerned, it is a palimpsest, as Hough claims, "one text mounted upon another, layer upon layer of meaning,"[43] and if the meaning or implications of the details are therefore frequently not intended but simply "gifts of the language—possibilities of multiple meaning that are built into the lexicon and syntax"[44] of a given language—then how could facts about an author's beliefs or attitudes ever suffice to rule out certain implications of a particular detail?

[41] *Ibid.* [42] *Ibid.*
[43] *Ibid.*, p. 240. See also pp. 233, 235, 238; and Tzvetan Todorov, "How to Read?", pp. 238f., 244.
[44] Hough, *ibid.*, p. 223.

Aesthetic Arguments

2.4 Paradise Lost
and the Text-As-Palimpsest Thesis

There is no doubt that most literary texts, as Hough rightly emphasizes, reveal "unrecognized assumptions and beliefs."[45] But they do not become part of the meaning of the work unless their disclosure in the text cannot be plausibly explained except on the assumption that the author, without being aware of it, intended to convey them.

As an example of the presence of unrecognized or unacknowledged attitudes and assumptions in literary works, Hough cites *Paradise Lost*. The interpretation according to which Milton was of the Devil's party without knowing it is well known and widely accepted, even though it "contradicts the expressed intentions of the author."[46] This illustrates, Hough contends, the nature of a literary text as a palimpsest. Its meaning always transcends and sometimes conflicts with what the author meant; it does so in virtue of "the presence in a literary text of earlier texts, some chosen by the author, some forced upon him by his culture, but always bringing with them consequences that go beyond his intention. . . ."[47] In support of this claim Hough quotes the following lines:

> Others more mild,
> Retreated in a silent valley, sing
> With notes angelical to many a harp
> Their own heroic deeds and hapless fall. . . .
>
> In discourse more sweet
> (For eloquence the soul, song charms the sense,)
> Others apart sat on a hill retir'd,
> In thoughts more elevate, and reason'd high
> Of providence, foreknowledge, will, and fate.[48]

Hough maintains that Milton did not intend to portray the fallen angels in so positive a light as they are presented here

---

[45] *Ibid.*, p. 235. [46] *Ibid.*, p. 236. [47] *Ibid.*, p. 238.
[48] *Paradise Lost* II, 11. 546-60; quoted by Hough, *ibid.*, p. 237.

Aesthetic Arguments

and elsewhere, that he did not intend to let so much "courage, nobility, and pathos [fall] to the defeated and the erring innocents."[49] How plausible is it to suppose that in writing the above lines Milton did not intend to convey that some of the fallen angels "sing/ With notes angelical . . . ," that their deeds were "heroic," their fall "hapless," that others sat "In discourse more sweet . . . In thoughts more elevate, and reason'd high/ Of providence . . ."? Barring his having been dazed, drugged, or intoxicated, how could Milton in writing these lines *not* have intended to express "a tender and elevated respect for these occupations"?[50] The same is true *mutatis mutandis* of the other passages which could be cited in support of the claim that "most of the courage, nobility, and pathos falls to the defeated and the erring innocents, most of the cruelty, implacability and deceit to the divine omnipotence."[51]

Surely, what we have here is not a clash between Milton's intention and the meanings which these lines have because they are derived from, or recall, earlier texts visible underneath them, as the text-as-palimpsest thesis has it. Surely, what clashes in *Paradise Lost* are two conflicting intentions. Milton clearly means to depict the society in hell in very positive terms. But at the same time he has another intention, in conflict with such a portrayal, which does not allow him to value the fallen angels so highly, and hence he "dutifully" undercuts the description of them "in the interests of his main design."[52] To suppose that "the details" are therefore unintentional is again to confuse intention with planning, premeditation, or due forethought. What makes the humanistic reading of *Paradise Lost* so plausible is not the presence, underneath the text, of "the scarcely erased lines"[53] of earlier texts—many of the phrases, descriptions, and stories which occur in Milton's epic expressing a humanistic worldview in those other texts—but rather their being the intentional expression of a "Christian human-

[49] *Ibid.*, p. 239. [50] *Ibid.*, p. 237. [51] *Ibid.*, p. 239.
[52] *Ibid.*, p. 237. [53] *Ibid.*, p. 238.

ism to which Milton with the better part of his mind aspired."[54]

Our problem has been how an author could have intended to convey the various meanings and implications of the details of his text even though (a) he could not have been thinking of all of them and (b) they may conflict with his larger design. I have tried to show that this problem arises from the assumption that what is intended or intentional is planned out in advance, premeditated, or done with due forethought. Armed with this notion of intention, one can readily show that much of the meaning of a work cannot have been intended. I have argued that this conception of intention is false and that once it is abandoned the problem dissolves.

3. The Rejection of an Author's Statement about His Intention

When we are confronted with a passage which we can easily construe without assuming that any of the sentences have been constructed according to very unorthodox syntactic or semantic rules, we are inclined to think that we would interpret the passage in that way regardless of what the author might say he meant. It is this kind of consideration which in large measure accounts for the temptation to suppose that it does not matter what an author means, that his intention stands in no logical relation to the meaning of his text. It is perhaps easy to overlook that what we are rejecting in this kind of case is not, or not necessarily, the author's intention, but rather a *statement* of his intention.[55]

[54] *Ibid.*, p. 239.
[55] See Close, "*Don Quixote* and the 'Intentionalist Fallacy'," in Newton-de Molina (ed.), *On Literary Intention*, p. 181: "declarations of intention . . . are subject to exactly the same checks as those by which we judge intentions in the absence of the author's disclosures; and because they are thus checkable we may occasionally wish to reject them." See also John Casey, *The Language of Criticism*, p. 149 and F. E. Sparshott, *The Concept of Criticism*, pp. 165-75.

Aesthetic Arguments

And what an author states he means or meant is not necessarily what he does or did mean.[56] A poet may, for example, fail to remember correctly what he meant, or he may for various reasons not be able or willing to admit his intention.

I have argued in the last two chapters that in appealing to coherence, to the context, or even to the rules of the language, we are in fact appealing to the author's intention. What I should like to suggest, then, is this: When we reject an author's statement about his intention and appeal in support of our interpretation to, say, the context, coherence, or what makes the most sense, we are giving preference to what we regard in this instance as better evidence of the author's intention than his explicit statement.[57]

A case in point is Beardsley's discussion of A. E. Housman's poem "1887." In an angry response to Frank Harris' interpretation of the poem as a sarcastic attack on church and state, Housman affirmed that he sincerely meant what he wrote and denied any irony or sarcasm.[58] Now Beardsley argues that Housman's (statement of his) intention does not impose any constraints on our interpretation of the poem, since its meaning cannot be identified with what the poet meant. He goes on to say:

> Of course, we must admit that in many cases an author may be a good reader of his own poem, and he may help us to see things in it that we have overlooked. But at the same time, he is not necessarily the best reader of his poem, and indeed he misconstrues it when, as perhaps in Housman's case, *his unconscious guides his pen more than his consciousness can admit.*[59]

[56] See Georg Henrik von Wright, *Explanation and Understanding*, pp. 112, 113, 197, and also Anscombe, *Intention*, pp. 41-45.

[57] See Cioffi, "Intention and Interpretation in Criticism," in Barrett (ed.), *Collected Papers on Aesthetics*, pp. 173-74.

[58] See Frank Harris, *Latest Contemporary Portraits*, p. 280.

[59] *Aesthetics*, p. 26 (italics added). For some arguments that unconscious intention is logically possible, see D. W. Hamlyn, "Unconscious Intentions," pp. 12-22, and MacIntyre, *The Unconscious*, Chs. 3 and 4.

Beardsley's point brings out very clearly our implicit notion of the meaning of a poem. How we interpret the poem depends logically on what we take the poet to mean. Thus when we reject a poet's statement of his intention, we are taking the poem to be better evidence of his intention, and we will say that he is mistaken about, or cannot admit, his intention.

Wimsatt's comments on the same poem provide a similar example:

> Mr. Beardsley has cited the nearly parallel instance of A. E. Housman's angry attempt to deny the irony at expense of state and church manifest in his poem for Queen Victoria's fiftieth anniversary. "Get you the sons your fathers got, And God will save the Queen." Here a statement made in retrospect and under provocation, a kind of profession of loyalty to a sovereign, stands in sharp contradiction not only to the cunning details of the poem in question but to the well-known skeptical and cynical cast of the poet's canon.[60]

Wimsatt clearly is not showing that Housman's intention is irrelevant; rather, he is casting doubt on the reliability of Housman's statement about his intention. Thus he speaks of "Housman's *angry attempt* to deny the irony . . . a statement *made in retrospect* and *under provocation,* a kind of *profession of loyalty* to a sovereign. . . ." In other words, Wimsatt is offering reasons why Housman is not likely to have in fact meant by the poem what (in retrospect) he said he meant.

Furthermore, in support of his own interpretation Wimsatt appeals not just to the text, but also to the "well-known skeptical and cynical cast of the poet's canon." If Housman's intention were irrelevant to what the poem means, then neither the question whether Housman's statement about his intention is likely to be correct nor the question what views Housman held or expressed in other works

[60] Wimsatt, "Genesis," p. 214.

Aesthetic Arguments

would have any bearing on what the poem means. What Wimsatt is doing, then, is taking the poem itself (or certain features of the text), in conjunction with Housman's typical views and attitudes, to be better evidence of Housman's intention than his statement.[61]

4. Can an Author Make His Text Mean Anything He Likes?

One of the main objections that has been raised against the thesis I am defending is the claim that if it were correct, an author could "just by fiat"[62] or "by his own say-so"[63] make his text mean whatever he likes. If, for example, Thomas Hardy

> (in a document just discovered) were to tell us that what he meant to convey in his novels is that humanity is nearing perfection, then this is implied in the novels, even though the novels seem to contradict such an assertion utterly at every point. If the poet says sincerely that what he meant to say in the poem is that reality is circular (and artists have said stranger things than this about their work), then this proposition is what is implied in the poem; and if the poet changes his mind and says that what he meant to convey is that blue is seven, then this (if it can be called a proposition at all) is implied.[64]

As I have already suggested, however, from the fact that a man asserts that he intended to convey m, it does not follow that he intended to convey m. Consequently, it does not follow from the thesis that the meaning of a work is determined by the author's intention, that an author can make his

---

[61] See also Chapter III, note 21.
[62] Beardsley, *Aesthetics*, p. 26.
[63] Isenberg, "Some Problems of Interpretation," in Callaghan et al. (eds.), *Aesthetics and the Theory of Criticism*, p. 209.
[64] Hospers, "Implied Truths in Literature," in Kennick (ed.), *Art and Philosophy*, pp. 313-14.

Aesthetic Arguments

work mean anything he likes simply by asserting that it means so-and-so.

Furthermore, the objection seems to be based on a mistaken notion of intention. It seems to imply that a person could, regardless of what he is doing, determine his intention by saying appropriate words to himself. Accordingly, it would seem that a person who (knowingly) replenished the water supply of a house with poisoned water could determine his intention by saying to himself: " 'What I *mean* to be doing is earning my living, and not poisoning the household'; or 'What I *mean* to be doing is helping those good men into power; I withdraw my intention from the act of poisoning the household, which I prefer to think goes on without my intention being in it'."[65] But obviously one cannot determine one's intention in this way.

An intention, as Wittgenstein has put it, "is embedded in its situation, in human customs and institutions."[66] It is partly for this reason that we can test (at least within limits) the truthfulness of an agent's statement of his intention. In order, for example, for the man who replenishes the water supply of a house with poisoned water to be able to claim (with any plausibility) that he is only doing his usual job, that it is not his intention to poison the inhabitants, it is clearly necessary that replenishing the water supply is in fact his usual job.[67] Similarly, as Wittgenstein remarks, I cannot "say 'bububu' and mean 'If it doesn't rain, I shall go for a walk'."[68] For it is only in a language that one can mean

---

[65] Anscombe, *Intention*, p. 42.

[66] Wittgenstein, *Philosophical Investigations*, § 337. See also §§ 592, 641-48, and p. 217; David S. Shwayder, *The Stratification of Behavior*, p. 192; Anscombe, *Intention*, pp. 41-45, 47-49; and von Wright, *Explanation and Understanding*, pp. 114-15. But cf. also Stuart Hampshire, "On Referring and Intending," pp. 129-42.

[67] For a more detailed discussion, see Anscombe, *Intention*, pp. 45f., and Melden, *Free Action*, pp. 100f.

[68] Wittgenstein, *Philosophical Investigations*, p. 18. See also § 510, and Stuart Hampshire, *Thought and Action*, pp. 136ff.

Aesthetic Arguments

something by certain sounds or marks. But this need not be the common language of a community. I may have an idiolect in which 'bububu' can be used to mean 'If it doesn't rain, I shall go for a walk'.[69] (See, for instance, the example given in section 4 of the last chapter.) I may even have a private language in the sense that as a matter of fact only I understand it, although others can with a little effort come to understand it as well.[70] What perhaps I cannot have, and what Wittgenstein was at some pains to show to be impossible, is a private language in the sense that only I *could* understand it.[71]

In his arguments against the intentionalist thesis, Beardsley sets in sharp contrast "the evidence of the poem itself" and "what the author intended," and he seems to equate the latter with what the author says he means.[72] Similarly, Hospers insists on a connection—which he assumes to be lacking on the intentionalist thesis—between what a work means or implies and "the words and sentences that are

[69] See Wittgenstein, *Philosophical Investigations*, §§ 160 and 508; Grice, "Utterer's Meaning, Sentence-Meaning, and Word-Meaning," in Searle (ed.), *Philosophy of Language*, p. 60; and Shwayder, *The Stratification of Behavior*, pp. 290f.

[70] See e.g. A. J. Ayer, "Can There Be a Private Language?" in Pitcher (ed.), *Wittgenstein*, pp. 251f.; and R. Rhees, "Can There Be a Private Language?," *ibid.*, p. 274.

[71] *Philosophical Investigations*, §§ 243, 256. See also e.g. Norman Malcolm, "Wittgenstein's *Philosophical Investigations*," in Pitcher (ed.), *Wittgenstein*, pp. 66ff., 70; and Alan Donagan, "Wittgenstein on Sensations," *ibid.*, pp. 338ff.

[72] Beardsley, *Aesthetics*, p. 26. See also p. 19, where Beardsley speaks of the need to distinguish "between the aesthetic object and the intention in the mind of its creator." See also Francis Noel Lees, "The Keys Are at the Palace," pp. 146f. Stegmüller has rightly emphasized that we cannot sharply distinguish between what a text means (or even how it is to be described) and facts or assumptions about its background, between 'what is in a text' and what the author intended. ("Der sogenannte Zirkel des Verstehens," pp. 42-44.) See also Cioffi, "Intention and Interpretation in Criticism," in Barrett (ed.), *Collected Papers on Aesthetics*, pp. 171f.

Aesthetic Arguments

actually to be found in the work."[73] And Isenberg, in the same vein, asks:

> What sort of context could compel us to interpret Thoreau as advocating absolute government? What kind or amount of external evidence would force us to read "that government is best which governs least" as meaning "that government is best which governs most"? Suppose we found Thoreau, elsewhere in his life or in his writing, admiring contemporaneous absolute monarchies or dictatorships. We would say that he had changed his mind, that he contradicted himself, or that he was ambivalent in his political attitudes. We would say that there were "conflicting strains of thought" in his work. We would say that he was speaking of different things (as Marxists speak of a *provisional* dictatorship and an *eventual* anarchy). We would say any of these things before conceding that the right interpretation of the passage in the text was the reverse of the apparent one.[74]

Isenberg is clearly right about what we would say in such a case. But it would be a mistake to infer from this that our interpretation of the passage is not linked to Thoreau's intention, for two reasons. (1) I have argued in section 4 of the last chapter that there *could* be external evidence which would make an interpretation of an utterance in a work very likely to be correct, even though the sentence used could not under the rules of the language bear that reading. Hence in excluding an interpretation ostensibly on the basis of the rules of the language, we are tacitly appealing to the author's intention.[75] (2) What makes it tempting to infer from

---

[73] Hospers, "Implied Truths in Literature," in Kennick (ed.), *Art and Philosophy*, p. 313.

[74] Isenberg, "Some Problems of Interpretation," in Callaghan et al. (eds.), *Aesthetics and the Theory of Criticism*, p. 208.

[75] If this is more difficult to see in Isenberg's example, it is because it is more difficult to make the assumption plausible that Thoreau

the kind of case illustrated by Isenberg's example that there is no logical connection between the author's intention and the meaning of a work is the erroneous identification of evidence of intention with external evidence. But as I have tried to show in Chapter IV, the text constitutes evidence for or against an interpretation if and only if it is evidence of the author's intention.

Thus given that Thoreau was a competent speaker of the language and did not in speaking about matters of government elsewhere use "least" when he meant "most," then the fact that he wrote "that government is best which governs least" together with other textual features is strong evidence that he meant what the passage has been taken to mean. By comparison, the hypothetical fact that Thoreau "elsewhere in his life or in his writing" admired "contemporaneous absolute monarchies or dictatorships" is relatively weak evidence that he meant "most" by the word "least" in the passage in question.

On the other hand, if it were clear that in making similar statements elsewhere, Thoreau always spoke ironically, I can imagine that we might not be quite as confident about our interpretation of the passage. Furthermore, if we construed the passage in the usual way, even though in other works and elsewhere in his life Thoreau expressed admiration and approval of contemporaneous absolute monarchies or dictatorships, then, as Isenberg notes, "we would say that he had changed his mind, that he had contradicted himself, or that he was ambivalent in his political attitudes. . . ." That we would say this shows that we then take the fact that Thoreau wrote "least," not "most," as well as other textual features to be better evidence of his intention than the (hypothetical) views he expressed elsewhere.

My claim that a text may be better evidence of a man's intention than his explicit statement might seem to make

---

meant "that government is best which governs most" in the passage in question. See Patton and Stampe, "The Rudiments of Meaning," pp. 11f.

my defense of the intentionalist thesis circular; for if the only evidence of what a man meant is what his text means, then the thesis that the meaning of a text is determined by the author's intention is trivially true. But this is not so. In the first place, the text at hand is not the only evidence of the author's intention. Secondly, other evidence that we might have of his intention, such as his beliefs, parallel passages in other works by him, an explicit statement, and so on, is not evidence of his intention only *by way of* being evidence of what the text means. Finally, when we do take the text to be better evidence of the author's intention, we do not appeal to the *meaning* of the text, but to certain *textual features* which, I have argued in Chapter IV, constitute evidence for the meaning of the text if and only if they are evidence of the author's intention.[76]

5. Conclusion

I have argued in the last four chapters that the meaning of a literary work logically depends on the author's intention; it follows that understanding a literary work necessarily involves recognizing what the author intended to convey. I have defended this thesis by examining the kinds of considerations and evidence commonly adduced in support of statements about the meaning of a work as well as the kinds of things which are taken to follow from such statements. In particular, I have tried to show:

(1) A speaker's or an author's statement about his intention constitutes at least *prima facie* evidence for the meaning of an utterance of a word sequence which has more than one linguistically possible reading.

(2) An interpretation which construes certain words in a literary work as an allusion or as ironic logically implies a corresponding claim about the author's intention.

[76] Ellis seems to have overlooked this point; see *The Theory of Literary Criticism*, p. 121.

Aesthetic Arguments

(3) An interpretation cannot account for the features of a text unless it is a statement about the author's intention. In other words, textual features can constitute evidence for an interpretation if and only if they are evidence of the author's intention. Thus textual features are evidence of what a work means in virtue of being evidence of what the author meant. The appeal to the text therefore turns out to be an implicit appeal to the author's intention. It follows that to appeal to coherence, complexity, or any other criterion of this kind in support of an interpretation is to appeal to the author's intention. For to say

> 'the text, or a certain part of the text, supports this interpretation rather than that since it is more coherent (or more complex, or anything else) on this interpretation than on that'

or to say (and this comes to the same thing)

> 'the text supports this interpretation rather than that since the former can account for the relevant features of the text more adequately than the latter'

is to appeal to evidence of the author's intention. It follows further that insofar as facts about the author's beliefs, values, concerns, and so on, as well as other external information, is evidence of what the author meant, it will be no less relevant to what the work means than textual features.

(4) The linguistic or nonlinguistic context is relevant to determining the meaning of an utterance in ordinary discourse or in a literary work only insofar as it constitutes evidence of what the author meant by the utterance.

(5) The distinction between the speaker or narrator and the author of a literary work does not support the claim that the meaning of a literary work is not what the author intended. For what the speaker means is what the author has him mean, that is, what the author intends the speaker to mean.

(6) Even an appeal to the rules of the language, in support of the claim that a particular interpretation is correct or incorrect, is an implicit appeal to the author's likely use of the words in question.

(7) That critics sometimes cite aesthetic considerations in support of an interpretation can be accommodated by the intentionalist thesis. For the force of aesthetic considerations frequently depends on assumptions about the author such that they are in fact evidence of his intention; in cases in which aesthetic considerations conflict with the evidence of the author's intention, they will be unacceptable; and aesthetic considerations which do not constitute evidence of the author's intention are not decisive even when the evidence of intention supports two or more interpretations to roughly the same degree.

(8) The intentionalist thesis can adequately account for the meanings and implications of a work's detail even though it is unlikely that the author was thinking of all or even many of them when he wrote the work. The claim that those meanings and implications are largely unintended rests on the mistaken assimilation of intending to planning.

(9) That we sometimes disregard an author's statement about his intention does not show that there is no logical connection between the meaning of a literary work and the author's intention. For when we reject an author's statement about his intention, we take certain features of the text (and possibly the author's other works, his general beliefs, and so on) to be better evidence of his intention than his explicit statement. Similarly, when we interpret a work contrary to beliefs or concerns which the author has expressed elsewhere, we take certain textual features, in conjunction with other facts about the author, to be better evidence of what he meant in the work in question.

It appears, then, that all the various kinds of evidence for the meaning of a literary work have one thing in common: they are evidence of the author's intention; and they are

Aesthetic Arguments

evidence of what a work means *because* they are evidence of what the author meant.

But although the anti-intentionalist thesis is false, behind it lies an important practical insight, namely, that by relying heavily on the historical and especially biographical background, one is easily led to overestimate the importance of the various events in an author's life to the understanding of his literary works. Wimsatt and Beardsley, among others, have emphasized the impersonal nature of a poem[77]; it is addressed to a wider, public audience and can thus be expected to be intelligible in terms of public conventions of usage and general human experiences. In other words, in insisting on an appeal to the text in confirming or disconfirming an interpretation, what the defenders of the anti-intentionalist thesis are doing is giving preference to one kind of evidence of intention over another; and what in effect they show is that sometimes textual features may be better evidence of what an author means than his explicit statement about his intention or facts about his life or beliefs.[78]

[77] Wimsatt, "Genesis," p. 194; Beardsley, *Aesthetics*, pp. 239f.; and Wimsatt and Beardsley, *The Verbal Icon*, pp. 5, 12. See also Robert Marsh, "Historical Interpretation and the History of Criticism," pp. 9ff.; Empson, *Seven Types of Ambiguity*, p. xv; and Culler, *Structuralist Poetics*, pp. 164-70.

[78] See e.g. Wellek and Warren, *Theory of Literature*, pp. 77ff., and Ellis, *The Theory of Literary Criticism*, pp. 123-28.

Ellis argues that "what [an intentionalist] does is to simplify what was made too complex for him to tolerate; he treats careful control both of connotation and denotation as error. He tries to seek out clear meanings that are delimited, (to use reference theory terminology) to reduce complex connotation to simple denotation, to remove ambiguity, and to supply simple answers from the poet's biography instead of from the more complex literary text" (p. 124).

It is interesting in this connection to note how Ellis justifies his claim that the intentionalist simplifies "what was made too complex for him to tolerate." First, he attributes the "unwillingness to let a literary work remain at the degree of openness that it actually has" to "an insecurity on the part of the critic when faced with a complex and

Although in general it is more probable that an author will use a word in the way he has typically used it in other works than in the way someone else uses it or the way it is generally used in the speech community, there are obviously exceptions. Similarly, an author may in a particular work express ideas or beliefs very different from, or even in conflict with, those he has expressed in most of his other works or in his private life. Although such considerations are certainly of importance in evaluating the *weight* of different kinds of evidence in a particular case, they have no bearing on the question whether there is a logical connection between what a work means and what the author meant.

---

challenging text" (p. 124). He goes on to say: "If we assume that poets are men who have a gift for using language to produce structures of words that will say what *they want to say*, have implications that *they wish to imply*, and leave carefully open what *they want to leave open*—in short, if we assume that the inexplicitness is *as controlled* as the explicitness, and that ambiguity or allusiveness is something that *the poet works with for his purposes*, then there is no temptation to proceed as an intentionalist does" (p. 124, italics added). In other words, Ellis justifies the claim that a critic ought not "to supply simple answers from the poet's biography" (*ibid.*) on the grounds that this is not what the poet meant—that is, on the grounds that the poet *did not intend* to convey something about his own personal life.

VII

Life, Literature, and the Implied Author
Can (Fictional) Literary Works Make Truth-Claims?

1. THE ISSUE

MANY LITERARY WORKS are commonly said to express, imply, suggest, or convey certain propositions: that man is a helpless victim of natural and social forces, for example, that he can achieve even a limited autonomy only by destroying himself, that man is capable of infinite self-perfection if he will only trust his innate sense of right and wrong, that modern man is fundamentally corrupted by his materialism and the increasing development of technology, that these have reduced him to the status of a beast or a cog in a machine, that man's only hope to regain his humanity is utterly to reject modern society, that "the essential barrier between man and his divine inheritance is the belief in a nonhuman God founded on the fallen vision of an objective nature,"[1] or "that mortality is the necessary condition for human greatness or the power of human art."[2]

Of course, a work need not express, imply, suggest, or convey a proposition at all; but when it does, the proposition will be part of the meaning of the work. Or that, at any rate, is the sense of "express," "imply," "suggest," and "convey" which I am concerned with. Although for the sake of convenience I shall often simply speak of propositions expressed

[1] Frye, *Fearful Symmetry*, pp. 270f.
[2] Harold Bloom, *The Visionary Company*, p. 399.

or conveyed by a work, what I shall say is intended to apply as well to propositions which a work suggests or implies.

These are the questions I want to explore: (1) What is the relation between the propositions expressed by some work and the author's beliefs? (2) If a proposition is expressed by a work, who is expressing it? (3) Can a proposition expressed by a work properly be said to have been asserted?

2. The Implied Author and the Connection between Literature and Life

The dominant trend in contemporary discussions in the theory of fiction has been to separate the actual person of the historical author from his work.[3] As a result, fiction has been divorced in a peculiar way from reality. As Northrop Frye has put it, there is "no clear line of connection between literature and life."[4] The distinction between the historical author and his poetic persona or between the living man and the aesthetic mask has become something of a dogma of literary criticism. According to a closely related view, a work of fiction, at least insofar as it consists exclusively of fictional discourse, cannot contain or make any bona fide assertions. In Jonathan Culler's words, literature is not "a version of the communicative speech act," it "is something other than a statement about the world."[5]

---

[3] For one of the best recent discussions of the relation between literature and life, see Foulkes, *The Search for Literary Meaning*, Ch. IV, and "On Wings of Fictionality," pp. 157-83. Foulkes argues convincingly that fictionality is not a necessary (or sufficient) condition of literature. Foulkes' treatment of the issue is particularly noteworthy for his emphasis on the educational effects of a rigid separation of life and art.

[4] *The Educated Imagination*, p. 93.

[5] *Structuralist Poetics*, pp. 131 and 130 respectively; see also pp. 131-33, 165f., 247ff., 259. The view that (fictional) literary works cannot make any genuine assertions is also held by Roman Ingarden, *Das literarische Kunstwerk*, pp. 182f., 321-25 (*The Literary Work of*

Life, Literature, and the Implied Author

Perhaps the most influential and widely accepted version of the distinction between man and mask is Wayne Booth's account of the relation between author and work in terms of the notion of an "implied author."[6] On Booth's view, an

---

Art, pp. 172-73, 300-304); Beardsley, *Aesthetics*, pp. 420-23, *The Possibility of Criticism*, pp. 57-61, and "The Philosophy of Literature," p. 323; Wolfgang Iser, *The Implied Reader*, p. 277, and "Die Appellstruktur der Texte," pp. 249-50; Richard Ohmann, "Speech Acts and the Definition of Literature," pp. 5f., 16f., 18; Johannes Anderegg, *Fiktion und Kommunikation*, pp. 30, 42, 44; Barbara Herrnstein Smith, "Poetry as Fiction," pp. 174, 177ff. Smith formulates the view as follows (p. 177): "The statements in a poem may, of course, resemble quite closely statements that the poet *might* have truly and truthfully uttered as an historical creature in the historical world. Nevertheless, insofar as they are offered and recognized as statements in a poem, they are fictive. To the objection, 'But I know Wordsworth meant what he says in that poem,' we must reply, 'You mean he *would have* meant them if he *had* said them, but he is not saying them.'" See also Käte Hamburger, *Wahrheit und ästhetische Wahrheit*, pp. 116-25, 135-45.

[6] *The Rhetoric of Fiction*, pp. 70-77, 137, 151f., 157, 200, 211-21, *et passim*. See also e.g. Louis D. Rubin, *The Teller in the Tale*, esp. pp. 3-23, 210, 211-17; Iser, *The Implied Reader*, pp. 30, 114f.; Ralph Freedman, "Intentionality and the Literary Object," in Krieger and Dembo (eds.), *Directions for Criticism*, pp. 137, 159; Uwe Japp, *Hermeneutik*, pp. 85-90, esp. 89-90; Rainer Warning, "Formen narrativer Identitätskonstitution im Höfischen Roman," p. 574 ("Erzählsubjekt, so stellt W. C. Booth in seiner immer noch unentbehrlichen *Rhetoric of Fiction* fest, ist weder der fiktive "narrator" noch ein "unmediated author," d.h. ein mit der biographischen Person kurzschlüssig gleichgesetzter Autor, sondern der Autor als eine im Text selbst sich konstituierende "implied version" dieser Person."), also pp. 575-76, 578; Karlheinz Stierle, "Die Identität des Gedichts—Hölderlin als Paradigma," p. 513; and Paul de Man's related distinction between an author's empirical and ontological self, *Blindness and Insight*, p. 50.

John Ross Baker has a brief critical discussion of Booth's "implied author" in his article "From Imitation to Rhetoric," pp. 142-44. See also Patrick Cruttwell's good discussion of the relations between the historical person of the author and the "maker" in "Makers and Persons," pp. 487-507.

Harald Weinrich ("Der Leser braucht den Autor," pp. 722-24)

author creates, in the act of writing a particular work, "an ideal, literary . . . version of the real man."[7] This "implied author," or the actual author's " 'second self,' " present in or

---

argues that we read a work with a picture of the real, historical author in mind. The reader, according to Weinrich, needs the (real) author because "Jedes Werk, das dem Autor gelungen ist, kann vom Leser als ein Dokument durchgehaltener Identität gelesen werden" (p. 724). Although this view is consistent with my own, I am concerned not so much with the psychology of the reading process as with the logic of interpretation and hence with the implications of statements to the effect that a work expresses or implies certain propositions. Furthermore, Weinrich gives an example which would appear to show that the author whom we have in mind in reading a text cannot be the real author: "Manche Philologen haben aus diesem Mangel an biographischen Daten den Schluß gezogen, es habe einen Dichter namens Homer nie gegeben. Und sie haben mit großem Aufwand an hermeneutischem Scharfsinn nachgewiesen, daß die Ilias und die Odyssee aus verschiedenen Teilen zusammengesetzt sind und daß diese Teile verschiedene Autoren haben und daß man von diesen Autoren erst recht nichts weiß. Die Leser haben alle diese Bemühungen nicht honoriert; sie sind—sofern sie überhaupt noch nach diesen alten Texten greifen—Homer-Leser geblieben. Die philologische Demontage des Autors Homer hat sich für die Homer-Rezeption als ganz wirkungslos erwiesen" (p. 722).

Now if in reading the *Iliad* or the *Odyssey*, readers have a picture of one particular person (Homer) as the author of the work, even though they are fully convinced that there was no such person and that the work was composed by a number of different people, then it would seem that their picture of the author cannot purport to be a picture of the *real* author. Consequently, it would seem that in construing the *Iliad* or the *Odyssey* as expressing or implying a certain proposition, readers are attributing the corresponding belief, not to the real author(s), but only to their imaginary one.

Weinrich's example does not, however, unequivocally support this conclusion. For if—and this is an open question as well—the readers Weinrich is referring to are indeed fully convinced that the *Iliad* (or the *Odyssey*) was composed not by Homer but by a number of different authors, it is not clear that those readers would not, in claiming that the work expresses or implies a certain proposition, attribute the corresponding belief to the people they in fact took to be the authors of the work.

[7] *The Rhetoric of Fiction*, p. 75.

behind a particular work, "is always distinct from the 'real man'"[8] and differs as well from the implied authors of his other works.[9] It is the implied author, not the real person, who is expressing the propositions which the work conveys. Consequently, the corresponding beliefs are properly attributable, not to the real author, but only to the implied author:

> Our sense of the implied author includes not only the extractable meanings but also the moral and emotional content of each bit of action and suffering of all of the characters. It includes, in short, the intuitive apprehension of a completed artistic whole; the chief value to which *this* implied author is committed, regardless of what party his creator belongs to in real life, is that which is expressed by the total form.[10]

From the fact that a work conveys certain propositions, it follows that the implied author holds the beliefs or attitudes corresponding to them. It does not follow, nor are we entitled to infer, that the real author holds those beliefs or attitudes. He may or may not share them. Whether he does is a biographical question. But since we are concerned with the implied author, not the real person, it does not matter whether the beliefs of the former are also those of the latter. The inquiry into the author's life may be of independent interest, but its results have no bearing on the proper interpretation of the work.[11] The real author's beliefs, attitudes, values, and so on are therefore irrelevant. He is responsible for the propositions expressed or conveyed by the work only in the sense that he intends us to understand the work in the light of these propositions.[12]

In the following I shall try to show that this picture of the relation between author and work is distorted. I shall argue that how we view the story, the situation, or the

[8] *Ibid.*, p. 151.   [9] *Ibid.*, p. 71.   [10] *Ibid.*, pp. 73-74.
[11] *Ibid.*, p. 137; see also Rubin, *The Teller in the Tale*, pp. 20, 21.
[12] Booth, *The Rhetoric of Fiction*, p. 73.

Life, Literature, and the Implied Author

events presented in a work, or what we take to be expressed or suggested, is determined, not by "our sense of the implied author,"[13] but rather by our sense of the real, historical person. In other words, I shall argue that implicit in our dealings with literature is a convention to the effect that, as in serious nonfictional discourse, the beliefs, attitudes, or values expressed or suggested by a work are properly attributable to the real author.[14] Hence, for propositions expressed or suggested by a work, the normal illocutionary commitments are *not* suspended. In a sense, then, my claim is that the connection between literature and life is a good deal closer than the implied-author doctrine or the nonassertion thesis would lead us to believe.

I have argued in Chapters III to VI that the meaning of a literary work is logically tied to the author's intention. Hence if a work expresses or conveys certain propositions, it follows that the author intended to convey them. I have not attempted to show, however, that if a work conveys or expresses certain propositions—in the sense in which literary works are commonly said to express or convey certain propositions—then the author has asserted these propositions. That is, I have not tried to show that if a work conveys or expresses certain propositions (in the sense indicated), then the author holds, or is seriously representing himself as holding, the corresponding beliefs and is committed to their truth. That this is also true is what I want to argue in this chapter.

It is important to distinguish between what a work conveys or expresses and what is conveyed or expressed by a character or the narrator of a work. If a work expresses certain beliefs, then there are three possibilities concerning the narrator's relation to them: he may be expressing or

---

[13] *Ibid.*

[14] For an illuminating analysis of the concept of expressing an idea in a work of art, see Guy Sircello, *Mind and Art*, pp. 156-81. On the difference between expressing a belief and asserting, see Alan Tormey, *The Concept of Expression*, pp. 68-71, 75.

implying those beliefs; he may be expressing or implying very different beliefs; or he may not be expressing or implying any beliefs of the sort expressed by the work. The propositions conveyed by so-called "reliable"[15] narratives—*Tom Jones*, for example—are expressed or implied by the narrator. On the other hand, the propositions implied by Camus' *La Chute*, for instance, or those conveyed, at least on some interpretations, by *The Turn of the Screw*, are not expressed or implied by the speaker or narrator at all. What I shall say in the following applies only to propositions which a *work* expresses or conveys and which are part of its meaning, not to propositions expressed or conveyed only by the narrator or a character in a work.[16]

I must add that in using the terms "literature" and "fiction" more or less interchangeably, I am not suggesting that all literary works are fictional and vice versa. Rather, I am restricting the discussion throughout this chapter to fictional literary works.

3. How One Might Arrive at the Notion of an Implied Author

Let us briefly consider how one might arrive at Booth's position. There are, no doubt, many literary works the main speaker or narrator of which we are not tempted to identify with the author. Nevertheless, it seems plausible to suppose

---

[15] On "reliable" and "unreliable" narratives, see Booth, *The Rhetoric of Fiction*, pp. 158-59, *et passim*. Booth calls "a narrator *reliable* when he speaks for or acts in accordance with the norms of the work (which is to say, the implied author's norms), *unreliable* when he does not" (pp. 158-59).

[16] On the distinction between what a work expresses and what is expressed by a character or the narrator in the work, see Tormey, *The Concept of Expression*, pp. 138-40.

For an instructive comparison between the narrator in a literary work and what Walton calls the "apparent artist" of a representational work in the visual arts, see Kendall Walton, "Points of View in Narrative and Depictive Representation," pp. 49-61.

that at least in some works the author may be telling the story himself. Couldn't I, the real person, tell a fictional tale about my adventures in some imaginary land? But appearances here are deceptive. A man who is telling his child a fairy tale is pretending to assert various things; in doing so, he is in effect an actor playing the role of someone who is really asserting those things.[17] For the narrator or narrative voice is not pretending; he is really saying what the author cannot be saying lest the story cease to be fiction. (Of course, the narrator may also be pretending if, for example, another fictional story is embedded in the first one; but then his pretense would be relative to the primary fictional world, not to the real world.)

Consider the difference between the following sentences:

(a) Alyosha kissed Ivan.
(b) In this (Dostoevsky's) novel, Alyosha kisses Ivan.

The narrator or narrative voice cannot use (b); if he does, the sentence will not be fictional. In other words, a narrator cannot make the pretense explicit; if he does, the corresponding sentence or sentences are no longer fiction. On the other hand, *we* cannot use (a) without becoming partici-

[17] Richard Gale has argued that while an author of a fictional work pretends to perform various illocutionary acts, he actually performs the locutionary acts that would ordinarily be performed by a use of the sentence or sentences in question. On Gale's account, a person who "makes a fictive use of a sentence . . . says [in the locutionary sense] exactly what he would say if he were to use it non-fictively." It follows that what is said in the former is true (or false) just in case what is said in the latter is true (or false). Gale also holds that what a referring expression denotes, if anything, "is independent of whether it is used . . . with the intention of referring to some existent." Hence Gale believes that fictional statements, not intended to refer to real persons or things, can nevertheless successfully refer (in the locutionary sense) to such persons and things. ("The Fictive Use of Language," pp. 324-40, esp. 324-35; the quotations are from pp. 327 and 328.) Beardsley has defended a similar view (*Aesthetics*, p. 442). But see also David Lewis, "Truth in Fiction," pp. 40, 41.

pants in the fictional world (or an extension of it).[18] Two qualifications are necessary: (a) is, of course, sometimes used by critics in talking about the novel; but in those cases (a) is elliptical for (b). Also, (b) could be used by a fictional speaker; but when it is, the phrase "In this novel" cannot refer to the novel we are reading, but must refer to a novel within the fictional world of the work. Thus when it does not, we get the sort of paradox exemplified by the following utterances from Beckett's novel *Watt*: "Haemophilia is, like enlargement of the prostate, an exclusively male disorder. But not in this work."[19]

In other words, the narrator of a fiction is always 'inside' the fictional world. It seems to follow that what we take a work to convey can properly be attributed only to a fictional speaker or narrator, not to the author. This is in fact the view urged explicitly by Wimsatt and Beardsley in "The Intentional Fallacy."[20] The problem with this position, however, is unreliable narrative. That is, fictional narrative differs from nonfictional narrative in that in fiction the story may be *about* the narrator in a sense in which the nonfictional narrative cannot be. A historian, a reporter, or a person writing his autobiography may all, of course, speak about themselves; they may present their own beliefs ironically and thus call them into question. But then the ironic perspective is still the perspective of the speaker.

If, for example, in a nonfictional story of his life and loves, a man says the sorts of things which the barber in Lardner's "Haircut" tells his customer, then it is not possible to interpret the story as a comment about the sort of person the

---

[18] For a more detailed discussion, see Kendall Walton, "Fearing Fictions," pp. 17f. I am grateful to David Lewis for calling this article to my attention. See also Wolfgang Kayser, "Wer Erzählt den Roman?," pp. 88-92, and *Entstehung und Krise des modernen Romans*, pp. 17-18.

[19] Samuel Beckett, *Watt*, p. 102n; quoted by Ohmann, "Speech, Action, and Style," p. 241.

[20] *The Verbal Icon*, p. 4.

speaker is without taking *him* to be implying this about himself. Furthermore, we could not take our nonfictional life-and-loves story as a comment about the speaker without assuming that the *author* was making this comment about *himself*. In nonfiction the perspectives of speaker and author are inseparable, because in nonfiction there is no distinction between speaker and author. In other words, the final perspective in an autobiography or any other nonfictional discourse is always that of the person speaking; whatever we take the work to mean or whatever propositions we take it to be conveying are attributable to the speaker. But precisely this, of course, is not true of works such as "Haircut" or Nabokov's *Pale Fire*. The propositions they convey are not expressed or implied by the speaker or narrator at all.

To whom, then, are these propositions to be attributed? Who is conveying them? There are several possibilities. One might assume (i) that the propositions expressed or conveyed by a work are expressed or conveyed by the (real) author. Or we might suppose (ii) that the author neither is expressing those propositions nor necessarily intends the work to be understood as 'expressing' or conveying them. Whereas in reliable narrative they are expressed, on this view, only by the speaker or narrator, in such works as "Haircut" or *Pale Fire* they are not expressed by anyone at all; they are conveyed or suggested by the work only in the sense in which the speaker's utterances or the story itself may suggest various things—what sort of person the speaker is, for example—regardless of his (and the author's) intention.[21]

Now if we assume that the propositions a work expresses or conveys are not tied to the (real) author's beliefs in the same way as a statement of his in a nonfictional context, then (i) does not recommend itself. If, on the other hand, we feel that those propositions are nevertheless 'expressed' or conveyed by the author in the sense that he intended to

[21] See Beardsley, *Aesthetics*, pp. 415-16.

'express' them or intended us to imagine someone (really) expressing them, then (ii) is ruled out as well.

The motivation, then, for introducing the notion of an "implied author" in contrast to either of the above alternatives is twofold: (1) It preserves an intuitively plausible connection between the real author and the propositions a work conveys. It is the real author who intends us to view the work in the light of those propositions; it is he who intends his work to convey them. But (2) the connection is such that external evidence of the author's beliefs, attitudes, and values is ruled out, and thus the autonomy of the work is preserved as well.

4. Assertion and the Implied Author

One important consequence of Booth's account is that a literary work cannot contain or make any genuine assertions. Writing a novel, for example, which expresses certain propositions cannot, given Booth's view, be an act of making a statement or of asserting something.[22] For an act of making a statement involves among other things the (serious) representation that one believes what one says. To put this point another way, if a given sentence or set of sentences is (or represents) an assertion, then we are entitled to infer that the author believes what he says. But from the fact that a work, or its implied author, expresses or suggests certain beliefs, we are not entitled, according to Booth's thesis, to infer that the real author holds those beliefs. Hence, given Booth's premises, the real author cannot by writing a work which expresses a certain proposition represent himself as believing what his work expresses. It follows that the work cannot be a statement.

[22] Booth wants to say, however, that "a novel is *both* autonomous (a concrete whole, a well-wrought urn) *and* . . . a statement of moral and philosophical truth," among other things. (*"The Rhetoric of Fiction* and the Poetics of Fictions," p. 82. The italics are Booth's.)

Life, Literature, and the Implied Author

Gottfried Gabriel has maintained that fictional texts may make genuine statements.[23] However, Gabriel wants to allow that the meaning of a work may not be what the author intended. Thus when a work conveys a proposition which the author did not intend, the statement is made, according to Gabriel, by an assumed speaker ("ein intentionales Subjekt"),[24] analogous to Booth's implied author. But how is it possible for an assumed and hence, I take it, fictional speaker to make a bona fide statement? To speak of a fictional subject or speaker as opposed to a real person would seem to imply that any utterance attributed to that speaker is *ipso facto* fictional; and the point of calling it "fictional" would seem to be that it is a pretended, not a real, speech act. From the fact that in *Hamlet* Hamlet makes certain statements, it no more follows that anything has

---

[23] *Fiktion und Wahrheit*, pp. 86-99. According to Gabriel, literary works can make "Aussagen" (roughly, statements) but not "Behauptungen" (assertions). The difference between the two is that a man who makes an "Aussage," unlike one who makes a "Behauptung," need not defend his statement upon request (pp. 87ff., 93, 95).

Gabriel claims that a fictional work makes a genuine statement if and only if what he calls "the primary speaker" of the text as a whole (p. 44) makes "(at least) one statement . . . on the level of reflection": "*Ein Wahrheitsanspruch fiktionaler Literatur liegt genau dann vor, wenn sich durch Interpretation (mindestens) eine Aussage des primären Sprechers auf der Ebene der Reflexion ausfindig machen läßt*" (p. 94).

Gabriel makes a number of subtle distinctions and perceptive observations and argues *inter alia* convincingly against the "Verdoppelungseinwand" (pp. 88ff., 65-82)—the objection that if it were the function (or one of the functions) of literature to provide truth, it would merely (and inadequately) reduplicate the sciences. But Gabriel does not actually offer arguments for the claim that—contrary to Beardsley, for example, to whom he refers fairly often—the primary speaker's reflective statements are not, like utterances which report or describe events in the story, to be construed as *pretended*, rather than genuine, speech acts. What Gabriel does show very well is 'where', if fictional works can properly be said to provide truth, the corresponding statements are to be located.

[24] *Ibid.*, p. 93.

164

been stated than that Hamlet exists. The only relevant difference between the usual fictional character and Gabriel's assumed speaker is that in the case of a character's utterances the *author* is pretending (or asking us to imagine) that these are real speech acts, whereas in the case of Gabriel's assumed speaker it is not the author but only we who would be pretending that his statement is a real speech act.

Suppose that a sentence in a philosophical text appears to be a statement of a certain proposition. Either the author has or he has not stated this proposition. But if we decide that he has not, then clearly we cannot take the proposition to have been stated *at all*. If a proposition which a work expresses or implies is properly attributed to the implied author or to some other fictional construct, then a literary work cannot make statements.

It may be worth noting here that the nonassertion thesis follows also from the view that the meaning of a literary work may change.[25] Suppose, for example, that the following utterance from Brecht's *Leben des Galilei* is a bona fide assertion (by Brecht):

"Ich halte dafür, daß das einzige Ziel der Wissenschaft darin besteht, die Mühseligkeit der menschlichen Existenz zu erleichtern."[26]

[25] This view has been defended by, among others, Wellek and Warren, *Theory of Literature*, pp. 153-56; Ingarden, *Das literarische Kunstwerk*, pp. 353-80, esp. 377-80 (*The Literary Work of Art*, pp. 331-55, esp. 352-55); Beardsley, *Aesthetics*, p. 156, and *The Possibility of Criticism*, pp. 19ff.; Gadamer, *Wahrheit und Methode*, pp. 280, 282, 373, 375, *et passim* (*Truth and Method*, pp. 263, 265f., 356f., 358); F. W. Bateson, "Linguistics and Literary Criticism," pp. 7ff.; H. E. Hass, *Das Problem der literarischen Wertung*, pp. 12-29; Ashok R. Kelkar, "The Being of a Poem," pp. 23-24; Culler, *Structuralist Poetics*, pp. 30, 132, 133, 248. It is also suggested by Ellis, *The Theory of Literary Criticism*, pp. 138-39. For a critical discussion, see P. D. Juhl, "Can the Meaning of a Literary Work Change?," pp. 133-56.

[26] Bertolt Brecht, *Leben des Galilei*, scene 14, p. 125.

("I hold that the only goal of science is to alleviate the hardship of human existence.")

Then we are entitled to infer that (the real) Brecht believes this. Now assume that, as a result of changes in the language, "erleichtern" ("alleviate") takes on the sense of "increase" and the meaning of the utterance is thereby changed. Then we are surely not entitled to infer that Brecht held the belief corresponding to the proposition which the utterance now expresses. Clearly, from the (hypothetical) fact that the meaning of the utterance has changed, we are not entitled to infer that Brecht has changed his mind about the goal of science. It follows that even if the utterance (or the sentence) was originally an assertion, it no longer is.

Furthermore, the speech act which a man performs by producing a certain word sequence cannot change at all, regardless of changes in the language, culture, or whatever; for it is uniquely determined at the time it is performed.[27] Thus if we take the sentence as an assertion by Brecht, it remains the same assertion, irrespective of changes in the language or culture. Hence, on the view that the meaning of a literary work may change, the propositions which a work expresses cannot be asserted.

But if the author of a work which conveys a certain proposition is not asserting it, what is he doing? On Booth's account, as we have seen, it is the implied author who is expressing the propositions conveyed by a work. Now the propositions expressed by the implied author stand in the same logical relation to the beliefs, attitudes, and values of the real author as the propositions expressed by the narrator. Which is to say that the propositions expressed by the implied author are no more attributable to the real author than the propositions expressed by the narrator.

The only essential difference between the implied author and the narrator of work is that whereas the narrator may

[27] See Cohen, *The Diversity of Meaning*, pp. 3-5.

be unreliable, the implied author cannot be unreliable, as reliability is defined in terms of the beliefs, attitudes, and values of the implied author. But this is immaterial to the question at issue, since the real author is not expressing the beliefs of the implied author any more than those of the narrator. Consequently, although the propositions expressed by the implied author, unlike those expressed by the narrator, are necessarily the propositions expressed by the work, they are no more attributable to the real author than the propositions expressed by the narrator. Thus in writing a fictional work which conveys certain propositions, and hence in creating an implied author who expresses them, the real author is *imitating* the expression of the corresponding beliefs. That is, he is *pretending* to express them.[28] In Monroe Beardsley's words, their expression is "part of the act."[29]

5. The Relation between Author and Work: Who Is Expressing the Propositions Expressed by a Literary Work?

Since I shall try to show that literary works can, and usually do, make genuine assertions, it will be helpful to state the rules governing the nondefective performance of an act of asserting a certain proposition:[30]

(i) The speaker presents the proposition in question as being true.

---

[28] See e.g. Ohmann, "Speech Acts and the Definition of Literature," pp. 13-14; Beardsley, *The Possibility of Criticism*, pp. 57-61; and Culler, *Structuralist Poetics*, p. 165. But see also Beardsley, "The Concept of Literature," pp. 31-35, 37-38.

[29] Beardsley, *Aesthetics*, p. 422.

[30] The statement of these rules closely follows Searle, *Speech Acts*, pp. 64-66, and "The Logical Status of Fictional Discourse," p. 322. See also Gabriel, *Fiktion und Wahrheit*, pp. 45f.; and, on the sincerity condition (iv), Shwayder, *The Stratification of Behavior*, pp. 375ff., esp. 377-79. Shwayder argues that (iv) is a necessary condition of assertion. See also J. L. Austin, *How to Do Things With Words*, pp. 22, 104.

(ii) The speaker has evidence, or reasons for supposing, that the proposition is true.
(iii) It is not obvious to both speaker and hearer that the hearer (or audience) knows the proposition to be true or does not need to be reminded of it.
(iv) The speaker holds the belief corresponding to the proposition expressed.

I shall argue that in interpreting a literary work as expressing (implying, conveying, or suggesting) a certain proposition, we assume that the author, though not necessarily the speaker or narrator, satisfies conditions (i) and (iv). I take it that this is sufficient to show that a proposition expressed by a work is asserted, although it does not show that such expression of a proposition is or can be non-defective assertion. I shall not argue that in interpreting a work as expressing a certain proposition, we also assume that (ii) is satisfied. If we assume that conditions (i) and (iv) are satisfied, however, it seems implausible that we do not also assume the satisfaction of (ii)—all the more, since the work itself will usually provide or suggest reasons for supposing the proposition true, because as a rule it "illustrates" or exemplifies in some way the propositions it expresses or conveys.[31] As for condition (iii), it seems that an

[31] One of the conditions given by Gabriel for the successful performance of an act of asserting ("behaupten") is that the speaker defend his assertion upon request (*Fiktion und Wahrheit*, p. 45). Gabriel holds that a work which expresses certain propositions makes "Aussagen" (statements), not "Behauptungen" (assertions), since the author is not obligated to defend those propositions upon request (pp. 87, 93, 95). But Gabriel's "Ernsthaftigkeitsbedingung" (p. 93) on assertions is not quite the same as (ii) above. A man who refuses to defend a statement he has made may nevertheless have evidence, or reasons for supposing, that it is true. Furthermore, I am inclined to believe that a man's refusal, for some reason, to defend an assertion he has made is not sufficient to render it defective. In any case, for my purposes nothing much depends on whether we construe the truth-claims which a work may make as *Aussagen* or *Behauptungen*.

Life, Literature, and the Implied Author

expression of belief which does not satisfy (iii) is just as defective or infelicitous in literature as in ordinary discourse.

Let us now look at a few concrete examples with the following questions in mind:

(1) Is the author committed to the truth of the propositions which a work expresses or conveys?
(2) If a work expresses or conveys a certain proposition, does anything follow regarding the author's beliefs?

Or to put these questions in terms of the distinction between the real author and the implied author:

(3) Who is expressing the propositions expressed by a work—the implied author or the real author?

5.1 *Empson on Housman*

In a discussion of I. A. Richards' theory of poetic value, William Empson makes some comments about A. E. Housman's poem "With seed the sowers scatter" (*More Poems* XXXII). Now Empson is scarcely one who as critic or theorist can be accused of flirting with intentionalism. And indeed Empson's considerations in the following passage look as though they have nothing to do with what the author may have believed or intended:

> [A]fter the first sentence (the lads are sowing) every one of the sentences contains an untrue assertion ('Tis little matter What are the sorts they sow, For only one will grow. . . . The charlock on the fallow . . . will not twice arise. The stinging nettle only Will still be sure to stand . . . It peoples towns, and towers About the courts of kings. . .). Apart from the absurdity of the literal meaning, the metaphorical meaning seems to me plainly untrue; but I also think it is one of his finest poems, which is saying a good deal. Of course you may say that my optimism is naive, and that Housman is

uttering the bitter truth which we recognise unconsciously but labour to ignore.[32]

It may seem as though what Empson is saying here is this:

(1) The speaker's assertions are plainly false.
(2) If the poem is expressing the beliefs or attitude corresponding to the speaker's assertions, then it is not a very good poem.
(3) But on at least one interpretation (namely, Empson's), the poem is quite good.
(4) Hence the poem is not expressing the speaker's beliefs or attitude.

One problem with this analysis is that Empson does not seem to be saying: 'There is at least one interpretation (Empson's) on which the poem is quite good; therefore, it cannot be expressing the speaker's beliefs.' Rather, he seems to be saying: '(I think that) the poem is quite good, therefore (I think that) it doesn't express the speaker's beliefs.' Or 'If I am right in thinking that this poem is quite good, then it cannot be expressing the speaker's beliefs.' The difference is important. The argument presented above presupposes the general principle: 'If a literary work is aesthetically better on some possible interpretation than on another, then the latter interpretation cannot be correct.' If this principle holds, then it would be implausible to suppose that the propositions expressed by a work are asserted. For it would be implausible to suppose, for example, that if Housman's poem is better on the assumption that it does not express the speaker's beliefs than on the assumption that it does, then Housman cannot be expressing (asserting) the speaker's beliefs.

But what I think Empson is in fact saying does not presuppose any such principle. It rests simply on the premise that if the poem expressed plainly untrue beliefs, it would

[32] William Empson, *The Structure of Complex Words*, pp. 11-12.

not be very good.[33] And this, unlike the argument sketched above, is quite compatible with the assumption that the propositions which a poem expresses are asserted. It does not have any implications for the issue one way or the other.

Another problem is that it is difficult to see how, on the above analysis, the conclusion which Empson draws, namely, that "Housman is [not] uttering the bitter truth" and thus not recommending the speaker's attitude,[34] can follow from the premises. For if those premises are construed as statements which have no bearing on what Housman may have believed or intended, then it is difficult to see how a conclusion about what Housman is or is not expressing can follow from them. Or could one take this argument the other way around and say that since Empson's conclusion is not based on considerations about what Housman believed or intended, that conclusion is not to be construed as a claim about what Housman is expressing?

To see that Empson's interpretation does depend on assumptions about the real Housman's beliefs, and hence that this suggestion is implausible, let us look at what else Empson says about the poem. The passage quoted above continues:

> It is also naive, I think I can retort, to imagine that in a 'pessimistic' poem such as this one the despairing assertions are meant to be accepted quite flatly.[35]

Why would it be naive to imagine that the pessimistic assertions are meant to be accepted? Surely because it would be naive to suppose that Housman held the corresponding beliefs. What Empson is saying is that it would be naive to suppose that Housman shares or endorses the speaker's beliefs and attitude.

Consider what would be involved in accepting the speaker's assertions "quite flatly." It would be to take the work

[33] See *ibid.*, p. 9. [34] *Ibid.*, p. 13.
[35] *Ibid.*, p. 12.

and hence Housman to be 'making these assertions'. The question is, what does that mean? Does it mean that Housman is really making these assertions, or does it mean that he is merely pretending to do so, as Booth's theory and the nonassertion thesis imply?

If Housman were pretending to make these assertions, then he is committed neither to the corresponding beliefs nor to their truth. Thus Housman would then not be wrong if those assertions are false, nor would it be odd if it should turn out that Housman never believed any such thing. Let us suppose, therefore, that Housman is not committed to the beliefs which the poem expresses, nor to their truth. Then the fact that the corresponding assertions are plainly false or unduly pessimistic would be no reason to suppose that they are not "meant to be accepted quite flatly."

For if the author is not committed to the beliefs which his work expresses, nor to their truth, then why should he want to 'express' beliefs which he holds? It would seem much more plausible to suppose that he would then use this freedom from the usual illocutionary commitments to explore, dramatize, and 'express', for various artistic purposes, precisely those beliefs which are not his own—beliefs, that is, the serious expression of which in nonfictional discourse, where the usual illocutionary commitments hold, might cause some problems. In other words, the force of the common argument that, say, a particular poem is not to be taken as an expression of certain beliefs (of the speaker) because those beliefs are, for example, plainly false, unduly pessimistic, unduly optimistic, immoral, or biased rests on the implicit assumption that if the poem expresses those beliefs, the author is committed to them and to their truth.

Empson makes two further comments which throw light on the connection between the author and what the poem expresses. He points out that, on the pessimistic interpretation, the poem is expressing "merely a sullen conviction that no effort is worth making, a philosophy for the village idiot."[36] What is the force of the claim that, on the pessimistic reading, the poem expresses "a philosophy for the village idiot"? Surely, it is that this is not Housman's philosophy, that Housman believed no such thing. For suppose that Housman did indeed believe that "no effort is worth making." Wouldn't it be implausible in that case to take the poem as repudiating such a view? Or suppose that the poem was written by the village idiot who dabbled in verse. Notice that we could then no longer take the "absurdity of the literal meaning" in the way Empson takes it in Housman's poem, namely, as "a positive help to the wilful pessimism of the metaphorical one"[37]; for it would then be more likely the result of the author's ineptitude. In that case, it would surely be difficult to argue that since, on the pessimistic reading, the attitude recommended by the poem is a "philosophy for the village idiot," that reading is not likely to be correct.

How is this to be explained if the real author's beliefs are irrelevant, if from the fact that the poem expresses certain beliefs it does not follow that the author is committed to those beliefs? One might try to account for this, on Booth's view, in terms of what the author intended. No doubt, the village idiot intends something different from Housman. But then the only evidence of what the author intended might be his beliefs and attitudes, what sort of person he is; but that should be immaterial on Booth's view.

That Empson's interpretation of the poem depends on an implicit assumption about Housman's beliefs is further confirmed by the following passage. It shows also that Housman is committed to the truth of the beliefs which the poem expresses.

> I remember a Japanese class of mine reading Housman in 1931, when they were liable to be conscripted to fight in Manchuria, indeed a man had already been drafted from the class and killed in Shanghai, and they wrote

[36] *Ibid.*, p. 13. [37] *Ibid.*, p. 12.

down pretty consistently "We think Housman is quite right. We will do no good to anyone by being killed as soldiers, but we will be admired, and we all want to be admired, and anyway we are better dead." To do the old gentleman justice, I fancy he would have been rather shocked by these bits of school work. So I think Housman is about as pure a case as you can get of a poet using untruths to excite attitudes. . . .[38]

Notice what is presupposed by the students' remarks: if they were not implicitly saying (or if it did not follow from their interpretation) that Housman is really asserting that "no effort is worth making," then it would be inappropriate to say that he was "quite right."

If to say that the poem expresses a certain belief were to say that Housman is pretending to express that belief, then one could not say that Housman was right or wrong. For in the sense of "say" in which what a man said can be called true or false, Housman would then not have *said* anything; and by 'expressing' the belief in question, he would then not be seriously representing himself as holding that belief. Hence to say that Housman is "quite right" presupposes that Housman holds the beliefs which the poem expresses and is committed to their truth and therefore will be wrong if the corresponding propositions are false. It follows that Housman is not pretending but really asserting those propositions.

Now one might argue that the assumptions the students make are in no way a reflection of the logic of interpretation, but simply indicate that the students are naive, that they have not yet grasped the fundamental convention of literature—namely, that if a poem expresses certain beliefs, that is not a case of assertion, but rather of pretended assertion. If this were true, however, Empson could surely be expected to challenge these assumptions immediately. Not only does he not challenge them, but his comment shows that these

[38] *Ibid.*, pp. 12-13.

assumptions underlie his own interpretive practice as well. For what Empson is suggesting is that his students' interpretation is wrong because Housman believed no such thing. ("To do the old gentleman justice, I fancy he would have been rather shocked by these bits of school work.")

That Empson does not mean by "these bits of school work" the assumption that Housman is (or could be) really asserting something, but rather the students' claim that Housman held the particular beliefs which the poem expresses on their interpretation, is clear from the fact that Empson goes on to say: "So . . . Housman is about as pure a case as you can get of a poet using *untruths* [that is, statements which Housman knew or believed to be untrue] to excite attitudes . . . " (italics added). If the implicit assumption here were not that Housman is committed to the beliefs which the poem expresses, then it would be difficult to see why it should matter that Housman did not hold the beliefs which, according to the students' interpretation, the poem expresses. Furthermore, this assumption is, as we have seen, implicit also in Empson's other arguments quoted above.

5.2 Crane on Swift

I want to discuss one further example which brings out more sharply some of the consequences of interpreting a work as expressing or conveying certain propositions, and which thus throws into greater relief our implicit assumptions about the status of those propositions. The example is R. S. Crane's interpretation of the fourth book of *Gulliver's Travels*, the "Voyage to the Country of the Houyhnhnms." I have chosen this particular example because Booth explicitly expresses his approval of Crane's arguments.[39]

Crane attempts to show that, contrary to the dominant interpretation since the 1920s, the view of man presented in the fourth Voyage is radically pessimistic and thus corre-

[39] Booth, *The Rhetoric of Fiction*, p. 321n.

sponds more or less to Gulliver's picture of human nature as utterly hopeless. I should mention that Crane's interpretation is offered as a "theory of [his] own about Swift's intentions."[40] But this should cause no problems. For Booth's theory as well as the nonassertion thesis is quite compatible with the claim that the meaning of a work is logically tied to the author's intention. (In fact, on Booth's view, the propositions which a work expresses are explicitly tied to the author's intention.) The question is: What follows from the fact that a work expresses certain beliefs? Or, in intentionalist terms: What follows from the fact that the author intended the work to express certain beliefs?

Now those critics who argued that the fourth book portrays human nature as not altogether hopeless

> sought to correct the misunderstanding of Swift's satiric purpose in the Voyage which had vitiated, in their opinion, most earlier criticism of it and, in particular, to defend Swift from the charge of all-out misanthropy that had been levelled against him so often in the past—by Thackeray, for example, but many others also—on the strength of Gulliver's wholesale identification of men with the Yahoos and his unqualified worship of the Houyhnhnms.[41]

It is interesting to note that Swift had been *charged* with all-out misanthropy and that the critics reacting to this interpretation wanted to *defend* him from this charge. For what this presupposes is that Swift did in fact by writing the fourth book *assert* something, namely, that man is incurably irrational and immoral. Otherwise, this view could hardly have been attributed to him on the basis of the fact or the assumption that the fourth book conveys it.

Of course, the critics who sought to defend Swift argued that the earlier writers had been mistaken in identifying

[40] R. S. Crane, "The Houyhnhnms, the Yahoos, and the History of Ideas," p. 231.
[41] *Ibid.*, pp. 231-32.

Life, Literature, and the Implied Author

Swift with Gulliver; but they did not suggest what, on the nonassertion thesis, one would have expected, namely, that even if the book's portrayal of human nature were radically pessimistic, no inference to the real Swift's beliefs is warranted. They did not suggest that Swift had not in fact asserted anything; rather, they argued that Swift had asserted something else. Is it really plausible to suppose that the critics who charged Swift with utter misanthropy as well as those who tried to defend him are just naive, that they failed to grasp the fundamental convention of literature, namely, that it is not "a version of the communicative speech act"?[42]

It is instructive to see what Crane takes to be the task of those who want to defend Swift:

> They would have to show that what Gulliver is made to say about human nature in the Voyage, which is certainly misanthropic enough, and what Swift wanted his readers to believe about human nature are, in certain crucial respects at any rate, two different and incompatible things. It would require them, that is, to draw a clear line between what is both Swift and Gulliver and what is only Gulliver in a text in which Gulliver alone is allowed to speak to us.[43]

The passage brings out very clearly the connection between the author's beliefs, "what is both Swift and Gulliver," and the propositions which the work conveys or "what Swift wanted his readers to believe about human nature." For to defend Swift, according to Crane, a critic would have to show that the beliefs of Gulliver and those of Swift diverge at crucial points. Similarly, to show that the book presents a more or less traditional view of human nature, a critic would have to show (among other things) that Swift held the corresponding beliefs. In other words, the implicit as-

[42] Culler, *Structuralist Poetics*, p. 131.
[43] Crane, "The Houyhnhnms, the Yahoos, and the History of Ideas," p. 232.

sumption is that if the work expresses certain beliefs, then the author is committed to those beliefs and to their truth.

Could one perhaps say that it is not the real Swift but only the implied author who is committed to the beliefs (and to the truth of the beliefs) which the work expresses? The problem with this is that the Swift Crane is talking about as well as the Swift who is charged with misanthropy by some and defended from this charge by others would seem to be the real Swift. Thus Crane frequently speaks of "Swift's intentions"[44] in writing the fourth book, of his "main design in the Voyage,"[45] of "what was in Swift's mind when he conceived the fourth Voyage"[46]; he speaks of "statements by Swift himself about *Gulliver's Travels*,"[47] of "that famous letter of Swift's"[48] to Pope, of his study of logic,[49] and of "Swift . . . remembering Marsh's logic as he composed the sentence, in his letter to Pope, about 'John, Peter, Thomas, and so forth.' "[50] In all these cases, it is clear that Crane is speaking, not of the implied author of the fourth book of *Gulliver's Travels*, but of its real author. Furthermore, that the reference in "what is both Swift and Gulliver and what is only Gulliver" is to the real author becomes clear from the kind of evidence Crane mentions for a claim about Swift's beliefs: facts about his education, his religious convictions, his political tendencies, and his inclinations in other matters.[51]

But the assumption implicit in Crane's remarks about Swift which I have quoted above—namely, that Swift is committed to the beliefs which the work expresses—is inconsistent with Booth's picture of the relation between the real author and his work. It may be worth noting also that those who argued against the pessimistic reading of the fourth Voyage did not suggest that while the real author may have thought that human nature was beyond hope, the

[44] *Ibid.*, p. 231.
[45] *Ibid.*, p. 235.
[46] *Ibid.*, p. 236.
[47] *Ibid.*, p. 238.
[48] *Ibid.*, p. 233.
[49] *Ibid.*, p. 249.
[50] *Ibid.*, p. 252.
[51] *Ibid.*, p. 237.

implied author did not. What they tried to show rather was that the real author did not believe this—thus the emphasis on the intellectual background of Swift's age, on biographical facts about Swift, and the appeal to the letter to Pope of November 26, 1725.

Now one of Crane's main points is that those who argued for the 'Christian humanist' interpretation of the Voyage in large measure on the basis of considerations concerning the intellectual and religious background of Swift's age have fallen victim to "a fundamental confusion in method."[52] It may appear, therefore, that what he is rejecting is evidence of the real author's beliefs as opposed to evidence, in the work, of the implied author's beliefs. That this is not what he is doing, however, is evident if one looks at what Crane objects to in the use of facts about the intellectual background. He points out that from empirical generalizations about the dominant beliefs, concerns, or doctrines of a particular period, one cannot infer that any given writer of the period shared those beliefs and concerns or subscribed to those doctrines. He suggests also that how a particular writer views the relationship between various doctrines of the time may have very little to do with the abstract schemes in terms of which later historians represent that relationship. In other words, Crane is not claiming that facts about the real Swift do not constitute any evidence that an interpretation of a work of his is correct, but rather that a certain type of fact—namely, "the generalizations and schematisms of the synthezising historians"[53]—do not constitute such evidence. What Crane denies, then, is not that the fourth Voyage expresses beliefs of the real Swift, but rather that facts or assumptions about the intellectual background can be used to suport a statement about what (the real) Swift believed.

Crane's own interpretation of the Voyage is based mainly on facts which are not directly evidence of Swift's be-

[52] *Ibid.*, p. 241.   [53] *Ibid.*, p. 242.

liefs: that Swift was quite familiar from his student days with the logicians' definition of man and their use of the horse as an example of a sentient creature which, unlike man, is irrational; and that in the first of two letters to Pope in 1725, in which he speaks of his intention in writing *Gulliver's Travels*, he appears to be alluding to a logic text he studied as an undergraduate at Trinity College. It is important to notice, however, that Crane does not rest his case solely on facts which are not direct evidence of Swift's beliefs. Crane also, no less than the critics whose interpretation he is challenging, appeals to Swift's beliefs. Thus he quotes a passage from the second letter to Pope which has been construed "as a retraction of the judgment on humanity expressed in the first letter" and goes on to say: "the final sentence makes clear, I think, that it was not so intended."[54] It does not matter, of course, for our purposes who is right; what does matter is that Crane, too, evidently felt it necessary to support his interpretation by an appeal to Swift's (the *real* Swift's) beliefs. But this would be odd unless the assumption that Swift did retract his judgment on humanity would count against Crane's interpretation.

5.3 *Booth on Fielding and Others*

Let us now look at some of the things which Booth himself says in discussing various novels. The purpose of this is not to show that Booth contradicts himself or that his theory is at variance with his practice and therefore unreliable. It is rather to show that despite his metacritical claims, the intuitions (about the relation between author and work) underlying his practical criticism are precisely what one would expect on the thesis I am defending but are difficult to account for on his theory. In other words, I shall argue that contrary to his theoretical views about the relation between author and work, Booth's practice reveals the same tacit conception as that brought out in the examples from Empson and Crane.

[54] *Ibid.*, p. 250.

Booth suggests that one of the advantages of drawing a distinction between the real author and the implied author is that this enables us to

> ... avoid pointless and unverifiable talk about such qualities as "sincerity" or "seriousness" in the author. Because Ford Madox Ford thinks of Fielding and Defoe and Thackeray as the unmediated authors of their novels, he must end by condemning them as insincere, since there is every reason to believe that they write "passages of virtuous aspirations that were in no way any aspirations of theirs." Presumably he is relying on external evidences of Fielding's lack of virtuous aspirations. But we have only the work as evidence for the only kind of sincerity that concerns us: Is the implied author in harmony with himself—that is, are his other choices in harmony with his explicit narrative character? If a narrator who by every trustworthy sign is presented to us as a reliable spokesman for the author professes to believe in values which are never realized in the structure as a whole, we can then talk of an insincere work. A great work establishes the "sincerity" of its implied author, regardless of how grossly the man who created that author may belie in his *other* forms of conduct the values embodied in his work. For all we know, the only sincere moments of his life may have been lived as he wrote his novel.[55]

Now, on Booth's view, it is not the real author, but rather the implied author who is expressing whatever the work expresses; and the relation between the real author's beliefs, values, or attitudes and those of the implied author is left unspecified inasmuch as no inference is warranted from the former to the latter and vice versa. It follows that by writing a work which expresses certain beliefs or aspirations, the (real) author is not seriously representing himself as hold-

[55] Booth, *The Rhetoric of Fiction*, p. 75.

ing those beliefs or having those aspirations. Consequently, it would be unintelligible to say of the real author that he is or is not sincere in a particular work. To put the point another way, if Booth is right, then it would be logically impossible for the (real) author to be sincere or insincere in his work.

It is noteworthy, therefore, that after the sentence "A great work establishes the 'sincerity' of its implied author, regardless of how grossly the man who created that author may belie in his *other* forms of conduct the values embodied in his work," Booth does not go on to say something like: 'Hence it is simply immaterial what the real author's values are.' For that seems clearly to be the implication. Instead, Booth says: "For all we know, the only sincere moments of his life may have been lived as he wrote his novel." This remark shows quite clearly, I think, that we do in fact take the real author to be seriously representing himself as holding the beliefs, attitudes, or values which the work expresses. For otherwise no sense could be given to the statement that the author was or was not sincere when he wrote the novel. Furthermore, it is difficult to see how an author can "*belie* in his *other* forms of conduct the values embodied in his work" unless the fact that they are embodied in his work commits the author to those values.

In his discussion of the implied author in *Tom Jones*, Booth quotes the following sentence: "For however short the period may be of my own performances, they will most probably outlive their own infirm author, and the weakly productions of his abusive contemporaries." And he comments: "Was Fielding literally infirm as he wrote that sentence? It matters not in the least. It is not Fielding we care about, but the narrator created to speak in his name."[56] This is indeed irrelevant, but it does not follow that we need to postulate an implied author. For the reason why it is irrelevant whether Fielding was or was not infirm is not that what is true of the real Fielding is just immaterial, but

[56] *Ibid.*, p. 218.

rather that this particular question does not affect the interpretation of the work.

To see that this is so, consider what Booth says about Céline's *Journey to the End of the Night*:

> Céline is never undeniably there, even in the long-winded commentary. But he is never undeniably dissociated, either, and therein lies the problem. The reader cannot help wondering whether Ferdinand's moralizing, of which there is a great deal, is to be taken seriously or not. Is this Céline's view? Should it be mine, at least temporarily, so that I can go along sympathetically with this hero? Or is it simply "life seen from the other side," as the epigraph has promised? Even assuming that the reader knows nothing of Céline's personal life, he must find it hard to believe, after a hundred or so pages of the following kind of thing, that Céline is merely dramatizing a narrator who is completely dissociated from him. . . .[57]

The implication clearly seems to be that if we *do* know something about Céline's personal life, we will then take the work as expressing the narrator's beliefs. In other words, we will then construe the work according to the narrator's beliefs *because* we know that they are Céline's.

It follows that if (we believe) the author does not share the views of the narrator or of a character, we will then reject the interpretation according to which the work expresses or implies those views.[58] A good example of this is found in Booth's discussion of Henry James' story "The Liar." He argues as follows against the interpretation according to which the character Lyon, the 'reflector', is " 'inspired by the Muse of Truth,' both as artist and as man."[59] First he quotes several passages which suggest that far from being "inspired by the Muse of Truth," Lyon acts from du-

---

[57] *Ibid.*, p. 380.
[58] This claim is qualified below, section 6.
[59] Booth, *The Rhetoric of Fiction*, p. 350.

bious motives at best. Booth goes on to say that Lyon's art is more and more perverted by these motives. In support of this claim, he cites a passage in which among other things we are told that as Lyon "saw nothing else [except the liar] in the Colonel today, so he gave himself up to the joy of 'rendering' nothing else."[60] But Booth does not leave it at that; instead, he adds:

> It is impossible to reconcile this picture of the artist's task with any notion James ever espoused; it is, in fact, James's portrait of what happens to art when it is made to serve 'interested,' or practical ends.[61]

This passage brings out very well the connection between what the story suggests or implies and James' beliefs. For, in the first sentence, Booth appeals to the beliefs of the real James in support of his claim that the story does not endorse Lyon's picture of the task of art; that is, he rejects the interpretation according to which the story (or the implied author) suggests that this is the artist's task, on the grounds that James never espoused a view compatible with Lyon's; and, in the second sentence, Booth links his own interpretation with a view which, he is suggesting, James did in fact hold.

Booth's brief comments on the novels of Henry de Montherlant reveal even more clearly the implicit assumptions we make about the author's beliefs:

> The aristocratic "ethic of quality," the "virtue of contempt," that his novels seem to advocate has led to widespread protest. Whether Montherlant himself really stands for what his characters advocate is hard to determine, but it is clear that to the extent he does so, our admiration for his work suffers. As a recent reviewer said, we cannot believe that a character like Pierre Costals in *Les jeunes filles* is intended to be sympathetic and at the same time fully respect the author. "Might

[60] *Ibid.*, p. 351. [61] *Ibid.*

it not be better," he suggests, "for M. de Montherlant's reputation as an intelligent writer if Pierre Costals were looked upon as a character who has as little of his author's complete approval as Georges Carrion, Alissa, or Jean-Baptiste Clamence?" (*T.L.S.*, January 6, 1961, p. 8). Surely it would be better. But must we not ask *of the novels themselves* whether they will justify the exoneration? In any case, the novelist's stature will rise and fall depending on what they tell us.[62]

But why should our admiration for Montherlant's *work* depend on whether he "really stands for what his characters advocate"? That is, why should it depend on Montherlant's (the real Montherlant's) beliefs? The reason appears to be that if Montherlant shares the views which his characters advocate, then we have no choice but to take his work as expressing or implying those beliefs. But why in turn should the fact that his work expresses or implies certain beliefs reflect on (the real) Montherlant? The reason which the passage suggests is that if Montherlant's work expresses or implies certain beliefs, then (the real) Montherlant is expressing or implying those beliefs—which is to say that then the real Montherlant is committed to those beliefs and to their truth. Of course, Booth is quite right in insisting that we must "ask *of the novels themselves* whether they will justify the exoneration." But as his earlier statement indicates, that involves determining "whether Montherlant himself really stands for what his characters advocate," even if we should in the end condemn the author or his work for not "making his moral orderings clear."[63]

6. THE PRESUMPTION THAT AN AUTHOR HOLDS THE BELIEFS WHICH HIS WORK EXPRESSES

Let us briefly summarize what emerges from these examples. I have been arguing that it is our picture of the

[62] *Ibid.*, p. 396n.   [63] *Ibid.*, p. 386.

real, historical author which determines how we construe a literary work. More specifically, if a work expresses or implies certain propositions, then the author is committed to the truth of those propositions and to the corresponding beliefs. It follows that by writing a work which expresses or implies certain propositions, the author is asserting those propositions; their expression is real, bona fide expression of belief, not pretense. To put this point another way, the propositions which a work expresses or implies are expressed or implied, not by a fictional "implied author," but by the real, historical person.[64]

[64] While I have argued that the propositions expressed or implied by a work are asserted, I have not tried to show *how* these propositions are asserted—that is, what the specific connection is between the work as a whole or individual sentences and the asserted propositions. For some arguments about how a work as a whole, or the individual sentences it contains, are not connected with the propositions said to be expressed by it as well as a proposal as to how the connection is to be construed, see M. J. Sirridge, "Truth from Fiction?," pp. 453-71, and "J. R. Tolkien and Fairy Tale Truth," pp. 81-92. See also D.E.B. Pollard, "M. J. Sirridge, Fiction, and Truth," pp. 251-56; M. J. Sirridge, "The Moral of the Story," pp. 257-59; Ronald Hepburn, "Poetry and 'Concrete Imagination'," pp. 3-18; and Mary Louise Pratt, *Toward a Speech Act Theory of Literary Discourse*, pp. 201-33.

Morris Weitz has defended the view that certain general statements in works of fiction are genuine assertions. He gives examples from Eliot and Proust (e.g., "In love we cannot but choose badly") and argues that it would be implausible to construe such "seeming general claims" as being "simply part of the story" since "[t]hese sentences, coming as they do, as reflections upon created, imaginary episodes are too similar to certain sorts of sentences outside of art that function as natural claims about the world." "Truth in Literature," in Hospers (ed.), *Introductory Readings in Aesthetics*, pp. 218, 219. See also Michael Scriven, "The Language of Fiction," pp. 185-96, esp. 185-91; Searle, "The Logical Status of Fictional Discourse," pp. 331-32; and Käte Hamburger's discussion of lyric poetry as a "reality statement" ("Wirklichkeitsaussage"), *Die Logik der Dichtung*, pp. 187-232, esp. 188, 193, 200, 215, 220f., 222, 227 (English trans. by Marilynn J. Rose, *The Logic of Literature*, pp. 232-92, esp. 233f., 240, 248f., 269f., 275-77, 278, 285).

Peter Mew has argued that "highly general universal factual state-

Life, Literature, and the Implied Author

It does not follow, however, that it is impossible for a literary work to express beliefs which the author does not hold. If it is possible for a man to express a belief he does not hold, then an author can express or imply such beliefs by or in his work.[65] But we do not on that account simply suspend judgment as to whether the author holds the beliefs which his work expresses. Nor, if a work clearly expresses certain beliefs, do we first look for evidence that the author holds those beliefs or that he generally holds the beliefs which his works express. Rather, as the examples I have given show, we *presume* that the author holds the beliefs which his work expresses unless and until strong evidence to the contrary is produced.[66] It is on this presumption that appeals to the author's beliefs rest.

---

ments in literature" are most naturally taken as hypotheses. Mew's view is compatible, however, with the claim that such statements are genuine assertions ("Facts in Fiction," pp. 329-37, esp. 332-34.) See also Hospers, "Implied Truths in Literature," in Kennick (ed.), *Art and Philosophy*, pp. 322f.

For the view that sentences in a (fictional) literary work which express general reflections do not constitute genuine assertions, see Martin Steinmann's lucid discussion in "Literature, Knowledge, and the Language of Literature," pp. 903-7, esp. 904, 907. See also Kingsley B. Price, "Is a Work of Art a Symbol?," in Coleman (ed.), *Contemporary Studies in Aesthetics*, pp. 53-69, esp. 62-63, 68-69; and Marcia M. Eaton, "The Truth Value of Literary Statements," pp. 163-74.

For a general discussion of the status of sentences in fiction, see Searle, "The Logical Status of Fictional Discourse," pp. 319-332; Margaret MacDonald, "The Language of Fiction," in Coleman (ed.), *Contemporary Studies in Aesthetics*, pp. 262-76; Gabriel, *Fiktion und Wahrheit*; and Felix Martinez-Bonati, "Die logische Struktur der Dichtung," pp. 185-200.

[65] See Sircello, *Mind and Art*, pp. 170-72 and also 168-69. But see also Shwayder, *The Stratification of Behavior*, pp. 375-79. Shwayder argues that a necessary condition of expressing a certain belief is that the speaker hold the belief in question. Hence if Shwayder is right, a man cannot properly be said to have expressed a belief which he does not hold.

[66] Isabel Hungerland has argued that there is a presumption of this kind in ordinary discourse ("Contextual Implication," pp. 223f., 233, 238, 250).

It does not follow from this presumption, of course, that if an author holds certain beliefs, then a particular work of his must express those beliefs. An author is likely to hold other beliefs as well, which he may have wanted to express.[67] Thus arguments based on the author's beliefs often take the form of giving reasons why it would *not* be likely that a work should express certain beliefs. (Good examples are Booth's claim that Lyon's view of the task of art, in "The Liar," is one which James never espoused, and Empson's argument that it would be naive to suppose that the pessimistic assertions in Housman's nettle poem are meant to be taken at face value.)

It is also possible, given our presumption, that a work expresses certain beliefs which the author has expressed nowhere else or which are inconsistent with the beliefs he has expressed elsewhere. After all, artists no less than other people change their minds, contradict themselves, or are ambivalent in their attitudes. Thus when a work clearly expresses certain beliefs which the author has expressed nowhere else or which are inconsistent with his (other) beliefs, we will nevertheless presume that the author held the beliefs which the work expresses rather than say that he is simply expressing beliefs he does not hold. It is conceivable, of course, that we should abandon the presumption that a particular author holds the beliefs which his work expresses if there is strong evidence, such as an appropriate statement by the author, that in the work in question he is expressing beliefs which he does not hold. But the fact that the author has expressed nowhere else the beliefs which the work expresses does not constitute evidence that our presumption is in this case unwarranted.

Furthermore, it does not follow from our presumption that if the speaker or narrator expresses beliefs, so must the work. If the speaker expresses certain propositions, it is

[67] See e.g. Crane's criticism of the 'Christian humanist' interpretation of *Gulliver's Travels*, "The Houyhnhnms, the Yahoos, and the History of Ideas," pp. 237f.

Life, Literature, and the Implied Author

conceivable that the author is neither expressing those propositions nor rejecting them. He may just be portraying a certain character or describing a certain situation. A case in point is T. S. Eliot's and Edmund Wilson's interpretations of Kipling's poem "Loot."[68] What is interesting about their remarks is that they do not argue that regardless of what Kipling believed or how he felt about the experiences of British soldiers in India, the poem just describes those experiences. Rather, they argue that *Kipling* is merely describing here, not passing judgment, and their contention is based on claims about (the real) Kipling's attitudes and concerns regarding the soldier's life in India, and in particular on the assumption that Kipling did not endorse the speaker's sentiments.[69]

7. Why Suppose That a Literary Work Has an Implied Author?

I should like to pursue one further question. What could have led Booth as well as the many other critics who have accepted his view, or who have taken a similar position, to suppose that the author we are dealing with in reading and interpreting a literary work is not the real, historical person, but rather a fictional version of that person, the "implied author"? What makes this view so attractive?

One reason may be that the beliefs which an author has expressed on this or that occasion of his life may not be the ones he is expressing in a particular literary work.[70] For it

[68] I am indebted to Cioffi for this example ("Intention and Interpretation in Criticism," in Barrett (ed.), *Collected Papers on Aesthetics*, pp. 178-79).

[69] T. S. Eliot, "Rudyard Kipling," pp. 244f.; Edmund Wilson, "The Kipling that Nobody Read," in Rutherford (ed.), *Kipling's Mind and Art*, p. 45. See also Edward Shanks, *Rudyard Kipling*, p. 81; George Orwell, "Rudyard Kipling," in Rutherford (ed.), *Kipling's Mind and Art*, p. 70; and Cioffi, "Intention and Interpretation in Criticism," in Barrett (ed.), *Collected Papers on Aesthetics*, pp. 178-79.

[70] See Booth, *The Rhetoric of Fiction*, p. 137, and Wimsatt, "Genesis," pp. 199, 203.

is perhaps tempting to infer from this that the author's beliefs are irrelevant. Although this is probably of minor significance as a motivation for introducing the concept of an implied author, it does make it easier to hold on to it, once one feels the need for such a notion.

To see what lies behind the implied-author thesis, it will be useful to look at Louis Rubin's version. Although it does not differ from Booth's in any essential respect, it brings out more clearly certain aspects of the thesis.

To illustrate the difference between the real author and "the authorial personality"[71]—Booth's implied author—Rubin gives two examples from Mark Twain's *Adventures of Huckleberry Finn*. When Huck Finn decides against the dictates of his conscience to rescue his black friend Jim from slavery and says to himself "all right then, I'll *go* to Hell," the authorial presence we are aware of "is as much a part of the fiction as Huckleberry Finn himself is."[72] But when Huck gets to Phelps Farm to save Jim and is taken for Tom Sawyer who is being expected there, "the coincidence is wildly improbable" and the authorial presence we become aware of here is "[t]he spectacle of Samuel L. Clemens figuring out a way to end his novel by reintroducing Tom Sawyer." No doubt, this "spectacle . . . is very different from that of Mark Twain instructing us about Huck's conscience through and above Huck Finn a bit earlier."[73] But why say, as Rubin does, that the difference is "the difference between fiction and biography"?[74] After all, to know that in the second episode the author "has wrenched his whole plot structure out of shape in order to get Tom back on to the scene," we need no more knowledge of the author's biography than we do to know that in the first episode Mark Twain "is saying . . . that Huck is not committing wrong, and that his so-called inner conscience is in reality only the arbitrary social values of his society."[75]

[71] Rubin, *The Teller in the Tale*, p. 21.
[72] *Ibid.*, p. 19.   [73] *Ibid.*
[74] *Ibid.*, p. 20.   [75] *Ibid.*, p. 18.

Life, Literature, and the Implied Author

One can admit that in the first case it is essential to understand what the author is doing—namely, suggesting certain things about the values of his society—in order to understand the work, whereas in the second case it is not. But why say that what the author does in the first case is not done by the real person? Rubin concedes that "the two [authors] may seem to come very close to being one and the same. Mark Twain talking about Huck Finn's conscience is also Samuel Clemens talking about himself as a child growing up in Hannibal, Missouri, and apologizing for once having accepted the divine right of slavery without question." But Rubin insists that "no matter how closely the two authors may coincide, they are not the same persons."[76]

Notice what Rubin is doing here. He is attributing statements which can be regarded as part of the meaning of the work to Mark Twain and certain other statements which cannot be so regarded and which are irrelevant to understanding the work to the real author. But surely it is quite implausible to take Clemens (here) to be talking about himself and apologizing for once having accepted slavery, although in a sense no doubt he is 'correcting' here his own behavior as a child. Even if this claim were plausible, however, notice how artificial it is to say that it is not the real author, Samuel Clemens, who is commenting on the values of his society.

One can readily admit that much of an author's personality and life has no bearing on what we make of his work. Few would be inclined to suppose that it mattered what the author believed to be the causes of hair loss or tooth decay. But what could be the point of giving a name ("implied author" or "authorial personality") to those aspects of the author which are relevant to our understanding of his work and another (the "real author") to those which are not and then saying that it is only the former we are concerned with? The point is that it gives us the illusion of being able to exclude in advance a certain set of facts as irrelevant. It

[76] *Ibid.*, p. 21.

gives us the illusion of reducing the considerations involved in determining how to view what is presented in a work to a strictly limited set of factors, namely, those and only those that pertain to the teller *in* the tale. In short, the insistence that the implied author is not the real author, Mark Twain not Samuel Clemens and Stendhal not Henri Beyle, creates the illusion of solving a highly complex problem by giving it a new name.

There is another reason why the implied-author doctrine seems so attractive. On the one hand, the real author is irrevocably expelled from the work, while the implied author, on the other, is wholly incorporated into the work. Thus one of the main points of Rubin's book is that "the author of a novel is a character in his fiction."[77] But notice again how strange it is to say this. For in the sense in which we ordinarily speak of a character in talking about fiction, it is certainly not a character in *Huckleberry Finn* who is telling us that Huck's "so-called inner conscience is in reality only the arbitrary social values of his society."[78]

Why, then, make the author into a "character in his fiction"? What lies behind this idea is a very common conception of a literary work, and of a work of art more generally, as a self-sufficient and perfectly self-contained whole. A literary work, as Ilse Graham has put it, is "a unique and self-sufficient organism, sealed off from every other work of art, and from life."[79] According to this view, a literary work creates a totally separate world complete in itself. On at least one interpretation of Mörike's "Auf eine Lampe," the last line of the poem epitomizes this view: "Was aber schön ist, selig scheint es in ihm selbst."[80] ("But what is beautiful

[77] *Ibid.*, p. 210.   [78] *Ibid.*, p. 18.
[79] Ilse Graham, *Schiller's Drama*, p. 46. See also Eliseo Vivas, *Creation and Discovery*, pp. 106, 112, 126.
[80] See the exchange of letters between Staiger and Heidegger published in Emil Staiger, *Die Kunst der Interpretation*, pp. 34-49. See also Staiger, "Die Kunst der Interpretation" in the same volume, pp. 17-29; and Heinz Politzer, "Das Handwerk der Interpretation," pp. 379-86.

blissfully shines in itself.") Ingarden similarly speaks of a literary work of art as "eine wunderbare Welt für sich" ("a miraculous world in itself") which gives our life "einen göttlichen Glanz"[81] ("a divine radiance"). It is obvious that to allow the real author, *any* real person, entry into this world is to profane, to defile it. It is to reduce a world which exists only for its own sake to a mere instrument, a means to an end, a tool for nonartistic purposes.[82] Thus Ingarden, for example, rejects emphatically the view that a literary work of art might make any genuine assertions as a misunderstanding of the essence of such a work.[83]

This picture of literature bears a certain resemblance to what Frye has called "the shivering virgin theory of art, according to which art is a fragile evocation of pure beauty surrounded by rough disciplines such as theology and morals, and in constant danger of being polluted by them."[84] For both are manifestations of a demand for an absolute: an absolutely pure art, an absolutely pure fiction.[85] The implied-author doctrine gives us the illusion that literary works, properly understood, satisfy this demand.

But the implied-author doctrine does even more. Unlike some of the more radical variants of the anti-intentionalist thesis, it acknowledges a need for the author's presence. Thus Rubin evidently feels that it matters whether what the narrator or a character "thinks and says to us is intended ... to tell the reader what he ought to think about the situa-

[81] *Das literarische Kunstwerk*, p. 400 (*The Literary Work of Art*, p. 373).

[82] See *ibid.*, p. 183n (*The Literary Work of Art*, p. 173n).

[83] *Ibid.*, pp. 182f., 325 (*The Literary Work of Art*, pp. 172f., 303).

[84] Frye, *Fearful Symmetry*, p. 418.

[85] As Stanley Cavell has pointed out in his discussion of what Cleanth Brooks called "the heresy of paraphrase," this kind of thing is relatively common in philosophy: "We impose a demand for absoluteness (typically of some simple physical kind) upon a concept, and then, finding that our ordinary use of this concept does not meet our demand, we accommodate this discrepancy as nearly as possible" ("Aesthetic Problems of Modern Philosophy," p. 77).

tion."[86] In other words, we do not feel satisfied unless we are convinced that the author stands behind what we take the work to mean or to express. Consequently, we face a dilemma. On the one hand, we feel a need for the author's presence; we "need to know where, in the world of values," we stand, "that is . . . where the author *wants* [us] to stand."[87] On the other hand, to the extent that the author is part of the real world, his presence destroys what is felt to be the essence of fictional literature. That the real author should be able to suggest things, to make statements by creating a fictional world, is incompatible with the picture of a literary work as a wholly separate, self-contained world which exists only for its own sake.

Now the implied-author doctrine—and herein, I think, lies its great appeal—appears to solve this basic dilemma in one fell swoop. By incorporating the author into the fiction it appears to achieve something of a major synthesis; it gives us the illusion of having reconciled the author's presence and the communicative function of literature with a fictional world which satisfies the demand for absolute purity.[88]

8. Conclusion

I have argued that if a literary work expresses certain propositions, then the author is committed to the corresponding beliefs and to their truth. I have tried to support this claim by examining a few representative examples of critical argument and commentary on the meaning of a text. That is, I have tried to make explicit some of the tacit assumptions

---

[86] Rubin, *The Teller in the Tale*, p. 212. But see also Rubin's insistence that the intentions of the historical author are irrelevant (p. 22).

[87] Booth, *The Rhetoric of Fiction*, p. 73.

[88] For a different attempt to reconcile the autonomy of a literary work with the need to "treat [the work] as an expression of the poet's consciousness," see Murray Krieger, *Theory of Criticism*, pp. 179-206; the quotation is from p. 194.

which underlie our interpretation of a literary work. If what I have said is true, then in one important sense (fictional) literature is not autonomous. At least as far as those propositions which a work expresses or conveys are concerned, the connection between language and the world is not severed in literature. This should hardly come as much of a surprise. For, I suppose, few of us, at least in our less guarded moments, would be inclined to believe otherwise. But when widely accepted and highly sophisticated theories of literature imply the contrary, it may be worth reminding ourselves of the homely truth that poets do after all actually say things.

VIII

Does a Literary Work Have One and Only One Correct Interpretation?

1. INTRODUCTION

EDMUND WILSON has claimed that the governess in Henry James' *The Turn of the Screw* "is a neurotic case of sex repression, and that the ghosts are not real ghosts but hallucinations of the governess."[1] Alexander Jones, on the other hand, insists that the ghosts are not hallucinations of the governess but are in fact quite real.[2] Christine Brooke-Rose has taken yet another view; she maintains that the question whether the ghosts are real or are hallucinations is left open.[3] If one of these statements about *The Turn of the Screw* is true, does it follow that the other two are false? Or could all three be true? Or if not true, at least acceptable? Could the ghosts be both real and mere hallucinations of the governess?

The existence of divergent interpretations such as these raises the general issue of whether a literary work has one and only one correct reading or whether it usually has several correct, acceptable or admissible readings. Can we in principle determine the correct interpretation of a work, or is it not just in fact but logically—that is, in virtue of our concept of a literary work or of its meaning—impossible to

---

[1] Edmund Wilson, "The Ambiguity of Henry James," in Willen (ed.), *A Casebook on Henry James's "The Turn of the Screw,"* p. 115.

[2] Alexander E. Jones, "Point of View in *The Turn of the Screw*," *ibid.*, pp. 316f.

[3] Brooke-Rose, "The Squirm of the True," p. 513.

find such a reading? Is the idea that one of the possible readings of a work is correct unintelligible?

Many structuralists reject the notion of literature as communication, representation, or expression. Interpretation, on this view, "is not a matter of recovering some meaning which lies behind the work and serves as a centre governing its structure; it is rather an attempt to participate in and observe the play of possible meanings to which the text gives access."[4] Although interpretation—at least on the moderate view defended by Culler—is governed by rules or conventions, they impose only relatively loose constraints on what a text can mean and hence allow a variety of different, equally acceptable interpretations of any given work. It is not difficult to see that, on this view, one cannot speak of 'the correct interpretation' of a text; nor can one say of an interpretation or an interpretive statement that it is true, inasmuch as the admissible interpretations of a given work may be incompatible.

Similarly, Joseph Margolis has maintained that "given the goal of interpretation, we do not understand that an admissible account necessarily precludes all others incompatible with itself."[5] Hence it would appear that the proper model of confirmation in literary interpretation is not truth and falsity, but rather plausibility and implausibility: "where his effort is interpretive, we cannot judge the critic's remarks to be simply true or false, accurate or inaccurate, but only that his interpretation . . . is 'plausible', 'reasonable', 'admissible', 'indefensible', 'not impossible', and the like."[6]

[4] Culler, *Structuralist Poetics*, p. 247.
[5] Margolis, *The Language of Art and Art Criticism*, p. 92. See also his "Works of Art Are Physically Embodied and Culturally Emergent Entities," in Aagaard-Mogensen (ed.), *Culture and Art*, p. 40, and "Three Problems in Aesthetics," p. 266.
[6] Margolis, *The Language of Art and Art Criticism*, p. 76. For a lucid and persuasive discussion of Margolis' claims, see Annette Barnes, "Half an Hour Before Breakfast," pp. 261-71.

Does a Work Have Only One Correct Interpretation?

The same holds true if we believe with Iser that the meaning of a text depends on the reader's creativity and imagination in filling in the so-called gaps in the text— in filling in, that is, what is left open or unspecified in a text.[7] For if these gaps can be filled in a number of different, equally legitimate and possibly inconsistent ways, then again one could not say of an interpretive statement that it is true or that a certain interpretation is the correct reading of the text.

In the following, I shall present a few considerations in support of the view that a literary work has one and only one correct interpretation.

---

[7] Iser, *The Implied Reader*, pp. 279ff. See also his essay "The Reality of Fiction," p. 35.

The view that a literary work has more than one 'correct' interpretation has also been defended by, among others, Umberto Eco, *Das offene Kunstwerk*, pp. 8, 11, 29f., 31, 37f., 56-59, *et passim*; Stuart Hampshire, "Types of Interpretation," pp. 101-8; Todorov, "How to Read?," pp. 238-39; Ricoeur, "The Model of the Text," pp. 103, 107f.; Tormey, *The Concept of Expression*, pp. 134-41; John F. Reichert, "Description and Interpretation in Literary Criticism," p. 290; Japp, *Hermeneutik*, pp. 46-58; András Horn, *Das Literarische*, pp. 37, 79-83; Smith, *On the Margins of Discourse*, pp. 38f., 74f., 124, and 137-54; and Matthews, "Describing and Interpreting a Work of Art," pp. 5-14. Matthews' argument for the claim that literary interpretations are typically neither true nor false (p. 13) rests on two crucial premises: (1) that a necessary condition for a person to be "able to interpret x . . . [is that he] *not* be in a position to know whether the statements constituting the interpretation are true of x" (p. 9); and (2) that external evidence is irrelevant (p. 12). He defends only the first premise, however. For a critical discussion of Matthews' claims, see Michael Hancher, "Describing and Interpreting Speech Acts," pp. 483-85.

That a literary work does not have one and only one correct reading also follows from C. L. Stevenson's theory, according to which interpretive claims are normative statements about how a text ought to be read ("On the Reasons That Can Be Given for the Interpretation of a Poem," pp. 121-39). See also Arthur Child, *Interpretation*, pp. 125ff., and Frank Kermode's interesting essay "Can We Say Absolutely Anything We Like?," pp. 159-72.

Does a Work Have Only One Correct Interpretation?

2. Multiplicity of Meaning and Incompatible Interpretations

Let us look a little more closely at the claim that there is not in principle one and only one correct interpretation of a literary work or that such interpretations are neither true nor false. Jonathan Culler has claimed that we "cannot ask [a theory of literature] to account for the 'correct' meaning of a work since we manifestly do not believe that for each work there is a single correct reading. . . . Indeed, the striking facts that do require explanation are how it is that a work can have a variety of meanings, but not just any meaning whatsoever. . . ."[8]

In order to clarify the issue, it will be useful to distinguish between two possible senses of the claim that a work can have a variety of meanings.

It may mean that a literary work usually suggests several different ideas, that it evokes or conveys a variety of different attitudes or feelings. For example, one might want to say that Wordsworth's poem "A slumber did my spirit seal" does not just convey, as Cleanth Brooks has maintained, "the lover's agonized shock"[9] at the death of the beloved, nor just a sense of pantheistic affirmation of "the grander dead-Lucy" who "is now a part of the life of Nature, and not just a human 'thing',"[10] as F. W. Bateson has contended. Rather, one might want to say that the poem conveys both agonized shock and a sense of affirmation. In this sense of the claim that a work can have a variety of meanings, it is perfectly consistent with the assumption that there is in principle one and only one correct interpretation of a work. If the various meanings of a work are logically compatible, then the corresponding interpretive statements can all be true.[11]

[8] *Structuralist Poetics*, p. 122.
[9] Brooks, "Irony as a Principle of Structure," p. 736.
[10] Bateson, *English Poetry*, p. 59.
[11] Accordingly, I do not deny, of course, that a literary work may,

Alternatively, the claim may be that a literary work can have a variety of mutually *incompatible* meanings. For instance, one might want to allow that the following interpretations of Wordsworth's poem are *jointly* acceptable: (a) that the poem conveys "the lover's agonized shock" at the death of the beloved and is not a pantheistic affirmation of "the grander dead-Lucy" who has become part of the life of nature; (b) that the poem does indeed celebrate "the grander dead-Lucy who has become involved in the sublime processes of nature"[12] and does not express grief or inconsolability; (c) that the poem is neither just an expression of the lover's agonized shock nor just a pantheistic celebration of the dead Lucy, but suggests both the lover's agony and affirmation.

In other words, in the second sense of the claim that a work can have a variety of meanings, it may be 'true' both that the poem expresses pantheistic affirmation and that it does not express pantheistic affirmation. This is an example of Margolis' principle of tolerance, that incompatible interpretations of a literary work can be jointly defended as plausible.[13] This interpretation of the claim, unlike the first, is indeed inconsistent with the assumption that there is one and only one correct reading of a work and hence with the assumption that literary interpretations are true or false.

---

in a sense, have several correct interpretations. For if a work has several correct interpretations, they must (if I am right) be logically compatible. Consequently, they will be *partial* interpretations of the work or interpretations of one or another of its different aspects. And these various (correct) partial interpretations—since they must be logically compatible—can be combined into one (comprehensive) interpretation of the work. It is important to notice, however, that when critics offer different interpretations of a given work, those interpretations are *in fact* usually incompatible. See Hirsch's excellent discussion, *Validity in Interpretation*, pp. 227-30, and also pp. 128-32.

[12] Bateson, *English Poetry*, p. 59.

[13] Margolis, *The Language of Art and Art Criticism*, pp. 91f. See also Hospers, "Implied Truths in Literature," in Kennick (ed.), *Art and Philosophy*, pp. 320-21.

Does a Work Have Only One Correct Interpretation?

It is important not to confuse the claim that a work may have a variety of logically incompatible meanings with another one which, unlike Margolis' principle of tolerance, is uncontroversial: namely, that for many works a variety of logically incompatible interpretations have been offered. For it does not follow from this that a literary work cannot have one and only one correct interpretation. It is *prima facie* quite conceivable that of the incompatible interpretations provided for a work only one is correct. Thus Culler and Margolis are not just saying that literary works are frequently construed in a number of incompatible ways. Rather, they are claiming that incompatible interpretations may be 'true' of the same work or, to put it another way, that we would be prepared to allow that if a work has a certain meaning x, it might also have another meaning y which is logically incompatible with x.

When confronted with two incompatible interpretations of a work, we could do several things: (1) We could say that each is (separately) plausible and the available evidence does not allow us to decide between them. (2) Or we could choose one and try to defend it and attempt to show that the other reading is inadequate or 'incorrect'. (3) Or we could modify the two interpretations so as to make them compatible and say, as in the case of Wordsworth's poem "A slumber did my spirit seal," for example, that it expresses both the lover's agonized shock at the death of the beloved and pantheistic affirmation. (This would be to opt for a third interpretation distinct from, and incompatible with, either of the original readings.)

But it would be very peculiar to say of Wordsworth's poem that it expresses the lover's grief and inconsolability *and* that it does *not* express the lover's grief and inconsolability but rather pantheistic affirmation. There is no evidence that in practice critics or other readers would be prepared to allow that logically incompatible readings could be jointly true. Nor does it help here, as Annette Barnes has pointed out,[14] to shift from truth to plausibility and to say that while logically incompatible readings cannot be jointly true, they can be jointly plausible. The conjunction 'the work means x and it does not mean x, but y' can no more be plausible than it can be true. If critics did allow logically incompatible readings to be jointly true or plausible, we would be forced to speak of different works corresponding to the various incompatible meanings of a given text.

But even if logically incompatible readings of a work cannot be jointly true or plausible, they may be *separately* plausible. Even if Wordsworth's poem cannot both express the lover's agonized shock and not express it, the reading according to which it expresses the lover's agonized shock may be just as plausible as the reading according to which it does not express this, but rather pantheistic affirmation. That any given work have at least two separately plausible readings is not quite sufficient, however, for a work not to have one and only one correct reading. We must also not in principle be able to say more than that a reading is plausible. Thus we can alternatively construe the claim that a work has several incompatible meanings as follows. For any given work there are several incompatible readings each of which is separately plausible and none of which can in principle be shown to be significantly more likely to be correct than any of the others.[15]

[14] "Half an Hour Before Breakfast," pp. 264f., 269. On logically incompatible interpretations, see also Shlomith Rimmon's clear and helpful discussion in *The Concept of Ambiguity*, pp. 7-11, 14, 17.

[15] Although this interpretation of the thesis that a work usually has several (incompatible) meanings precludes the possibility that there is one and only one correct reading of a work, it does not allow us, strictly speaking, to say that a work *has* several (incompatible) meanings. All we can say of a work now is 'it *could* mean x and it *could* mean y, not x'. One might object that since it is in principle impossible to say more than that the work *could* mean x, in the sense that x is a plausible, admissible, or acceptable reading, to say that the work

Does a Work Have Only One Correct Interpretation?

3. POSSIBLE READINGS AND CRITICAL CHOICES

The conception of the meaning of a literary work which underlies the view that a literary work may have several or many logically incompatible meanings seems to be something like this. An interpretation of a literary work is analogous to a statement about the meaning of a word or sentence in a particular language; it is in important respects like a statement about the meaning of the word "man" in English, for example, or about the meaning of, say, the English sentence 'He almost killed the dragon' in abstraction from its use by a speaker on a particular occasion. Culler, for instance, writes:

> The meaning of a sentence, one might say, is not a form or an essence, present at the moment of its production and lying behind it as a truth to be recovered, but the series of developments to which it gives rise, as determined by past and future relations between words and the conventions of semiotic systems. . . .[16]

> The written word is an object in its own right.[17]

> Interpretation is . . . an attempt to participate in and observe the play of possible meanings to which the text gives access.[18]

---

could mean *x* *is* to say that it means *x* or that the work *has* the meaning *x*. But this would be to miss the point. It is not because we cannot say of any reading that it is correct, as opposed to being plausible or admissible, it is because a work cannot both mean *x* and not mean *x* that we cannot say it *has* the meaning *x* if a reading according to which the work does not mean *x* is also plausible or admissible.

[16] *Structuralist Poetics*, pp. 132. See also pp. 123-24.

[17] *Ibid.*, p. 133.

[18] *Ibid.*, p. 247. See also Smith, *On the Margins of Discourse*, pp. 51ff., 59, 69f., 74f., 124, and Siegfried Schmidt, *Elemente einer Textpoetik*, p. 87. Schmidt holds (pp. 41ff.), however, that a work can have only logically compatible meanings which must be capable of

Does a Work Have Only One Correct Interpretation?

The sign has a life of its own which is not governed by any *arché* or *telos*, origin or final cause, and the conventions which govern its use in particular types of discourse are epiphenomena: they are themselves transitory cultural products.[19]

Of course, Culler does not want to go quite as far as Derrida or Kristeva; for he insists that "at any one time the production of meaning in a culture is governed by conventions."[20] The main differences between the meaning of a sentence (*in abstracto*) in a given language and the meaning of a literary work would seem to be these: the sentences of a natural language are not typically ambiguous in as many ways as are literary works; and the relevant conventions differ inasmuch as there is a special set of rules for the interpretation of literature (in addition to the semantic and syntactic rules of ordinary language) whose mastery constitutes literary competence.[21]

In this and the following section I shall try to show that this model, even if it is modified in certain respects, fails to account adequately for some central facts about the interpretation of literary works. These facts provide strong evidence that a literary work has one and only one correct reading. They support the view that the meaning of a literary work (rather than being like the meaning of a sentence *in abstracto*) is like the meaning of a person's *utterance* of

---

being integrated into a coherent whole ("Textgesamtgestalt"). But see also Schmidt, "Text und Bedeutung," p. 49.

Ricoeur claims that although a text will have several meanings, "the kind of 'plurivocity' which belongs to texts as texts is something other than the polysemy of individual words in ordinary language and the ambiguity of individual sentences" ("The Model of the Text," p. 107). This is no doubt true. But since the ambiguity of individual words or sentences is used here only as an analogy, the objections raised below apply to Ricoeur's thesis as well.

[19] Culler, *Structuralist Poetics*, p. 248.
[20] *Ibid.*, p. 249.
[21] See *ibid.*, pp. 113-30, *et passim.*

a sentence in a certain context—that is, like the meaning of a speech act.[22]

Consider the sentence

>   Cary saw the girl laughing at John.

Provided we know that the sentence is ambiguous and in what ways it is so, it would not make sense to say, in specifying the meaning of this sentence in English, that it just means

(i) Cary saw the girl as she (the girl) was laughing at John.

or that it just means

(ii) Cary saw the girl who is laughing at John.

In other words, under these circumstances it would not make sense to *choose* one of the linguistically possible readings of the sentence and say that it means (i), not (ii), or vice versa. On the other hand, if we are interpreting a person's utterance of the sentence on some particular occasion, then it would make sense to choose one of its possible readings even if we cannot in fact tell whether the utterance means (i) or (ii) or possibly both.

Consider now the following poem:

>   The shooting of the hunters she heard;
>   But to pity it moved her not.

It has at least three possible readings:

(1) She heard the hunters shooting (at animals or people), but she had no pity for the victims.
(2) She heard the hunters being shot but did not pity them.

---

[22] For a detailed and illuminating application of speech act theory to literature, see Pratt, *Toward a Speech Act Theory of Literary Discourse*. See also Michael Hancher's critical appraisal of the book in "Beyond a Speech Act Theory of Literary Discourse," pp. 1081-98.

(3) She heard the hunters shooting at someone or something, and she heard the hunters being shot (at), but did not pity either.

If the meaning of a literary work is like the meaning of a sentence *in abstracto*, then we should have to say that the poem means (1), (2), and (3). But it would not make sense to decide between these readings, just as it would not make sense, in specifying the meaning of the sentence 'Cary saw the girl laughing at John', to choose one of its possible readings and to say it means (i) and not (ii). If someone did say this, we would be inclined to think either that he does not know that the sentence is ambiguous or that he is talking, not about the sentence, but about an utterance of the sentence on some particular occasion. In other words, on the model we are considering, it would be *unintelligible* to suppose that the poem could, for example, mean (1) and not also (2) and (3).

If we look at the practice of literary interpretation, however, we find that critics do in fact choose between the possible readings of a given text. For example, each of the three readings of the poem by Wordsworth mentioned above is, as far as the linguistic rules of English as well as Culler's conventions of literary interpretation are concerned, a possible reading of the text. Nevertheless, most of the critics who have offered an interpretation of the poem have chosen one of its possible readings and have claimed that it is the most probable interpretation, whereas the other possible readings which they have considered are incorrect, improbable, or implausible.

Of course, we do not always choose between the various possible readings of a work. Sometimes a critic will say of a particular work that it could mean so-and-so or that it could equally well mean such-and-such. But in saying this, a critic is not implying that it would not make sense to choose one of the possible readings; rather, he is saying that the evidence we possess is not sufficient to allow us to determine which of the possible readings is most probably correct.[23] Similarly, even if we believe that a particular work is ambiguous in the sense that the textual evidence provides more or less equal support for two or more interpretations, it would not be unintelligible to suppose that only one of the readings in question is correct.

A good example is R. S. Crane's interpretation of the fourth book of *Gulliver's Travels*. Crane believes that there is nothing in the text which would allow us to decide between the reading of the fourth Voyage as presenting a radically pessimistic picture of man and the reading according to which human nature is portrayed as not altogether hopeless.[24] Yet he does not go on to suggest that therefore it would be unintelligible to suppose that only one of the two interpretations might be correct. Rather, he proceeds to argue that the former interpretation is more likely to be correct.

Of course, he does so on the basis of 'external' evidence of what Swift intended to convey. But then the anti-intentionalist needs to explain how Crane and the vast majority of other critics could be so utterly misguided in their interpretive *practice* as to suppose that what they were offering in producing evidence of the author's intention is evidence of what the text means. Surely, the task of a theory of interpretation is to account for the most central aspects of critical practice, such as the kinds of evidence which the vast majority of critics implicitly accept as relevant, the kinds of things critics do in trying to establish that a work means so-and-so, and the kinds of inferences they draw from the fact or the assumption that a certain interpretation is 'correct'. Now, on the anti-intentionalist thesis, it is difficult to see how standard interpretive practice could be explained except as being the result of an enormous conceptual confusion. What I am referring to here are not metacritical pro-

[23] See Beardsley, *The Possibility of Criticism*, p. 44.
[24] Crane, "The Houyhnhnms, the Yahoos, and the History of Ideas," pp. 234ff., 237f., 243f.

nouncements about the nature of literary interpretation, but rather the facts of actual interpretive practice and its implicit assumptions. And it is precisely these facts and assumptions that a theory of interpretation needs to account for.[25]

I have claimed that critics commonly choose between the possible readings of a text and say that it means this rather than that; they do so, as we have seen, at least occasionally even if they believe that on the basis of the textual evidence several interpretations are equally possible or plausible. Consequently, it would appear to be intelligible to suppose that only one of the possible readings of a given text is correct.

4. Critical Disagreements and Acceptable Readings

On the view that the meaning of a literary work is like the meaning of an ambiguous sentence *in abstracto*, it is difficult to account for the fact that in interpreting a work we usually choose one of its possible readings. This could be explained, however, on something like the following hypothesis.[26]

In order to be possible, plausible, or admissible, an interpretation of a literary work must satisfy linguistic constraints, certain requirements of textual coherence, and general rules or conventions of literary interpretation (such as Culler's). For any given work there are usually several readings which meet these conditions. Our concept of a literary work or of its meaning is such that there are no further constraints which an interpretation must or could satisfy in order to qualify for the more restrictive status of

[25] See on this point Cavell, "A Matter of Meaning It," p. 227. See also Lyas, "Personal Qualities and the Intentional Fallacy," pp. 199, 209.

[26] For some suggestions along these lines, see Joseph Margolis, "Critics and Literature," p. 378; Hungerland, "The Concept of Intention in Art Criticism," pp. 738ff., and *Poetic Discourse*, pp. 168-71, 175; Eaton, "Good and Correct Interpretations of Literature," p. 231.

being true rather than merely plausible or admissible. That it is plausible or admissible is the most that could be said of an interpretation. So far the hypothesis introduces nothing new.

We now assume further that a critic may impose additional restrictions corresponding to his interests or his purpose in reading a work. He may, for example, want to read it in the way the author's contemporaries construed it; he may want to interpret it as a study in abnormal psychology; or he may want to give a Freudian or an existentialist reading; and so on. But since no such supplementary restriction is derivable from our concept of the meaning of a work, the fact that only one of the admissible readings of a given text satisfies a certain additional restriction of this sort does not make the interpretation in question correct. The most one might be able to establish is that a certain interpretation is 'the correct — reading' of a particular text, where the blank is filled in by a suitable specification of the additional restriction imposed. But that an interpretation is the correct — reading of a work does not imply, of course, that it is the correct reading of the work. Nor does it have any bearing on the (objective) plausibility of that reading relative to other admissible interpretations of the work.

The fact that in interpreting a work we usually make a choice between its possible readings could then be explained by assuming that when we do so, we have imposed further restrictions of this kind corresponding to our interests. There is another problem, however, which this hypothesis cannot eliminate so easily.

If a literary work has a variety of plausible or "acceptable"[27] readings, then we should expect that the critics who have examined a particular text *agree* that the various (incompatible) interpretations, which are "acceptable" according to the model, are indeed acceptable interpretations of the text. But such agreement is extremely rare. It is not just

[27] Culler, *Structuralist Poetics*, pp. 124f., 127.

Does a Work Have Only One Correct Interpretation?

that critics do not agree on an interpretation. That, as we have seen, could be accommodated by the view that for any work there is a variety of plausible or acceptable readings—namely, if the critics in question simply preferred, for whatever reason, different interpretations of the set of "acceptable" readings but did not deny that the other readings are (objectively) equally 'correct' or acceptable. It is the fact that they do almost invariably deny this which is difficult for this thesis to explain.

I have suggested in section 2 that critics are not prepared to allow that logically incompatible readings of a given work could be *jointly* plausible or acceptable. The point here is that although critics do allow that logically incompatible readings could be separately acceptable, they do not agree in most cases which reading or readings of a particular work *are* separately acceptable. In particular, they deny as a rule that readings incompatible with their own are also (separately) acceptable. It is important to notice that the crucial test of this claim is not whether a critic is prepared to assert that certain readings incompatible with his own might also be (separately) acceptable, but rather whether *when actually confronted* with readings incompatible with his own, he is in fact willing to concede that those readings are equally acceptable.

Culler, for example, maintains that "the claim is not that competent readers would agree on an interpretation but only that certain expectations about poetry and ways of reading guide the interpretive process and impose severe limitations on the set of acceptable or plausible readings."[28] But if the fact that competent readers hold different interpretations of the same text shows that it has several equally 'correct', plausible, or acceptable readings, then what is it that these readers are disagreeing about when each of them denies that the others' interpretations are acceptable?

Let us consider a parallel in ordinary discourse.

[28] *Ibid.*, p. 127.

Does a Work Have Only One Correct Interpretation?

The sentence

> The boys are lying about the house.

is ambiguous and hence has more than one correct reading. Competent speakers of English will recognize at least two different interpretations of this sentence *in abstracto*:

(1) The boys are lying around in the house.
(2) The boys are not telling the truth about the house.

Now suppose that competent speakers of English disagreed about whether the proper reading of the sentence is (1) or (2). In that case, one could not expect a grammar of English simply to assign two readings to the sentence without qualification. Rather, the two readings would have to be marked as relative to certain dialects, so as to exhibit the fact that the sentence is not ambiguous in either of the relevant dialects. Thus, on the face of it, if a literary work has several 'correct' or acceptable interpretations, one would expect that competent critics are in agreement about this, as competent speakers are in the case of a sentence which has several readings.

If we are to retain the view that for every work there is a variety of equally 'correct' or acceptable interpretations, then we need to account for the fact that competent critics nevertheless disagree about which of those 'correct' or acceptable interpretations is indeed correct. The explanation suggested by the hypothetical example of a disagreement over the proper reading of the sentence 'The boys are lying about the house' would seem to be implausible in the case of a literary parallel. For it would be difficult to show, for example, that the dispute about Wordsworth's poem is rooted in the different dialects of the critics involved. Furthermore, if this were the right explanation, the controversy could be expected to dissolve as soon as the critics became aware of this.

Nor can disagreements about the meaning of a work be explained by assuming that usually each of the participants

Does a Work Have Only One Correct Interpretation?

in a dispute has imposed a different supplementary restriction corresponding to his interests or purpose in interpreting the work. For, on the hypothesis sketched at the beginning of this section, such further restrictions have no bearing on the question whether a certain reading is or is not acceptable. Hence each of the critics could be expected to agree that the other readings are (objectively) equally acceptable. Nevertheless, a disagreement about the meaning of a work could be due to the fact that each critic has imposed a different supplementary restriction—if, for example, each has tacitly assumed that the others have imposed the same supplementary restriction. But this should become obvious fairly quickly in the course of the dispute. One would therefore expect the critics to acknowledge that each of their readings is 'correct' given the corresponding supplementary restrictions. Hence the dispute should dissolve.

One might argue, however, that disagreements about which reading or readings are acceptable could be explained as follows. Let us assume that the acceptability of a reading is determined in the way postulated by the above hypothesis so that any given work will have several acceptable readings. Nonetheless, in practice critics might generally impose one further restriction, say, correspondence to the author's intention. Thus a reading that is acceptable might be regarded as unacceptable by the critics who conform to the general practice. Disputes about the meaning of a work could then be explained as disputes about what the author intended.

But, by hypothesis, any given work has some acceptable readings other than the one which the author intended. Suppose then that a critic refuses to adopt this restriction and chooses one of the acceptable readings of a particular work which does not correspond to what the author intended. One would expect, on the hypothesis under consideration, that critics who, in conformity to the general practice, reject that reading as unacceptable would nevertheless admit that it is acceptable, provided one does not adopt the author's intention as a supplementary restriction. The problem, however, is that as a rule critics are not prepared to relativize in this way their claim that a certain reading is unacceptable. What they are claiming in rejecting a reading as unacceptable is that it fails to account (or account adequately) for certain facts which *any* interpretation must (satisfactorily) account for, regardless of what supplementary restriction a critic may decide to impose.

I am not suggesting that a literary work has only one possible reading. Clearly, for virtually any work there are a number of possible and perhaps plausible interpretations; and this is brought out by the fact that critics who disagree about the meaning of a given work will generally, or can be gotten to, admit that the interpretations with which they take issue and reject are nonetheless in some sense possible or have a certain plausibility. What I am suggesting is that a theory of interpretation must account for the fact that we do draw a distinction between a possible and a correct interpretation, even if we may not agree in any given case what the correct reading is.[29]

Critics who propose and defend an interpretation of a work do not usually claim merely that their reading is possible or plausible; rather, they typically claim implicitly, if not explicitly, that it is more likely to be correct than the various other interpretations which they have considered in determining what the text means.[30] Consequently, al-

[29] Culler's use of the terms "possible," "plausible," and "acceptable" in characterizing "correct" interpretations (*ibid.*, pp. 243, 124, 127f., 120) blurs this distinction—not surprisingly, since he believes no such distinction can be drawn. (See also e.g. Hampshire, "Types of Interpretation," p. 108, and Margolis, *The Language of Art and Art Criticism*, p. 76.)

[30] This conclusion is confirmed by a series of empirical studies of literary interpretations conducted by Savigny (*Argumentation in der Literaturwissenschaft*), Grewendorf (*Argumentation und Interpretation. Wissenschaftstheoretische Untersuchungen am Beispiel germanistischer Lyrikinterpretationen*), and Georg Meggle and Manfred Beetz (*Interpretationstheorie und Interpretationspraxis*). See esp. Savigny, p.

Does a Work Have Only One Correct Interpretation?

though a literary work usually has several possible or even plausible readings, there is strong evidence that it has one and only one correct interpretation.

The facts I have presented here do not constitute conclusive evidence, however, since it remains conceivable that we should be mistaken in drawing a distinction between a possible or plausible and a correct interpretation of a work.[31] If it turned out to be in principle impossible to determine which of the possible or plausible readings of a work is correct, then we might have to assume that this distinction is illusory. I shall argue in section 9 below, however, that the relevant facts can be adequately explained without assuming that it is in principle impossible to determine the correct interpretation of a work.

5. Parallel Passages

Another consideration which supports the view that a literary work has one and only one correct reading concerns the use of parallel passages in critical interpretations.

When the meaning of a particular word or passage in a text is not clear or in dispute, critics frequently appeal to passages similar in relevant respects in other works by the same author or by authors of the same period. Even structuralists, who, one might suppose, would dismiss arguments based on what the author intended, do not reject parallel passages out of hand. In their interpretation of Baudelaire's sonnet "Les Chats," Roman Jakobson and Claude Lévi-

---

41, and Grewendorf, p. 80. For a list of the interpretations analyzed, see Savigny, pp. 9-12.

In claiming that a particular interpretation is more likely to be correct than various alternative readings, a critic is not necessarily, nor typically, claiming "finality" for the interpretation in question. See Hampshire, "Types of Interpretation," p. 108; also Beardsley, "The Limits of Critical Interpretation," pp. 73-74.

[31] For a parallel in ethics, see J. L. Mackie, *Ethics*, pp. 34-35.

Does a Work Have Only One Correct Interpretation?

Strauss, for example, mention that Crépet and Blin, in their edition of *Les Fleurs du Mal*, have cited two parallel passages—in Sainte-Beuve and in Brizeux—to the phrase *puissants et doux*, which qualifies *Les Chats*, and to their comparison to the stars. They continue:

> That would confirm, if there were a need to, that for Baudelaire, the image of the cat is narrowly linked to that of the woman, as it is shown explicitly in two other poems entitled "Le Chat" and pertaining to the same collection.[32]

After quoting the relevant lines, they say:

> This motif of vacillation between male and female is subjacent in "Les Chats" where it shows through under intentional ambiguities. . . .[33]

In addition, Jakobson and Lévi-Strauss appeal in support of their interpretation to another poem from *Les Fleurs du Mal* as well as to passages from Baudelaire's *Foules*.[34]

Nor does Michael Riffaterre, in his well-known reply to Jakobson and Lévi-Strauss, deny the relevance of parallel passages; rather, he argues that the particular parallels adduced by Jakobson and Lévi-Strauss are unconvincing. Riffaterre's view concerning evidence of the author's intention might appear to support the thesis that interpreting a poem is essentially like interpreting a text *in abstracto*. For he maintains that though a poem is an "act of communication," it

> is a very special act . . . for the speaker—the poet— is not present; any attempt to bring him back only produces interference, because what we know of him we

---

[32] Roman Jakobson and Claude Lévi-Strauss, "Charles Baudelaire's 'Les Chats'," in de George and de George (eds.), *The Structuralists*, p. 145.
[33] *Ibid.*   [34] *Ibid.*, pp. 144n., 144-45.

Does a Work Have Only One Correct Interpretation?

know from history, it is knowledge external to the message, or else we have found it out by rationalizing and distorting the message. The message and the addressee—the reader—are indeed the only factors involved in this communication whose presence is necessary.[35]

Yet in criticizing Jakobson and Lévi-Strauss as well as in arguing for his own interpretation of the poem, Riffaterre certainly appears to make use of knowledge of the poet "external to the message."

He challenges the parallels (from the two poems both entitled "Le Chat") cited by Jakobson and Lévi-Strauss as follows. He claims that

> there is nothing in "Le Chat" [*Les Fleurs du Mal*, LI] that imposes upon the reader the image of a woman. The descriptive details claimed for femininity apply as aptly to felinity; all the passages that might be alluding to love can be taken just as satisfactorily as mystical. . . .[36]

Riffaterre's argument is not that the cited parallel passage, being external evidence, could not provide support for Jakobson's and Lévi-Strauss' reading of "Les Chats"; rather, he claims that as a matter of fact it does not, because it is not clear that the cat in the 'parallel' poem is associated with a woman. As for the other parallel (*Les Fleurs du Mal*, XXXIV), Riffaterre admits that "it does conjure up a woman," but he argues that it is nevertheless unconvincing: for "the description of the cat in itself does not bring to mind a woman so long as the comparison is not made formal and explicit. . . . But then the structure is entirely different from that of 'Les Chats'. . . ." Riffaterre mentions another poem of Baudelaire's, "L'Horloge," in which he compares a

[35] Riffaterre, "Describing Poetic Structures," in Ehrmann (ed.), *Structuralism*, p. 202.
[36] *Ibid.*, pp. 224-25.

mistress with a cat; again, Riffaterre contends that "form and emphasis are completely different: in fact, the structure of our sonnet seems to be *pointedly* avoided."[37]

In other words, Riffaterre's rejection of the parallels cited by Jakobson and Lévi-Strauss is not a wholesale rejection, in principle, of parallel passages, but is based on specific features of the particular passages in question. Furthermore, Riffaterre appeals in support of his own interpretation of "Les Chats" to passages in several other poems of Baudelaire's in which the hypothesized "symbolic structures . . . and . . . modes of contemplation . . . implemented [in "Les Chats"] with a *cat-code* . . . can be readily verified."[38] There is no doubt that Riffaterre does not simply accept Jakobson's and Lévi-Strauss' assumption about the relevance of parallel passages for the sake of the argument; for he notes that "[i]f the structures determined from the data of the sonnet are correct, there should be other codes actualizing them."[39] That Riffaterre's arguments, no less than the claims of Jakobson and Lévi-Strauss, rest on assumptions about what Baudelaire meant becomes quite clear when Riffaterre remarks:

> Of course Baudelaire is perfectly capable of perceiving the cat in the woman, the woman in the cat. He occasionally uses the one as a metaphor of the other. But not always. Whatever the role of the cat in his private erotic imagery, it was not such as to make him write "chat" when *he meant* "femme": whenever he does, we have seen he feels obliged to provide the reader with an explanation.[40]

Whether or not this is "knowledge [of the poet] external to the message,"[41] it is clear, at any rate, that the use of

---
[37] *Ibid.*, p. 225 (italics added).   [38] *Ibid.*, p. 227.
[39] *Ibid.*
[40] *Ibid.*, p. 226 (italics added). See also p. 211.
[41] *Ibid.*, p. 202.

parallel passages in confirming or disconfirming an interpretation is an implicit appeal to the author's intention.

One may well agree with Riffaterre that in their reading of "Le Chat" (*Les Fleurs du Mal*, LI) many critics have been misled by biographical data whose relevance in this case is questionable.[42] One may agree, too, that the eyes in "Les Yeux de Berthe" are "not the eyes of Baudelaire's mulatto paramour"[43]; but nothing follows from this as to the 'absence' of the poet if this means that biographical facts about the author are *in principle* irrelevant. For, after all, the biographical facts in these cases constitute at best inconclusive evidence that indeed Baudelaire is here speaking of, or intends us to see these poems as conveying, his private erotic experiences. Thus in rejecting the identification of the cat with a woman in "Le Chat" (*Les Fleurs du Mal*, LI), Riffaterre does not simply point out that the biographical data which have been adduced in support of it could not in principle have any bearing on what the poem means; rather, he suggests that those facts are "by no means certainly applicable here."[44]

All this is difficult to explain if we assume, as Culler and others do, that a literary work is not a speech act or that the author's intention is irrelevant to its meaning. Of course, few critics would deny the relevance of other texts; for, as Culler has put it,

> A work can only be read in connection with or against other texts, which provide a grid through which it is read and structured by establishing expectations which enable one to pick out salient features and give them a structure. And hence intersubjectivity—the shared knowledge which is applied in reading—is a function of these other texts.[45]

The difficulty, however, as far as the use of parallel passages in literary interpretation is concerned, is this. If a literary

[42] *Ibid.*, p. 225.   [43] *Ibid.*, p. 228.   [44] *Ibid.*, p. 225.
[45] Culler, *Structuralist Poetics*, p. 139.

Does a Work Have Only One Correct Interpretation?

work is not a speech act, if its meaning is like the meaning of a word or sentence in a particular language, then one would expect that it does not matter whether or not a parallel passage adduced in support of an interpretation of a given text was written by the same author. Thus in interpreting a line in a poem by Sidney, for example, a parallel in another of his poems should in principle have no more bearing on what the line means than a 'parallel' in, say, Wallace Stevens or T. S. Eliot. What is difficult to account for, on this view, is the fact that (other things being equal) a parallel passage in a work by the same author always has greater weight than a parallel passage in the work of another author of the same period; and, similarly, that (other things being equal) a parallel in an author of the same period always carries greater weight than a parallel in an author of a different period. On the other hand, if we assume that a literary work is a speech act, this is quite easily explained.

6. Poetry and the Expression of Attitudes: Culler's Rule of Significance

One of Culler's main claims is that there is an important difference between understanding the words and sentences of which a poem consists, in the sense that one can provide a translation, and understanding a poem. To illustrate the difference, Culler quotes the following poem and the concluding remarks of Harold Bloom's interpretation.[46]

> Ah, Sun-flower! weary of time,
> Who countest the steps of the Sun,
> Seeking after that sweet golden clime
> Where the traveller's journey is done:
>
> Where the Youth pined away with desire,
> And the pale Virgin shrouded in snow
> Arise from their graves, and aspire
> Where my Sun-flower wishes to go.

[46] *Ibid.*, p. 115.

Does a Work Have Only One Correct Interpretation?

Here is Bloom's reading:

> That sweet golden clime is both the daily sunset and the timeless heaven where the Sun-flower, weary of the mechanics of its natural cycle, wishes to follow the sun. The poem's leading irony is in the absolute identity of the three illusory "wheres" of lines 4, 5, and 8. The Youth and the Virgin have denied their sexuality to win the allegorical abode of the conventionally visualized heaven. Arriving there, they arise from their graves to be trapped in the same cruel cycle of longings; they are merely at the sunset and aspire to go where the Sun-flower seeks his rest, which is precisely where they already are. The Sun-flower must live a merely vegetative existence, being bound into nature, but the lovers trap themselves in the limitations of the natural world by refusing the generative aspects of their state. By an increase in sensual fulfillment they could break out of cycle, but their minds are bound as the Sun-flower is literally bound. Blake's dialectical thrust at asceticism is more than adroit. You do not surmount nature by denying its prime claim of sexuality. Instead you fall utterly into the dull round of its cyclic aspirations.[47]

But instead of supporting Culler's thesis that a literary work is not a speech act, that "literature is something other than a statement about the world,"[48] Bloom's interpretation would seem to confirm that a literary work is indeed a speech act. For Bloom is attributing to Blake a statement which both Bloom and Culler see as central to the meaning of the poem, namely, that "You do not surmount nature by denying its prime claim of sexuality. . . ." Surely, it is not just a persona who, on Bloom's reading, is saying this. Bloom speaks explicitly of "*Blake's* dialectical thrust at asceticism"

---

[47] Bloom, *The Visionary Company*, p. 46. The poem is quoted from Bloom (*ibid.*). Culler quotes the last three sentences of Bloom's interpretation.

[48] *Structuralist Poetics*, p. 130; See also pp. 131, 165f.

Does a Work Have Only One Correct Interpretation?

(my italics). Isn't Blake then making a statement about man and nature? Isn't he, on Bloom's reading, performing a genuine speech act?

Culler's "primary convention"—illustrated by Bloom's interpretation—enjoins us to read a poem "as expressing a significant attitude to some problem concerning man and/or his relation to the universe."[49] Even if this rule is not constitutive, in the sense of being a necessary condition for reading a text as literature, it certainly applies to a very large number of works.[50] Now this convention would seem to ensure that a poem is, or is regarded as, a speech act. For it is difficult to see how one can construe a poem as expressing a certain attitude toward anything without taking it as a speech act of its author.

One might object here that this convention commits us only to the claim that the *speaker* is expressing an attitude. But, as I have argued in Chapter VII, the beliefs or attitudes which a work expresses are expressed neither by the "implied author" nor (or not just, depending on the case) by the speaker, but rather by the real, historical author. But of several logically incompatible claims about what attitude an author is expressing, only one can be correct. It is not logically possible for an author both to express the belief that "You do not surmount nature by denying its prime claim of sexuality" and *not* to express this belief. If a literary work is a speech act, it cannot have logically incompatible meanings; it would then also appear to be possible in principle to determine whether a certain reading of a work is or is not correct. I take it that it would be in principle possible to determine, for example, whether in the poem "Ah! Sun-flower" Blake is or is not expressing the belief that "You do not surmount nature by denying its prime claim of sexuality."

Culler does admit that in order to understand a work we

[49] *Ibid.*, p. 115.
[50] See Beardsley's discussion of this rule in "The Philosophy of Literature," p. 332.

Does a Work Have Only One Correct Interpretation?

need to restore it "to a communicative function." But since this is not easily explained on the view that a literary work is not a speech act, it is not surprising that he sees this as

> the fundamental paradox of literature: we are attracted to literature because it is obviously something other than ordinary communication; its formal and fictional qualities bespeak a strangeness, a power, an organization, a permanence which is foreign to ordinary speech. Yet the urge to assimilate that power and permanence or to let that formal organization work upon us requires us to make literature into a communication, to reduce its strangeness, and to draw upon supplementary conventions which enable it, as we say, to speak to us. The difference which seemed the source of value becomes a distance to be bridged by the activity of reading and interpretation.[51]

Culler appears to be suggesting here that a literary work is a speech act or that in order to understand it we must take it as such. Nevertheless, in his detailed discussion of the conventions underlying the interpretation of poetry and elsewhere, he clearly rejects such a view.[52] But, as I have indicated in the preceding chapter, in order to be able to say that a literary work is a speech act, we need neither suppose that it is a case of "ordinary" communication nor deny that "its formal and fictional qualities bespeak a strangeness, a power, an organization, a permanence which is foreign to ordinary speech."

Could we not say, one might wonder, that while we seek to limit the meaning of a work, it is always necessarily richer than any restrictive individual reading?[53] Could we not say that a poem constitutes not just one, however complex, speech act but many such acts, including incompatible

[51] Culler, *Structuralist Poetics*, p. 134.
[52] See *ibid.*, pp. 165ff. and pp. 30, 130, 131, 243, 247, 248f.
[53] See e.g. Iser, "Die Appellstruktur der Texte," pp. 229, 233f., 249f., and *The Implied Reader*, pp. 280, 285.

Does a Work Have Only One Correct Interpretation?

ones?[54] Could we not say that Blake's "Ah! Sun-flower," for example, does not just make the statement which Bloom attributes to Blake but many other 'statements' as well, corresponding to the various possible readings of the poem? The difficulty is that this proposal in effect denies that a work is a speech act at all.[55] It simply reiterates the claim that the meaning of a work is essentially the meaning of the text *in abstracto* or, to put it another way, that a work is a set of possible speech acts each of which corresponds to an "acceptable" reading.[56]

I have tried to show that this is not the way we in fact speak or think of a literary work. On this view, we cannot adequately account for, among others, the following facts: that we do not agree as to which of the various possible readings of a given work is acceptable or 'correct'; that we draw a distinction between a possible or plausible and a correct reading of a work; that in defending an interpretation we claim implicitly that it is more likely to be correct than any of the alternative readings we have considered; and that parallel passages in works by the same author always carry greater weight than parallels in other authors.

Furthermore, that most literary works have received several (incompatible) interpretations constitutes no evidence that they have several meanings, since this can be explained quite adequately (as I shall try to show in section 9) on the view that a literary work has only one correct interpretation. Nor does the fact that a work has a number of possible readings, or that none of a certain set of interpretations can *in fact* be shown to be significantly more likely

---

[54] Of course, an author may contradict himself and thus make logically incompatible statements or attributions; but that, I take it, is not what those who claim that a work has many meanings have in mind. On logically inconsistent intentions, see Aschenbrenner, "Intention and Understanding," pp. 249-51, and Jack W. Meiland, *The Nature of Intention*, pp. 46-47.

[55] See Hirsch, *Validity in Interpretation*, pp. 45f.

[56] See in this connection also Searle, "Reiterating the Differences," p. 202.

to be correct than any of the others, support the claim that the work in question has all of the corresponding meanings.

7. The Survival of Literary Works

I want to deal now with a few potential problems for the view that a literary work has one and only one correct interpretation. I shall try to show that we can account for the relevant facts without abandoning this assumption.[57]

Literary works are, as a rule, not "expendable"[58] like a piece of scientific explanation once it is understood. We reread certain works many times; even when we have understood them (or believe that we have), they continue to be of interest and value to us. We do not grow tired of many quite familiar texts; some never cease to fascinate us.

Now one possible explanation for this is that we continue to value these works because, as we reread them, we often discover meanings we had not suspected before. Even if this explanation is correct, however, it does not follow that literary interpretations are not true or false. For it is possible that the new meanings we find in the work upon rereading it are consistent with the way we construed it earlier; that is, those new meanings may complement, enrich, or deepen our previous understanding of the work and hence may be quite compatible with it. If they are, then the proposed explanation can be accommodated by the view that there is only one correct reading of a work.

But there is another at least equally plausible explanation which does not depend on the discovery of new meanings in a work at all. Kendall Walton has argued that in becoming "emotionally involved" or getting "caught up" in a fic-

[57] I am ignoring here minor difficulties such as the fact that an author's intention may change in the course of writing a work, a problem which is particularly acute in the case of texts written over a long period of time, such as *Faust*.

[58] Wollheim, *Art and Its Objects*, p. 75; see also pp. 72-76, 103, 120f.

Does a Work Have Only One Correct Interpretation?

tional story, we are participating in a game of make-believe.[59] He suggests that many fictional texts do not lose their interest for us, create the same excitement and suspense even after we are thoroughly acquainted with them, because each time we hear or read them, we participate again in a game of make-believe. "The point of hearing *Jack and the Beanstalk*," for example, "is to have the experience of being such that, *make-believedly*, one realizes with trepidation the danger Jack faces, waits breathlessly to see whether the giant will awake, feels sudden terror when he does awake, and finally learns with admiration and relief how Jack chops down the beanstalk, killing the giant."[60] We play the same game again and again because it continues to satisfy persistent emotional needs in much the same way as do certain types of psychotherapy which employ techniques of role playing.[61]

8. The Inexhaustibility of Literary Works

Walton's theory provides a plausible explanation of the continued interest and value which many literary works hold for us. No doubt, there are other reasons as well for this, notably and most obviously perhaps the aesthetic pleasure they afford. Furthermore, it is reasonable to assume that at least some works survive not only because they are still capable of satisfying certain emotional needs, but also because they continue to 'say something' to us.

It is often claimed, with some justification, that the great literary works are inexhaustible, that we can always find

---

[59] Walton, "Fearing Fictions," pp. 5-27, and "How Remote are Fictional Worlds from the Real World?," pp. 11-23. See also Walton's paper, "Pictures and Make-Believe," pp. 283-319.

[60] Walton, "Fearing Fictions," p. 27.

[61] *Ibid.*, pp. 27, 24-25. For another explanation why stories bear repeating—which is also consistent with the view that they have only one correct interpretation—see Louis O. Mink, "History and Fiction as Modes of Comprehension," pp. 120f.

new meaning in them. I have suggested earlier (Chapter II, section 5) that this can be explained without assuming that the meaning of a literary work changes, namely, in terms of Hirsch's distinction between meaning and significance.[62] I shall briefly state the explanation and then discuss an example which should help give some substance to it.

Given a certain meaning, a work may be inexhaustible in that readers of many different periods are able to relate that meaning to their own personal experiences or to changing historical, social, or political circumstances. We may, for instance, perceive parallels between certain developments of our own time and those portrayed in an older work. We may be able to discern affinities between certain beliefs, feelings, attitudes, or aspirations expressed in a work and our own. As a result of having experienced the horrors of war, for example, readers of a certain time may be able to appreciate parts of a work which others had neglected. Or the way in which an author deals with a particular problem may raise a number of pertinent questions for us. Thus a work may have one and only one correct interpretation and yet be inexhaustible in that its *significance*—that is, the relation of its meaning to the changing problems and concerns of its readers—is in principle unlimited. That this is clearly a possible explanation shows that it does not follow from the inexhaustibility of a literary work that it has many meanings. But the possibility of this explanation offers only slight reason for supposing that when critics reinterpret a work, they are in fact often saying something about its significance, rather than its meaning.

To see that this explanation, though possible and plausible, is not just speculative fancy, let us look at a recent reinterpretation, or rather proposal for a reinterpretation, of Goethe's *Iphigenie auf Tauris* by Hans Robert Jauss.[63]

A new interpretation of Goethe's *Iphigenie* is needed, ac-

[62] Hirsch, *Validity in Interpretation*, pp. 62, 138, 140-44, and *The Aims of Interpretation*, pp. 1-8, 79-81, 85-88, 146.
[63] Hans Robert Jauss, "Racines und Goethes Iphigenie," pp. 1-46.

Does a Work Have Only One Correct Interpretation?

cording to Jauss, if the play is not to lose its meaning and value for us, if it is to be able to say something to us again. Jauss argues first that the work seems irrelevant today in part because of inadequate traditional interpretations which overlooked or ignored the social significance of the work, its rejection of the subjectivism of the *Geniezeit*. He goes on to give his own reading of the work as an answer to questions posed by Racine's *Iphigénie*, in particular the problem of reconciling human freedom and divine authority.[64] Despite the emancipatory aspects of Goethe's *Iphigenie*, however, Jauss believes that the work imposes unalterable limits on its possible relevance for us; these limits are set by the fact that the transformation from barbarism to civilization is achieved at the price of a new myth, namely, that of the pure woman, which guarantees the realization of the ideal of *Humanität*.

Wherein, then, does the relevance of *Iphigenie* lie? Jauss sees it in the questions raised by our dissatisfaction with "Goethe's solution"[65]—whether, for example, emancipation through enlightened reason must necessarily lead to new injustice or else to a new mythology. Is there perhaps, Jauss suggests, a parallel between Goethe's solution, the myth of female purity, and our own: that is, have we overcome "the old myth of nature only at the price of submitting to the new myth of society as an ineluctable second nature"?[66] Thus Jauss calls for the creation of a new *Iphigenie* (like Plenzdorf's new *Werther*), "eine weitere, wiederum 'erstaunlich moderne' Iphigenie"[67] ("another, again 'astonishingly modern' *Iphigenie*") in which the conflict between *Humanität* and historical reality, which Goethe concealed or suppressed, is brought out into the open.

What is important here for our purposes is that, contrary to what one would expect on the view that a work has a

---

[64] For a lucid analysis and criticism of Jauss' arguments for his interpretation, see Michael Kunze, "Probleme der rezeptionsästhetischen Interpretation," pp. 133-44.

[65] Jauss, "Racines und Goethes Iphigenie," p. 28; see also p. 27.
[66] *Ibid.*, p. 29.   [67] *Ibid.*

Does a Work Have Only One Correct Interpretation?

variety of meanings and, in particular, that its meaning may change from one historical period to another, Jauss does not argue that as a result of historical, social, or political developments *Iphigenie* no longer means what it meant in Goethe's time. In fact, he tries to determine what Goethe intended and argues on the basis of his interpretation, as we have seen, that the myth of female purity (what Goethe meant), by restricting the emancipatory meaning of the play, limits its possible relevance for us.[68]

Now if the meaning of *Iphigenie* has in fact changed, then one would expect Jauss to argue either (a) that the nineteenth-century interpretations which he criticizes were quite correct or adequate then but have *become* inadequate today as a result of social, historical, or cultural changes, or (b) that these interpretations were already inadequate at the time they were proposed because the critics in question ignored or overlooked social or cultural changes as a result of which the work had, already at that time, taken on a different meaning. But Jauss claims neither (a) nor (b). Rather, he contends that these interpretations are inadequate because the critics overlooked evidence of Goethe's intention.[69] There is not the slightest indication in Jauss' discussion of *Iphigenie* that the work could acquire meanings which Goethe did not intend. This is all the more significant, since it appears to follow from Jauss' metacritical position that the meaning of a work may indeed change "unter veränderten geschichtlich-gesellschaftlichen Rezeptionsbedingungen"[70] ("when the socio-historical conditions

[68] *Ibid.*, pp. 9, 26.   [69] *Ibid.*, pp. 7-9, 26.
[70] *Ibid.*, p. 3. The passage reads as follows: "Die virtuelle Struktur des Textes bedarf der *Konkretisation*, d.h. der aneignenden Erfahrung durch seine Empfänger, um sich als Werk zu entfalten; das Werk "aktualisiert die Spannung zwischen seinem 'Sein' und unserem 'Sinn' " derart, daß sich *Bedeutung* erst in der Konvergenz von Text und Rezeption konstituiert, mithin der *Sinn* des Kunstwerks nicht mehr als überzeitliche Substanz, sondern als historisch sich bildende Totalität zu fassen ist. Den Begriff 'Konkretisation' verwende ich nicht im

Does a Work Have Only One Correct Interpretation?

of its reception change"). When Jauss does mention what might conceivably look like a meaning which the work acquired as a consequence of historical or cultural developments—namely, its emancipatory aspects—he quickly adds that this is part of its "lost character as a 'verteufelt humanes Wagestück'."[71]

Jauss' new interpretation (or new *Iphigenie*) does not imply, then, that the text no longer means what Goethe intended—that, for instance, Iphigenie's farewell speech is now a veiled criticism of the injustice against Thoas,[72] that *Iphigenie* now deals with the conflict between *Humanität* and historical reality, or that it calls "the idealist solution"[73] into question. The assumption implicit in Jauss' discussion is that Goethe's *Iphigenie* can acquire new 'meaning' only in the sense that what Goethe meant, what he expressed or suggested ("the idealist solution") has become problematical for us; hence we must reexamine his solution in the light of our own knowledge and experience and must ask, for example, whether Iphigenie's faith can be justified in the face of historical reality.[74] In short, Jauss' new interpretation

---

engeren Sinne von R. Ingarden, als Ergänzung der Lücken und imaginative Auffüllung von Unbestimmtheitsstellen in der schematischen Werkstruktur, sondern bezeichne damit im Einklang mit der ästhetischen Theorie des Prager Strukturalismus den immer neuen Charakter, den das Werk in seiner ganzen Struktur unter veränderten geschichtlich-gesellschaftlichen Rezeptionsbedingungen erhalten kann." See also pp. 33-35, 37.

[71] *Ibid.*, p. 23. In a well-known letter to Schiller (of January 19, 1802), Goethe described *Iphigenie* as "verteufelt human" ("devilishly humane") and spoke of it as a "Wagestück" ("bold venture"). (Hans Gerhard Gräf, *Goethe über seine Dichtungen*, Zweiter Teil, Bd. 3, p. 202.) Jauss quotes the passage earlier (p. 8).

[72] Jauss, "Racines und Goethes Iphigenie," p. 27. See also Theodor W. Adorno's interpretation ("Zum Klassizismus von Goethes Iphigenie," p. 26), which Jauss quotes on this point.

[73] Jauss, "Racines und Goethes Iphigenie," p. 29.

[74] *Ibid.*

229

Does a Work Have Only One Correct Interpretation?

is an attempt to relate the meaning of the text, Goethe's meaning, to the problems and concerns of our time.

This example provides support for the explanation proposed above. It confirms that a literary work is indeed inexhaustible, not in the sense that it has a virtually unlimited number of meanings, but rather in the sense that its significance, the relation of its meaning to changing historical circumstances, is potentially unlimited.[75]

A reinterpretation of a work need not, of course, be a claim about its significance rather than its meaning. Many reinterpretations are attempts to determine what a work means, not how its meaning relates to the problems and concerns of a particular age. Jauss' paper, as we have seen, presents a reinterpretation in this sense as well. It does not follow, however, that the meaning of a work can change. Jauss' discussion confirms, on the contrary, that what changes in such cases is not the meaning but only our *understanding* of a work.

---

[75] For a perceptive discussion of the inexhaustibility of literary works, see Jones, *Philosophy and the Novel*, pp. 181-206, esp. 181-94. He proposes a theory of "creative interpretation" (p. 189) and explains reinterpretations of literary works in terms of "the *use* to which interpreters find they can put particular works" (p. 188). What Jones calls 'putting a work to a new use' is, on my view, largely what we do when we find a new significance, as opposed to meaning, of a work by 'applying', for example, Swift's "A Modest Proposal" to what we regard as a parallel situation. It will then be illuminated for us by the way Swift portrayed or characterized his own time or a general situation. The fact, however, that we would not say that "A Modest Proposal" is *about* our situation—about the Vietnam war, for example—brings out the distinction we make between the meaning of a work and its significance, or relevance, to our problems, concerns, or interests. Of course, we might in a sense say that "A Modest Proposal" is about, or also about, the Vietnam war. But what we mean then is that it is about a certain *type* of situation of which the Vietnam war is an instance. And that is quite compatible with the assumption that the meaning of the work is logically tied to the author's intention, since Swift no doubt intended to say something not *just* about a situation of his own time, but about certain general human tendencies.

Does a Work Have Only One Correct Interpretation?

9. Why Are There Several Interpretations for Most Literary Works?

If a literary work has one and only one correct interpretation, then we must account for the fact that most works which have received any attention have been interpreted in a number of different (incompatible) ways. (The interpretations in question here are statements about the meaning of a work, not about its significance.) It might seem that this could be more readily explained on the assumption that a work has many (incompatible) meanings. I shall try to show that we can account for this quite as easily on the view that a literary work has one and only one correct interpretation.

If we look at the various interpretations of Henry James' *The Turn of the Screw*, for example, it is undeniable that there is some evidence for each of them. One might be inclined to say that all or most of the readings can account in a more or less plausible way for the central features of the text. This may be to admit more than the facts warrant, however; for it is not clear that the critics who have offered interpretations of the work, or for that matter critics who are thoroughly familiar with it but who have not committed themselves to a particular reading, would be prepared to accept this claim. But we can say at least this much. Given the available evidence, there are several interpretations none of which can, in such a way as to command general assent, be shown to be correct or to be incorrect. The relevant facts allow more than one reading.

Now this is no more surprising on the assumption that a work has one and only one correct interpretation than on the view that it has a variety of meanings. For to say that a work has one correct reading is not to say that we can *in fact* determine what the correct reading is. It is to say rather that it is intelligible to suppose that an interpretation is not just plausible but correct, that although a certain reading may be plausible given the evidence we possess, it could nevertheless turn out to be wrong. It is to say that we can imagine what it would be like for an interpretation to be correct or incorrect. The discovery of evidence which would show beyond reasonable doubt that a certain reading of *King Lear*, for example, is correct, and all other interpretations wrong, is no doubt highly unlikely. But from the fact that such evidence is not forthcoming, it does not follow that there could not in principle be such evidence. Nor does this assumption provide a more satisfactory explanation of the fact that a literary work can usually be construed in a variety of ways. This can be explained quite adequately on the assumption that although it is in principle possible to determine the correct reading of a given work, we do as a matter of fact lack the necessary evidence.

Whether a work means this or that frequently depends on precisely what associations certain words have in a particular passage; it depends on the significance of a gesture, an image, of an obscure antithesis or parallel, on the implications of a metaphor or the symbolic import of certain objects. It depends on the explanation of a character's actions, on his motives, attitudes, feelings. It depends on the narrator's reliability—the extent, that is, to which the narrator's beliefs, feelings, attitudes, and the like provide the proper frame of reference for interpreting the work.[76] Is the work to be taken as expressing or suggesting the narrator's beliefs, or does it call them into question? Does the narrator distort events? Is the governess in *The Turn of the Screw*, for example, suffering from delusions, or can we generally trust her reports?

Given questions such as these, it is not surprising that even where we know a great deal about the period and the author of a certain work, such evidence should leave considerable room for disagreement. Facts—when we have them—about the author's knowledge, beliefs, idiolect, and

[76] See Booth's discussion of some of the problems of interpreting impersonal narrative in *The Rhetoric of Fiction*, pp. 311-74.

such usually provide only inconclusive evidence for the significance of certain images, for example, or the explanation of a character's action. Even explicit declarations of intention, as I have suggested earlier, do not constitute incontrovertible evidence.[77] In some cases, we do not have enough evidence to say, for instance, what the precise associations of a word in a given passage or line are; in others, we have a great deal of evidence, but it conflicts, different sets of facts supporting different conclusions.[78] Hence, on the view that a literary work is a speech act, one could not in practice expect facts about the author and the period of a certain work to rule out more than some of the readings which might conceivably be proposed or which purely 'internal' considerations might appear to allow.

Furthermore, given inconclusive evidence about what the author intended to convey by having a character commit suicide or murder, for example, our own beliefs about such matters come to play a much larger role. Because a certain view of the situation seems clearly right to us, it is often difficult to believe that the author could have thought otherwise. Thus when the evidence is inadequate, it is often easy to convince oneself that the author 'must have' meant a certain passage in the way that our own beliefs would require.

That literary works are interpreted in a variety of ways is also in part due to the fact that literary interpretations satisfy two different demands. An interpretation is logically tied, as I have argued, to what we take to be the author's intention and hence must tell us what the author was up to in writing a particular work. It can usually be expected to answer a further demand as well. It does so, however, not in virtue of our concept of what it is for a work to mean

[77] See Close, "Don Quixote and the 'Intentionalist Fallacy'," in Newton-de Molina (ed.), *On Literary Intention*, pp. 180-81; and Chapter VI, section 3, above.

[78] For some examples and a detailed discussion of some of the difficulties involved in reaching a decision in such cases, see Hirsch, *Validity in Interpretation*, pp. 181-98.

so-and-so, but rather in virtue of its social function. We read literary works because they satisfy certain of our interests, needs, or values. We therefore expect an interpretation to show us, among other things, that and how a work does so; we expect it to tell us why a work is worth reading.[79] Now when the relevant facts allow a number of different assumptions about what the author intended, it is not surprising that, as a result of this demand, critics should make different choices. When it is difficult to tell objectively whether there is more evidence for one or another of a certain set of readings, it is easy to persuade oneself that the more relevant, interesting, or aesthetically more satisfying reading is at least as plausible as any of the alternatives.[80] This also explains why aesthetic considerations occasionally have some appeal.

I have suggested in Chapter IV that an interpretation is an explanation of a complex human action. If this is true, then one cannot expect questions of interpretation to be decidable in quite as straightforward a way as matters of description. It does not follow, however, that such explanations cannot in principle be shown to be true or false. If explanations of complex actions in other areas of life are correct or incorrect, then it is implausible to suppose that literary interpretations are not. There is a good deal of per-

---

[79] Frequently, this demand is satisfied in the way I have suggested in considering the inexhaustibility of literary works, namely, in terms of the relation between the meaning of a work and our problems and concerns. But the meaning of a work, as opposed to its significance, may of course also answer many different interests; whether it can continue to do so depends on the readings which the available evidence allows.

[80] See on this point Alastair Fowler's pertinent remarks ("Intention Floreat," p. 253): "An interpretation faithful to every proportion of the original, but lacking in relevance or interest, would be of little use. The bearing of this truth on habits of construction is incalculable. How often do we unconsciously meet the choice between falsifying the construct or neglecting the work? It is repugnant to admit that we are temporarily or permanently incapable of receiving anything from what nevertheless was once a great work. But this may often be so."

Does a Work Have Only One Correct Interpretation?

sistent disagreement in the interpretation of the major philosophical works, for example. Yet, I take it, one would not want to say that, therefore, such interpretations are not true or false. That there are more disagreements over literary works is no reason to suppose that literary interpretations differ in this respect from interpretations of philosophical texts; nor is it surprising in view of the kinds of considerations involved in determining what a literary work means and the lack of sufficient evidence of the appropriate sort.[81]

I have tried to show that we need not assume that a literary work usually has a variety of logically incompatible meanings in order to account for the fact that for most literary works a variety of logically incompatible interpretations have been offered. Why, then, say that a literary work has several or many meanings?

Those who hold this view usually claim either that external evidence is irrelevant or that, though relevant in some sense, it is always and necessarily compatible with more than one reading of the text and, in particular, with more than one of the readings which the 'internal' evidence permits. Here is an example. Pierre Menard's *Don Quixote* (let us assume that he completed the work), written in the early twentieth century, has a different meaning from Cervantes' *Don Quixote*, although the two are textually identical. This shows that external evidence is relevant in the sense that it can rule out certain interpretations permitted by the text.

---

[81] For detailed analyses and discussions of interpretive controversies, see Meggle and Beetz, *Interpretationstheorie und Interpretationspraxis*. On the reasons why it may seem that confirming an interpretation involves the 'hermeneutic circle', see Stegmüller, "Der sogenannte Zirkel des Verstehens," pp. 21-46, and Hirsch, *Validity in Interpretation*, pp. 164-68.

On the question whether interpretations of people's behavior in ordinary life are true or false, see Jonathan Glover, "Introduction," in Glover (ed.), *The Philosophy of Mind*, pp. 1-3; and, on the status of psychoanalytic interpretations, see B. A. Farrell, "The Criteria for a Psycho-Analytic Interpretation," pp. 15-34.

Does a Work Have Only One Correct Interpretation?

But, one might argue, although the assumption that *Don Quixote* was written in the twentieth century would rule out various readings of the text, it would also make room for several new ones. This is true, no doubt, inasmuch as all we have done is to transpose *Don Quixote* from the seventeenth to the twentieth century. There is no reason to suppose, however, that more restrictive assumptions about the author could not rule out all but one interpretation of the text. If the meaning of a work is logically tied to the author's intention, as I have argued in Chapters III to VI, or what a work expresses is linked to the author's beliefs in the way suggested in Chapter VII, then there is good reason to believe that any interpretation of a given text can in principle be shown to be correct or incorrect.[82]

I want to emphasize that this thesis does not reduce or eliminate multiplicity of meaning in the usual sense. It is perfectly consistent with this view that the various elements of a work should suggest or express a number of different ideas, attitudes, feelings, and so on, that the words of a poem should have multiple associations and connections, and that a work as a whole should convey a variety of things. What I am denying is that a work can have logically incompatible meanings in the sense that it could both express the idea that man is doomed to destroy himself, for example, and not express this, or that it is in principle impossible to determine which of these readings, if any, is correct.

Nor am I claiming that we can in fact resolve any significant number of interpretive controversies. The reason is that we lack the necessary evidence to rule out more than a few of the possible readings of most works. Also, as even a cursory glance at the critical literature about virtually any text will show, critics are generally aware of a great deal of external evidence and use it quite freely to support one interpretation or to cast doubt on another. It is possible, of course, that on occasion someone should discover further

[82] For a detailed defense of this view, see Appendix.

evidence which shows a particular reading to be wrong beyond reasonable doubt. But the discovery of such evidence for all but one interpretation of any given text is unlikely. Nevertheless, as long as it is in principle possible that there should be such evidence, a work will have one and only one correct interpretation.

10. Conclusion

I have given a few arguments for the claim that a literary work has one and only one correct interpretation. If it does, then a work cannot have logically incompatible meanings. It is consistent with this claim, however, both (a) that a work may express or convey a number of different things, and (b) that literary works are typically construed in a variety of logically incompatible ways.

(1) I have argued that on the assumption that a literary work has a number of logically incompatible meanings, it is difficult to account for several central facts which are easily explained on the view that a work has one and only one correct interpretation: (i) Critics are not prepared in practice to allow that logically incompatible readings can be jointly plausible or acceptable. (ii) Critics usually choose one of the possible readings of a text; at least occasionally, a critic will do so even if he believes that on the basis of the textual evidence several readings are equally plausible or acceptable. Hence it appears to be intelligible to suppose that only one of the possible readings of a work is correct. (iii) Critics generally do not agree about which readings of a particular work are or are not acceptable. In particular, a critic will typically deny in practice that readings incompatible with his are also (separately) acceptable. Furthermore, a critic who defends a certain interpretation of a work does not as a rule claim merely that his interpretation is possible or plausible, but rather that of all the alternative readings he has considered, it is the most likely to be correct.

(2) I have presented further evidence in support of the claim that the meaning of a literary work is not like the meaning of an ambiguous sentence *in abstracto*, but rather like the meaning of a person's utterance or speech act: (i) Parallel passages in works by the same author always carry greater weight than parallel passages in the works of other authors. As we have seen, even structuralist critics, who might be expected to reject arguments involving an appeal to the author's intention, tacitly accept this rule. (ii) I have also considered an interpretation which Culler cites to illustrate his claim about the difference between understanding the words and sentences of which a poem consists and understanding a poem. The interpretation certainly appears to imply that the work is a speech act. Culler gives no reason for thinking otherwise. In fact, his "rule of significance," according to which a poem should be read as expressing some significant attitude toward man or his relation to the universe, ensures that a poem is, or is construed as, a speech act. But if a work is a speech act, then it cannot have logically incompatible meanings, and it would appear to be possible in principle to determine whether a certain reading is or is not correct.

(3) Finally, I have dealt with three considerations which might appear to support the view that a literary work has many meanings: the survival of such works, their inexhaustibility, and the fact that they are usually construed in a variety of ways. I have tried to show that we can adequately account for these facts without abandoning the assumption that a work has one and only one correct interpretation.

APPENDIX

The Doctrine of *Verstehen* and the Objectivity of Literary Interpretations[1]

1. INTRODUCTION

AT LEAST since Wilhelm Dilthey an influential German tradition in philosophy has claimed that there is a fundamental difference between the natural sciences (*Naturwissenschaften*), on the one hand, and the humanities and social sciences (*Geisteswissenschaften*), on the other.[2] The difference between them is held to be one of basic methodology: whereas, in the former, phenomena are explained by being subsumed under general laws, in the latter, phenomena are 'understood' by means of an experience of a certain sort, depending upon the object of study. The difference has come to be associated with the notions of *Erklären* in the natural sciences and *Verstehen* in the humanities and social sciences. In order to 'understand' a particular religious rite (say, baptism), for example, or a work of art, it is necessary to have a certain experience (or close approximation thereof), namely, the experience expressed by the particular work of art, or the experience (or kind of experience) involved in performing the religious rite in question. The gen-

[1] This is a revised version of a paper which originally appeared in *Deutsche Vierteljahrsschrift für Literaturwissenschaft und Geistesgeschichte*, Vol. 49 (1975). I should like to thank the publisher for permission to reprint the article.

[2] There has been (in Britain and America) a revival of interest in this question; see e.g. Winch, *The Idea of a Social Science*, von Wright, *Explanation and Understanding*, and Alan Ryan, *The Philosophy of the Social Sciences*, Chs. 6 and 7.

Appendix

eral paradigm for these cases appears to be that of understanding a person's action by means of an imaginative mental 'reconstruction' of the factors (reasons, motives, beliefs, intentions) that led to or are involved in the performance of the action in question. The application of this general doctrine to literary criticism has been particularly prominent in Germany. Peter Szondi, among others, has defended such an application.[3]

The purpose of this essay is to consider some of the typical claims of proponents of the doctrine of *Verstehen* in regard to the interpretation of literary works. I have chosen to examine Peter Szondi's version of this doctrine not only because it is representative of fairly widely held views concerning the understanding of literary works and the verification of interpretive statements, but also because Szondi, unlike most of those who have defended the same thesis, focusses on specific examples of problems and methods of literary interpretation and thus makes explicit the implications of the doctrine of *Verstehen* for the theory and practice of literary criticism.

In Chapter VIII, I offered a few considerations on behalf of the view that a literary work has one and only one correct interpretation. My contention has been that the meaning of a literary work is essentially like the meaning of a person's speech act. Now one may allow that this is true and yet deny that a literary work has one and only one correct interpretation. For one might challenge this claim on the grounds that any attempt to determine what a particular work means—even if its meaning is essentially like the

[3] "Zur Erkenntnisproblematik in der Literaturwissenschaft," *Die Neue Rundschau*, Vol. 73, 1962, pp. 146-65. Reprinted in *Universitätstage*, 1962, pp. 73-91; K. O. Conrady, *Einführung in die Neuere deutsche Literaturwissenschaft*, 1966, pp. 155-62 (excerpts); P. Szondi, *Hölderlin-Studien. Mit einem Traktat über philologische Erkenntnis*, 1970, pp. 9-34; R. Grimm and J. Hermand, eds., *Methodenfragen der deutschen Literaturwissenschaft*, 1973, pp. 232-54. All page references to Szondi's essay, which will be given in parentheses in the text, are based on the Suhrkamp edition (1970).

Appendix

meaning of a speech act—is necessarily circular. If this view is correct, no sense could be attached to the statement that a particular interpretation is correct or incorrect, true or false.

The central issue with which I shall, therefore, be concerned is whether an interpretation of a literary work can in principle be objectively confirmed or whether any attempt at such confirmation is hopelessly misguided, because it is necessarily circular. This issue is of some importance for the discipline of literary criticism, for it is quite simply the question whether there can be any knowledge about the meaning of literary works or whether their interpretation is no more than a matter of subjective experience, personal preference, or individual taste.

Szondi argues (roughly) that an interpretation of a literary work cannot be objectively confirmed or disconfirmed because (a) any fact (f) that a critic might adduce for or against an interpretation (J) must itself be interpreted ('understood'); in other words, before he can offer f in support of J, a critic must establish (or be able to assume) that f is in fact evidence for J; and (b) it is impossible to establish that f is evidence for J independently of establishing J— that is, in order to establish that f is evidence for J, it is necessary to establish that J is correct. It is clear that if (b) is true, then a critic who purports to offer objective evidence for an interpretation is simply begging the question, since in appealing to such evidence he is in effect appealing to the very interpretation which the evidence is intended to support.

I shall argue in the following (1) that Szondi is right in claiming that the facts relevant to an interpretation of a literary work must be interpreted— 'understood'—in a way (in terms of someone's intentions) in which facts relevant to a claim in the natural sciences are properly left uninterpreted because it would make no sense to interpret the latter in this way; but (2) that Szondi's premise (b) and hence his thesis that an interpretation of a work or an interpretation

Appendix

of a fact cannot be objectively confirmed or disconfirmed is false.

2. Szondi's Conception of *Verstehen* and Its Role in the Verification of Interpretive Claims

What does the 'understanding' of a literary work, according to Szondi, consist in? And how does it follow that an interpretation cannot be objectively supported?

Szondi claims that knowledge of literary works differs fundamentally (*grundsätzlich*) not only from knowledge in the natural sciences but from historical knowledge as well. The difference between historical and philological knowledge lies in the fact that the latter does not exist except in the actual process (the mental act) of understanding:

> Philological knowledge is characterized by a dynamic element not only because, like any other body of knowledge, it is constantly changing as a result of new points of view and new insights, but because it can exist only in the continual confrontation with the text, only in the continual process of tracing back this knowledge to insight, to the understanding of the poet's word. (11)

The critic must continually return to the text and (in his imagination) reconstruct for himself the experience, mental states, or beliefs which the work expresses or of which it is the result; not, or at least not primarily, in order to check what he knows already, but because philological knowledge, knowledge of a literary work, consists in the process of understanding, in the concrete experience of what the work expresses. Knowing what a literary work means, understanding it, is having a certain experience[4]; without such a concrete experience the kind of understanding Szondi has in mind would be impossible.[5] Thus knowledge of a literary

---

[4] Emil Staiger holds a similar view; see *Die Kunst der Interpretation*, pp. 9-33.

[5] See also Horst Rüdiger: "Während die Naturwissenschaften ihre Gegenstände mit Hilfe rationaler Mittel, also durch Beobachtung,

Appendix

work is not, once acquired, a permanent possession; in order to have it, we must constantly reacquire it, we must continually reenact the experience in which it consists, namely, the concrete process of "cognition and understanding" (*Erkennen und Verstehen*, 14). For this reason, philological knowledge is "perpetual re-cognition" (*perpetuierte Erkenntnis*, 11).

It is important to notice that although we may not be able to understand a work or a passage from a work properly without having a certain experience, it does not follow that an interpretive claim based on such understanding is properly verified, or can only be verified, by having the experience in question when reading the work or the passage. For example, it may be that we cannot understand—in the relevant sense of 'understand'—a person's action, say, committing suicide, without a certain degree of empathy, without, that is, knowing or imagining what it is like to have the kind of feelings, desires, or thoughts the person in question is presumed to have had; but it does not follow that a statement about the person's feelings, desires, motives, or intentions is properly verified by checking whether I can produce the relevant mental states (or an approximation thereof) in myself on the basis of a mental reconstruction of the situation in which the person in question is known or presumed to have been. Any such test relies on *my* reaction or imagined reaction to certain facts; but, clearly, that I might react to them in a certain way does not guarantee that someone else reacted or was even likely to have reacted to them in the same way.[6] I might be thoroughly mistaken. The only

---

Experiment und Berechnung analysieren, gehen die Geisteswissenschaften von einem nicht weiter reduzierbaren persönlichen Erlebnis des Forschers aus; durch den Akt des Verstehens begreift der Geisteswissenschaftler die ihm gemäßen Gegenstände, zu denen vor allem die Literatur gehört" ("Zwischen Interpretation und Geistesgeschichte," (p. 103). Though Rüdiger here paraphrases Dilthey, the passage is a fair statement of his own views as well.

[6] For a more detailed discussion of the method of *Verstehen* in historiography and the social sciences, see Wolfgang Stegmüller, *Pro-*

Appendix

reliable way to find out what a person is likely to have felt, wanted, or intended in a certain situation is to check the factual evidence about the person's reaction in a similar situation or to utilize or establish empirical generalizations about the likely reactions in such a situation of people similar in relevant respects to the person in question. Hence the method of *Verstehen* may be a useful heuristic device for producing hypotheses, but it does not eliminate the need for empirical facts and generalizations in the verification of statements about another person's mental states.

Since, however, Szondi does appear to believe that interpretive statements about a literary work are properly verified by a critic's subjective *Verstehen*, it might be worthwhile to consider the possibility that he sees the nature of interpretive claims somewhat differently. Szondi says:

> Dilthey's claim that explanation in the natural sciences corresponds to understanding in the humanities and social sciences holds for empirical research in philology as well. *As soon as it attempts to bracket out the investigating subject for the sake of a putative objectivity, it runs the risk of falsifying the subjectively moulded facts by inappropriate methods without being able to recognize the error.* By surrendering to empirical evidence, philological research cannot appeal to subjective insight even as a mere instrument of validation. [15, italics

---

bleme und Resultate der Wissenschaftstheorie und Analytischen Philosophie, Bd. 1, pp. 360-75. Stegmüller cites Gardiner's apt example: "From the fact that, if I did x, it would be because I wanted y, i.e. would have been satisfied if y occurred, would have given y as my aim if asked, &c., it does not follow that when a medieval baron did x he wanted y. To find out whether y was really the reason for someone's doing x, we need more facts, not more intuition." Patrick Gardiner, *The Nature of Historical Explanation*, p. 130.

See also Ernest Nagel, *The Structure of Science*, pp. 481-85; Carl G. Hempel and Paul Oppenheim, "The Logic of Explanation," in Feigl and Brodbeck (eds.), *Readings in the Philosophy of Science*, pp. 330-31; and Theodore Abel, "The Operation Called *Verstehen*," *ibid.*, pp. 677-87.

Appendix

added] . . . This is not to recommend resignation, let alone to open the door to an unscientific arbitrariness. It is arbitrary, rather, to attribute to the facts, for the sake of a scientific ideal derived from other disciplines, an ability to provide objective evidence which they lack in this field. (27)

Szondi appears to be claiming that the individual cannot be "bracketed out" because what the facts are—"the subjectively moulded facts" (*die subjektiv geprägten Tatsachen*) —is at least in part determined by him, and thus may be different for someone else.

This view of interpretation would require us to construe interpretive claims as statements (at least in part) about the individual who makes them, rather than about some independent state of affairs or about someone else's mental state. If, as Szondi maintains, the proper interpretation "attempts to reestablish dynamically, in the reconstruction of the process of composition, the static connection of the facts which is severed in the process of producing individual pieces of evidence" (27), then an interpretive claim based on the experience resulting from the successful mental reconstruction of the process of composition (*des Entstehungsvorgangs*) is essentially a statement, not about the author's mental state, experience, intention, or whatever, but about the critic's own personal experience or understanding as a result of his "reconstruction of the process of composition" (27). Only if we construe interpretive statements in this way does it follow that "self-evidence" (*Evidenz*)—and not empirical tests, which are certainly in principle always possible—is the proper criterion for their verification:

> For this reconstruction, the facts serve to indicate the right direction as well as to warn us where we might go astray. None of the facts must be overlooked if the reconstruction is to be self-evident. But self-evidence (*Evidenz*) is the proper criterion to which philological knowledge must submit. When the reconstruction is

self-evident, the significance of the facts is neither missed nor in their hypostatization misunderstood, but grasped as *subjectively conditioned and in the process of understanding subjectively conveyed,* in other words, first and foremost in its true objectivity. (27, italics added)

The criterion then, on Szondi's view, for determining the truth or falsity of an interpretive claim is whether the latter is "evident,"—that is, intuitively obvious or self-evident on the basis of a critic's subjective understanding.

In order to avoid confusion, it is important to contrast this criterion with scientific verification. A conclusion based on or confirmed by an examination of a certain set of facts together with appropriate empirical generalizations may or may not be self-evident to a scientist, but nothing as to the truth value of the conclusion depends on its being self-evident; a scientist may believe the conclusion to be highly probable or even virtually certain on the basis of the relevant evidence, even though it is by no means self-evident or intuitively obvious to him. Scientific methodology is objective in the sense in which Szondi believes that the appropriate methodology of literary criticism is not: namely, the results of scientific experiments or other empirical tests do not depend on the person who carries them out.[7] The latter (Szondi's "erkennende Subjekt" [15]) can be and indeed is "bracketed out."

Now if a statement by a critic P about the meaning of a literary work is essentially a claim about the experience of the work which P has (or about his subjective understanding) as a result of his mental reconstruction of the process of composition, then it is clear that my claim that a particular work means, say, m, is properly verified by my having the relevant experience or understanding; if I have it, then the truth of my statement will be self-evident to me. It is also

[7] This formulation is slightly oversimplified. For some qualifications, see Thomas S. Kuhn, *The Structure of Scientific Revolutions,* esp. pp. 111-35.

Appendix

obvious that what a work means cannot be objectively verified or confirmed; we can objectively verify (or confirm) only what it means to P, or what it means to Q. P's claim, C_1, that a work means m is properly verified if C_1 is self-evident to him on the basis of his understanding, while Q's claim, C_2, that the work means n is properly verified if C_2 is self-evident to Q on the basis of his understanding. Hence if P claims that the work means m, not n, while Q claims it does not mean m, but means n, then it does not follow that one of them must be mistaken; both may be right and indeed will be if the two claims are self-evident to P and Q respectively.

Suppose P thinks that a certain passage, p, in which a woman and a rose are mentioned, in a literary work by author A, is metaphorical, while Q denies this. Q may offer as evidence, in support of his denial, the fact that the passage p does not have a certain characteristic c, say, an explicit identification of the woman with the rose, which Q has observed to be generally associated with similar passages (in the works of A) which Q considers metaphorical. Now P may agree that p does not have characteristic c and yet not change his mind about what p means, because whether it does or does not have c simply does not affect his understanding and hence his interpretation of p. If his experience or subjective understanding is the proper test, then he can rightly dismiss the fact adduced by Q as irrelevant. But suppose that whether p has c or not does affect P's experience or understanding and hence interpretation of p. It is conceivable that P could rightly claim that p has c, while Q could be justified in maintaining that it does not; that is, it is possible that whether a particular passage has c is not objectively decidable because, for example, it depends on what experience a person has when reading the passage.

In other words, there are two ways in which an interpretive claim may be subjective: it may be (1) that we do not (or need not) agree on the relevant criterion to be applied

Appendix

in order to determine whether a work or passage means m. Or, if we do agree about the relevant test, it may be (2) that we do not agree about whether the condition specified by the test is satisfied; we may, for example, agree that p means m (say, is metaphorical) if p has characteristic c, but we may not agree whether in fact p has c.

In order to show that an interpretive statement cannot be objectively confirmed, it is necessary to establish either (1) or (2); but if we choose (2), then it is necessary to show that there is some difficulty in principle (not merely one of lack of relevant facts) about deciding whether the condition specified by the test is satisfied—whether p has c, for example.

If the relevant general test for determining whether a passage p means m is, for instance, to ascertain whether the author intended to convey m by p, then it must be shown that a judgment about whether the author intended m by p is irreducibly subjective (depends, say, on the particular critic's experience or his subjective understanding). Now if a statement by critic P about the meaning of a work is a statement about P's experience or understanding of the work and hence is properly verified by appealing to this understanding, then we can see why it should be impossible to confirm or disconfirm an interpretive statement objectively. For then a fact will be relevant to an interpretive claim only insofar as it affects the critic who makes it. And since the same fact may affect the experience or subjective understanding of different critics differently—the individual being the ultimate judge—it is obvious that no fact can be objective evidence; what it proves or confirms will depend on the person who considers it. We have seen, then, how this conclusion follows from Szondi's view that the proper test for determining the truth or falsity of an interpretation consists in checking whether that interpretation is intuitively obvious or self-evident to a critic on the basis of his subjective understanding (*Verstehen*) of the work or passage in question.

Appendix

3. Is It Possible to Establish without Circularity that a Fact Is Evidence for an Interpretation? The Doctrine of the 'Hermeneutic Circle' as a Quest for Certainty

I have indicated above the two ways in which an interpretive claim might be irreducibly subjective. Szondi's first general argument is intended to show that even if there is a criterion for determining what a work means (the author's intention), a claim that a work means, say, m (or that the author meant m) is properly verified by a critic's subjective understanding. (As we shall see later, Szondi denies as well that the meaning of a work is determined by what the author meant.) How, then, does Szondi attempt to show that the proper criterion for determining the truth or falsity of an interpretation is its *Evidenz* or lack of it—that is, whether the latter is self-evident or intuitively obvious to a particular critic on the basis of his understanding of the work in question? Szondi attempts to justify this thesis by showing that there is no other way in which we could verify or confirm an interpretation. His argument is this. An interpretation of a fact (f) as evidence for an interpretation (J) of a work or passage cannot be verified or confirmed independently of J. This is what Szondi calls "the interdependence of evidence and understanding" (*Interdependenz von Beweis und Erkenntnis*, 26); in order, that is, to establish that f is evidence for J, we need to establish J. If this is true of any fact, then it is clear that no interpretation can be objectively established or confirmed, since to do so would be to adduce some fact as evidence for it. It would follow that interpretive claims are irreducibly subjective:

> Philological argumentation thus depends upon understanding in a very different way from, say, a mathematical proof. For not only must the steps of the argument be understood, but *the character of the facts as evidence is only revealed by the interpretation*, while conversely the facts point the way for the interpretation.

Appendix

This interdependence of evidence and understanding is an instance of the hermeneutic circle. Those who deny that only insofar as a fact is interpreted can it confirm the correctness of an interpretation falsify the circle of understanding by mistakenly supposing that understanding moves along a straight line which leads directly to knowledge. But since there is no such straight line in philology, the facts ought to be regarded as *hints* (*Hinweise*) rather than as objective evidence. (26-27, italics added)

Lest Szondi's remark that the facts are "hints" (*Hinweise*) —or should be so considered—rather than (objective) evidence prove misleading and suggest a residue of objectivity where in fact there is none, the following should be borne in mind. If a fact (f) cannot constitute objective evidence for a particular interpretation J_1 and against another interpretation J_2, because whether it supports J_1 or J_2 depends on which of the two is self-evident to a particular critic, then f cannot be an objective "hint" or "indication" (*Hinweis*) either, because whether it will 'point to' J_1 or to J_2 depends on which interpretation a particular critic happens to hold.

3.1 *Can the Meaning of an Earlier Reading Be Objective Evidence for the Meaning of a Later Reading?*

Szondi gives two examples to illustrate his conception of how a fact is related to an interpretation for which it is evidence; "the hermeneutic analysis of interpretation on the basis of variant readings" (*die hermeneutische Analyse des Interpretierens auf Grund von Lesarten*, 26) provides the first one:

> Someone who is unable to recognize the meaning of "Tischen" in the line "Von tausend Tischen duftend" ["Fragrant with a thousand tables"] from the later version of "Patmos" will therefore go back to the earlier version, "Mit tausend Gipfeln duftend" ["Fragrant with

250

Appendix

a thousand peaks"]. He will support the metaphorical interpretation of "Tischen," which he is now able to give, by appealing to the reading of the earlier version. For the fact that the earlier version has "Gipfeln" in place of "Tischen" shows that in the later version 'Tische' stand metaphorically for 'Gipfel'. But does it really show this? Another of Hölderlin's hymns begins with the lines: "Wie wenn am Feiertage, das Feld zu sehn/Ein Landmann geht, des Morgens...." In the prose draft the beginning read: "Wie wenn der Landmann am Feiertage das Feld zu betrachten hinausgeht, des Abends...." From the fact that the first version has "Abends" where the later version has "Morgens," no one would infer that in the metrical version "Morgens" means "Abends"; rather, one will assume that Hölderlin changed the time in the later version. This shows that in "Patmos," too, one cannot speak of the first version as constituting objective evidence. For the critic contributes something of his own to this evidence by construing the change from "Gipfeln" to "Tischen" as a metaphorical process, as a transference, and by inferring from this that the meaning has remained the same. It is only within this framework, provided by the understanding, that the fact appears as evidence. (26)

Szondi argues that the change from the words "Mit tausend Gipfeln duftend" to "Von tausend Tischen duftend" is not objective evidence for the claim that the latter is meant metaphorically; and this is, of course, true if Szondi means (as I think he does) that the mere fact that an author changes a particular word or word sequence from w_1 to w_2 is not *per se* evidence that the author means by w_2 what he meant by w_1. The reason is that there are always at least in principle two possibilities: the author may have wanted to convey the same meaning differently (say, metaphorically), or he may have wanted to convey something else. Hence if a critic held that "Von tausend Tischen duftend" is not

Appendix

meant metaphorically, the change *per se* from the earlier to the later version would not be evidence against his view, since Hölderlin may have wanted to change the meaning of the passage.

Let us call the earlier reading

"Mit tausend Gipfeln duftend" 'G'

and the later reading

"Von tausend Tischen duftend" 'T'

and let

'f' stand for the fact that Hölderlin changed G to T.

Now the critic who supports his metaphorical interpretation of T by appealing to f is clearly assuming one of the two possible 'interpretations' of f; namely, that f is evidence for the metaphorical interpretation of T. This assumption is what he contributes "of his own" to f. But why should what the critic contributes "of his own," namely, his interpretation of f, be irreducibly subjective? Is it not possible in principle to determine objectively whether f is or is not evidence for the metaphorical reading of T?

The problem here is this. We cannot simply assume that because an author changed a particular reading, r_1, to another reading, r_2, he must have, or is likely to have, wanted to convey by r_2 what he meant by r_1. Before f (the fact that Hölderlin changed G to T) can be adduced in support of the claim that Hölderlin meant G by T, we need a generalization such as the following: whenever Hölderlin changed a reading r_1, in specified respects similar to G, to another reading r_2, in specified respects similar to T, he consistently intended to convey the same meaning by r_2 as by r_1. In other words, we need a generalization correlating occurrences of changes in readings like that from G to T with an intended metaphorical (or figurative) interpretation of the later reading. Such a generalization would give us reason to believe that if Hölderlin changed G to T, then he would be likely to

Appendix

have intended to retain the earlier meaning. In virtue of a generalization of this kind, f would be evidence that Hölderlin meant G by T. Hence it would appear to be possible to establish that f is evidence for the metaphorical interpretation of T. Let us call this interpretation J_1. Why, then, should Szondi believe that whether f is or is not evidence for J_1 depends on a critic's subjective understanding?

Szondi's contention is this. In order to establish that f is evidence for J_1, it is necessary to establish that J_1 is correct, since f will be evidence for J_1 only if J_1 is correct; or in Szondi's words, "the method of variant readings" (*die Lesartenmethode*) is valid only under the condition "that the change in the passage does not also correspond to a change in what is meant" (*daß der Änderung der Stelle nicht auch eine Änderung des Gemeinten entspricht*, 28). This means: f is evidence for J_1 only if J_1 is correct, for the assumption "that the change in the passage does not also correspond to a change in what is meant" cannot be true unless J_1 is correct—that is, unless Hölderlin meant G by T. Hence the only way in which a critic can establish or confirm that f is evidence for J_1 (the metaphorical interpretation of T) is by 'showing' that J_1 is correct. This indeed appears to be the way in which the critic in Szondi's example is arguing:

> For the critic contributes something of his own to this evidence [the fact that Hölderlin changed G to T] by construing the change from "Gipfeln" to "Tischen" as a metaphorical process, as a transference, and by inferring from this that the meaning has remained the same. It is only within this framework, provided by the understanding, that the fact appears as evidence. (26)

Somewhat more explicitly:

(1) Hölderlin changed G to T.
(2) Hölderlin meant T metaphorically—that is, meant G by T. [(1) and (2) constitute the reconstruction of the change from G to T "as a metaphorical process."]

Appendix

(3) If Hölderlin changed G to T, he must have intended to retain the earlier meaning. [This follows from (2).]
(4) Hölderlin intended to retain the earlier meaning when he changed G to T. [This is the 'inference' from (1) and (3) "that the meaning has remained the same."]
(5) Hölderlin meant G by T. [This follows from (4).]

It is obvious that this argument begs the question; for the only basis on which the critic concludes that Hölderlin intended to retain the earlier meaning when he changed G to T (and hence meant G by T) is the critic's assumption that Hölderlin meant G by T. We can, of course, infer (4) from the assumption that Hölderlin meant G by T, if we are reasonably sure of the latter. But then our assurance that Hölderlin intended to retain the earlier meaning when he changed G to T logically depends on our assumption that Hölderlin meant G by T. Consequently, if we choose this way of establishing (4), we cannot without obvious circularity infer from it that T stands metaphorically for G. More generally: an inference from (4) to (5) will be circular if whatever evidence we have for (4) is evidence for it only by way of being evidence for (5). For example, among the contextual features which leave little doubt that T is meant metaphorically are the references to "Länder" ("countries") and "Asia" ("Patmos," later versions, lines 24 and 31 respectively). Suppose a critic adduced these references in support of J_1 (the metaphorical reading of T) and hence for (4), the claim that Hölderlin intended to retain the earlier meaning when he changed G to T. Then the critic cannot without circularity appeal to (4) in support of J_1, because the only evidence he has produced for (4) is the probability (based on the references to "Länder" and "Asia") that J_1 is correct—that is, that Hölderlin meant G by T.

One problem with Szondi's contention is this. Even if we knew that J_1 is correct, that Hölderlin meant G by T, it does not follow that f is evidence for J_1. For the fact that Hölderlin intended in this case to retain the earlier meaning when

Appendix

he changed G to T and hence meant G by T simply has no bearing on the question whether f (the fact that Hölderlin changed G to T) is evidence that he meant G by T. In other words, that Hölderlin changed G to T does not in virtue of the fact that he meant G by T become evidence for the claim (J_1) that he meant G by T. (But if it did, it would be superfluous, since we would have to know that J_1 is true in order to know that f is evidence for it.) On the other hand, if f is evidence that Hölderlin meant G by T (in a case in which we have a generalization of the kind indicated above), it does not follow necessarily that Hölderlin meant G by T. To suppose that it does would be to imagine that from the fact that Hölderlin changed G to T we could ever *infer with certainty* that he meant G by T; and this is in principle, not merely in fact, impossible. Hence Szondi's claim that we need to establish J_1 in order to establish that f is evidence for J_1 is clearly false.

I have suggested that it is indeed possible to establish without circularity that f is evidence for J_1. To complete the argument I shall give an illustration of the conditions under which f would be evidence for J_1. Suppose that Hölderlin consistently marked changes in his manuscripts in red when he intended to convey a different meaning by the new words, but did not do so when he wanted to retain the earlier meaning. Suppose further that the change from G to T was not marked in red. Would not the fact that Hölderlin changed G to T and did not mark the change in red be, under these circumstances, objective evidence for the claim (J_1) that Hölderlin meant G by T? It is, of course, not conclusive evidence; it remains possible that T is not meant metaphorically. Hölderlin may, for example, have forgotten in this case to mark the change in red, or he may have decided to stop marking changes in red which are not intended to retain the earlier meaning. But unless there is reason to believe that something of this sort happened, the fact that Hölderlin changed G to T and did not mark the change in red would clearly constitute objective evidence against the lit-

Appendix

eral interpretation of T, even though one might be able to produce possibly stronger evidence in support of this reading—that there is some particular feature of the text, for example, which indicates that T is not meant metaphorically, or that Hölderlin commented on the passage in, say, a letter to the effect that he did not mean T metaphorically. This example illustrates the conditions under which f and a further fact (that Hölderlin did not mark the change in red) would be evidence for J_1. But it is easy to see under what kind of conditions f alone would be evidence for J_1: namely, if, for instance, there were a number of passages in which Hölderlin changed the word "Gipfel" to "Tische" and if in all (or virtually all) of these he meant "Tische" metaphorically. (We might know this from direct statements by Hölderlin about these passages, or the context might in those cases make it clear that Hölderlin meant "Tische" metaphorically.)

I have not, of course, shown that the conditions under which f is objective evidence for J_1 (the metaphorical interpretation of T) are in fact satisfied. I have shown only that there are such conditions and that consequently it is possible to determine objectively, without appealing to the meaning of T, whether f is evidence for J_1 or not. This is sufficient to show that f can be objective evidence for J_1.

We have seen, then, that what the critic in Szondi's example contributes "of his own" to the fact (f) to which he appeals in support of the metaphorical reading of T—namely, the claim that f is evidence that Hölderlin meant G by T—is by no means irreducibly subjective, as Szondi claims, but can be objectively confirmed or disconfirmed and in particular without appealing to the meaning of T.

Is there any reason to believe that what I have shown for f does not hold for other kinds of fact? Suppose a critic adduced in support of the metaphorical reading of T the references to "Länder" ("countries") and "Asia" ("Patmos," later versions, lines 24 and 31 respectively). Would these not be objective evidence for his interpretation? In order to

Appendix

show that they cannot be objective evidence, Szondi would have to show that no matter under what conditions these references were made, it would always be not only possible, but equally justifiable, to construe them as evidence for the metaphorical reading or as evidence against it (or to dismiss them as irrelevant). If this could be shown, a critic would be perfectly justified in disputing that the references to "Länder" and "Asia" objectively confirm the metaphorical reading of T even if he did not offer any reason whatever why they should not *in this particular case* support the metaphorical interpretation of T. But unless there is at least some evidence that Hölderlin used the words "Länder" and "Asia" metaphorically (or at least figuratively) in "Patmos," or unless there is some other reason why these references do not in this particular case support the metaphorical reading of T, the claim that they are not objective evidence for the metaphorical interpretation of T would be clearly unjustified.

To say that, for any fact f, f cannot be objective evidence for an interpretation J is to say that there are no objective conditions under which f would be evidence for J. Hence a critic could always (under any objective conditions) justifiably dismiss f as irrelevant to the truth or falsity of J without offering any reason why f should not in a particular case be (objective) evidence for J, since it would make no sense to ask whether the (objective) conditions under which f would be evidence for J are or are not satisfied in this (or any) particular case. But as the above example shows, it certainly does make sense to ask such a question. What is more, in any serious controversy about the relevance of some fact f to the truth or falsity of an interpretation J, a critic clearly could not justifiably dismiss f as irrelevant (or construe it as disconfirming J) without offering evidence as to why f should in the case or cases in question be irrelevant to (or disconfirm) J. (That the relevance of f in a particular case is not self-evident or intuitively obvious to a critic obviously does not qualify as evidence here.)

Appendix

But why should Szondi want to say that a fact f cannot be evidence for an interpretation J unless J is correct? What Szondi appears to want to say is that f cannot be evidence for J unless f entails J. In other words, unless we can infer from f *with certainty* that J is correct, f cannot be evidence for J.

This seems to be the point of his stipulation that the "method of variant readings" (*Lesartenmethode*) is valid only if "the change in the passage does not also correspond to a change in what is meant" (*der Änderung der Stelle nicht auch eine Änderung des Gemeinten entspricht*, 28). For if we *assume* this, then we can of course infer *with certainty* that if an author changed reading r_1 to r_2, he must mean by r_2 what he meant by r_1. The problem is that the price we pay for the certainty of our conclusion is the inevitable circularity of the argument (for to know "that the change in the passage does not also correspond to a change in what is meant" *is* to know that the author means by r_2 what he meant by r_1). But if we must assume "that the change in the passage does not also correspond to a change in what is meant" in order to have any evidence at all that the author means by r_2 what he meant by r_1, then there are only two alternatives: subjective certainty at the price of total (objective) scepticism or no 'knowledge' at all.

More generally: if a fact or set of facts f cannot be evidence for J unless f logically entails J, then there can be *no* factual evidence for J; for no fact or set of facts ever logically entails the truth of an empirical claim (that an author meant so and so, for example) in the humanities and social sciences or in the natural sciences. Consequently, if we can have any evidence (and hence knowledge) that J is correct, it must be evidence of a different kind. Since it cannot be factual evidence, it must be an intuitive insight (*Verstehen*) that J is correct; and if that is evidence, as Szondi claims, then we can be *certain* that J is correct. Szondi's central claim turns out to be a disguised demand for certainty. Not satisfied with factual evidence, which would at most confirm

Appendix

an interpretation probabilistically, Szondi rejects such evidence *in toto* and substitutes for the discredited appeal to facts a direct, intuitive understanding (*Verstehen*) which provides subjective certainty.

3.2 Can an Interpretation of a Given Passage Be Objectively Confirmed or Disconfirmed by an Appeal to Other Passages?

Szondi's conception of the relation between a fact and an interpretive claim for which it is 'evidence' is also illustrated by his remarks about the so-called method of parallel passages (*Parallelstellenmethode*, 27). If we are not sure about the meaning of a particular word—let us call it 'w'—in some passage (p) of a literary work, we look at other passages of the same work (or of other works by the same author) in which w occurs; if it turns out that w in all these other passages means, say, m, then it is, on the basis of this evidence, likely that w also means m in p. In other words, our conclusion that w in p means m will be based on the fact that in most or all of its other occurrences w means m.

Now Szondi claims that a passage (p_1) is parallel to another passage (p), only if p_1 has the same meaning as p; or, to put it slightly differently, p_1 is evidence for the meaning of p only if p_1 and p have the same meaning. It is readily apparent that this—just like the analogous claim in regard to the method of variant readings (*Lesartenmethode*) —is an instance of the more general thesis that in order for some fact to be evidence for an interpretation J, J must be correct. Thus Szondi says, speaking of the *Parallelstellenmethode*:

> The meaning of a word is clarified here, not with the help of other words which stand in the same place in earlier versions, but by other passages in which the same word occurs. Of course, the word must be used everywhere with the same meaning, the passages must be parallel passages in this strict sense. That is the

Appendix

crucial constraint on this method, just as it is a condition of the applicability of the method of variant readings that the change in the passage does not also correspond to a change in what is meant. Consequently, the method of parallel passages, like the other method, comes up against the question which facts are able to establish that the passages are parallel. . . . *Whether a passage is properly regarded as a parallel passage can, therefore, be determined neither by the organization of the text nor by other facts, but depends solely on the meaning of the passage.* [*Ob eine Stelle als Parallelstelle anzusehen ist, kann darum nicht etwa der Gliederung des Textes, auch nicht einer anderen Faktizität, sondern ausschließlich dem Sinn der Stelle entnommen werden.*] Like any other piece of evidence, a parallel passage must first establish its character as evidence. But that happens in the interpretation. However valuable parallel passages are for an interpretation, it cannot rest upon them as though they were independent evidence for it, for whatever force they have as evidence depends on the interpretation. This interdependence is one of the basic facts of philological knowledge which no ideal of science can afford to ignore. (28-29, italics added)

It is easy to see that if Szondi's statement about parallel passages is correct, then any attempt to confirm an interpretation of a passage (p) by adducing other passages will necessarily involve circular reasoning. For if in order to know that a particular passage or set of passages is parallel to p and hence evidence for a certain interpretive claim (J) about p I need to know that J is true, then obviously any appeal to such evidence must *presuppose* the truth of the very conclusion which such evidence is intended to confirm. Hence if Szondi is right, then parallel passages cannot constitute objective evidence for the meaning of a passage (p) the interpretation of which is in dispute. And if we need to

Appendix

know what p means in order to know that certain passages are parallel to p and hence evidence for its meaning, then such 'evidence' is clearly useless.

But why must a word, w, in passage p have the same meaning as in another passage or set of passages (ps) in order for ps to be parallel to p and hence evidence for what w in p means? If this were necessary, then, of course, a set of passages ps in each of which w means m could be evidence for the claim that w in p means m only if that claim is true; that is, we could not adduce ps as evidence for the claim that w means m in p unless we knew that w means m in p. It would follow that if ps and p are parallel (and hence ps constitutes evidence for the meaning of w in p), then we could *infer with certainty* from the fact that w in each of ps means m that w means m in p as well. This consequence appears to be what motivates Szondi's curious constraint on parallel passages.

In my example above, I have specified the parallel passages (ps) simply in terms of the occurrence of the word w. I have said that if there is a fairly large number of such passages, and if in each of them w means m, then it is likely that w in p also means m. Now a judgment based on this generalization is, of course, less reliable than a judgment based on a generalization which correlates passages more similar to p, in terms of contextual features, with a certain meaning of w. For example, we can specify the similarity which a passage must bear to p in terms of words in the immediate context of w, in terms of the syntax of the sentence in which w occurs, or in terms of imagery, ideas expressed, and so on, in the context of w. (We can certainly specify at least some features of this kind without appealing to the meaning of w.) If in each of the passages (ps) similar to p in the specified respects (say, in terms of the words forming the immediate context of w) w means m, then this correlation will allow a more reliable judgment about the meaning of w in p than the correlation between occurrences of w, irrespective of its contextual features, and a certain

Appendix

meaning of w. The reason is that it is (generally) more likely that an author should use w in p in the way he has used w in passages more similar to p than in the way he has used w in passages less similar to p. In general: the greater the similarity, in terms of contextual features of w, between each of ps and p, the more reliable is a judgment about the meaning of w in p based on the meaning of w in ps. But it is clear that no matter how great the degree of similarity (in terms of contextual features of w) between ps and p, the fact that w in each of ps means m never logically implies that w means m in p as well; it is always *possible*, though not always likely, that the author should have meant by w in p something other than what he meant by w in each of ps.

It is equally clear, however, that if ps and p are similar to a high degree in terms of contextual features of w, then the probability that w has the same meaning in p as in ps (assuming that w has the same meaning in each of ps) is relatively high. This probability is based on the assumption that if an author has used w to mean m in all the passages highly similar (in the specified respects) to p, then it is very likely that he meant m by w in p as well. This assumption is, in Szondi's words, one of the "rules of rhetoric" (*Regeln der Rhetorik*, 28). The reason Szondi rejects arguments based on it appears to be that the only way we can be *certain* that the assumption is borne out in a particular case would be to know what w in p means:

> The solution [the appeal to the rules of rhetoric] was illusory in Schleiermacher's time as well, since the question whether or not these rules of rhetoric have been followed in a given case always leads back to hermeneutics. (28)

This is, of course, true. But the conclusion Szondi draws from it does not follow, namely:

> Whether a passage is properly regarded as a parallel passage can therefore be determined neither by the

Appendix

organization of the text nor by other facts, but depends solely on the meaning of the passage. (29)

For certainty that the "rules of rhetoric have been followed in a given case" (*diese Regeln der Rhetorik in einem gegebenen Fall befolgt sind*)—which is to say that w in p means m—is not what justifies the inference that w in p means m.

Szondi's thesis about parallel passages seems to be based on a confusion of two distinct questions: (1) Under what conditions are we justified in regarding certain passages ps as parallel to another passage p and hence as evidence for the meaning of w in p? (2) Under what conditions can we be *certain* of what w in p means? Szondi seems to be assuming that the answer to (2) is also the answer to (1). The answer to (2) is that we cannot be certain that w in p means m unless we could have direct, intuitive knowledge that w in p means m (or that the author meant m by w in p). But such intuitive 'knowledge' is not what justifies the claim that ps and p are parallel and hence that ps is evidence for the meaning of w in p.

The claim that ps and p are parallel is justified if ps and p are similar in terms of the occurrence of w and more or less restrictively specified contextual features of w. If ps and p are similar in these respects, then we can adduce ps as evidence for the meaning of w in p. Now if w means m in each of the passages ps, then we are justified in inferring that w is likely to mean m in p as well. And this is true irrespective of any "rules of rhetoric," for the very fact that w consistently means m in a specified context is evidence that the author is following a rule of some sort or has come to associate w with m habitually in the context in question. It is, of course, possible that in some of the passages of the set ps, w means m, and in others (of the same set) w means n. We would then have conflicting evidence: the passages (of ps) in which w means m make it likely that w in p means m, while the passages (of ps) in which w means n make it likely

Appendix

that w in p means n. In such a case, the evidence may not warrant either conclusion.

But the fact that parallel passages can never *guarantee* that w means m in p does not entail that such passages do not constitute (objective) evidence for the meaning of w in p. For it remains perfectly true that if w means m in each of a set of passages ps, and if the latter are parallel (in the sense indicated above) to another passage p, then the fact (f) that w means m in each of ps is evidence that w means m in p as well; or, to put the point differently, then it is likely, on the basis of f, that w means m in p—even if it should turn out that w does not mean m in p. What the latter possibility implies is that f is never *sufficient* evidence, in the sense that f cannot logically entail or *prove conclusively* that w means m in p. In other words, it is always possible that there is stronger evidence (e) for a different conclusion—a direct statement by the author, for instance, to the effect that he meant n by w in p—such that on the basis of *all* the available evidence, in this case e and f, it is more likely that w in p means n than that it means m. Hence even if w does not mean m in p (or if, on the basis of all the evidence, it is not likely that w means m in p), we are nonetheless justified in claiming that f is evidence that w means m in p, or—what is the same thing—that *on the basis of f* it is (objectively) likely that w means m in p.

Szondi's argument has been the following: no passage or set of passages, ps, is parallel to another passage p and hence evidence of what w in p means unless w has the same meaning in p as in each of the ps. Thus a set of passages ps which are parallel—in the sense I have indicated above—to p and in each of which (ps) w means m does not constitute evidence that w in p means m unless w in p means m (or unless on the basis of ps we can be certain that w means m in p). Therefore, if it turns out that w in p does not mean m, then ps would not be evidence that w in p means m. As I have suggested, however, this would be to confuse the conditions under which passages similar to p are *evidence* that w in p

Appendix

means *m* with *certainty* that *w* in *p* means *m*; and, indeed, it would be to misconstrue the nature not only of an inference from parallel passages but of all empirical knowledge, for no empirical claim is logically entailed by the evidence for it.[8] But to deny that passages parallel to *p* can be objective evidence that *w* in *p* means *m*, because such evidence does not entail that *w* in *p* means *m*, is to trade reasonable assurance for total scepticism out of a misguided desire for certainty where it is not to be had; and to conclude, as Szondi does, that *Evidenz* is the proper criterion for determining the truth or falsity of an interpretive claim would be to turn this (objective) scepticism by a sleight of hand into subjective certainty based on an intuitive *Verstehen*.

I have so far argued that although on the basis of passages parallel to *p* we cannot be certain of what *w* in *p* means, it does not follow that such passages do not constitute objective evidence for the meaning of *w* in *p*. I have claimed further that passages parallel to *p* are indeed objective evidence of what *w* in *p* means. I want to show now that although this claim is not quite as unproblematical as I have so far assumed, it is nevertheless correct.

Consider the following case. *P* and *Q* disagree about the meaning of a particular word *w* in passage *p*. *P* thinks that *w* means *m*, while *Q* holds that it means *n*. Let '*a*' and '*b*' stand for words or word sequences which form the immediate context of *w*; *a* precedes *w* and *b* follows it; this relation shall be denoted by '*awb*.' Suppose *P* and *Q* find a set of passages *ps* such that $p_1 = (...cawbd...)$, $p_2 = (...eawbf...)$, $p_3 = (...gawbh...)$, and so on, where '*c*,' '*d*,' '*e*,' etc., again stand for words or word sequences which form the immediate context of *awb*. We assume further that *P* and *Q* agree that *w* in each of these passages means *m*. Let '*f*' then denote the fact that, in each of the passages *ps*, *w* means *m*.

If Szondi is right in claiming (a) that whether our passages *ps* are parallel to *p* depends on the meaning of *w* in

[8] See Friedrich Waismann, "Verifiability," in Flew (ed.), *Logic and Language*, pp. 122-51.

265

Appendix

p, and (b) that there is no objective way in which we can determine what w in p means, then the question whether the ps are parallel to p depends on a critic's subjective judgment about the meaning of w in p. If it does, then a critic who held that w means, say, n in p would *always* be justified in denying that ps and p are parallel, while a critic who held that w in p means m would *always* be equally justified in maintaining that ps and p are parallel. I want to show: whether ps and p are parallel and hence whether f constitutes evidence that w in p means m does not depend on a critic's subjective judgment about the meaning of w in p but on objective characteristics of the ps and p and on certain facts about the author. I shall attempt to support this claim by arguing that Q cannot always justifiably deny that ps and p are parallel and that in cases in which he can deny this, it is not equally justifiable (for another critic) to assert that ps and p are parallel.

On Szondi's view, Q should always be able to deny (in fact, given Q's assumption about the meaning of w in p, he could not but deny) that ps and p are parallel, for the simple reason that Q thinks w in p means n, while (*ex hypothesi*) w in each of ps means m. But, clearly, if Q's only reason for denying that ps and p are parallel is his claim that w does not have the same meaning in p as in ps (since Q holds that w means n in p), then he is simply begging the question what w in p means; for that is precisely what is not known and upon which the passages ps are to shed light. Or if Q denies that ps and p are parallel, because the specified respects in which they are similar (namely, the occurrence of ...*awb*...) are not sufficient to *guarantee* that w will have the same meaning in p as in ps, then—as we have seen—Q is misconstruing the nature of an inference from ps to the meaning of w in p and is asking in effect for something which by its very nature an argument from parallel passages cannot provide, namely, that the conclusion follow necessarily from the premises. But, as I have suggested, it does not

Appendix

follow that the *ps* are not objective evidence for what *w* in *p* means.

Since the meaning of *w* in each of the passages *ps* is undisputed, since, that is, each of the *ps* is a clear case (and obviously must be, if the *ps* are to provide objective evidence), there will always be some contextual feature which distinguishes each of the *ps* from *p*. So it looks as though Q can always appeal to this difference in support of his denial that *p* and *ps* are parallel. Or can he?

Q's argument will be implausible at best unless he can show that the feature which distinguishes each of the *ps* from *p* is the same in all of the *ps*. For suppose the contextual features, say, $c_1, c_2, c_3, ...c_n$, which distinguish $p_1, p_2, p_3, ...p_n$, respectively, from *p* are different from one another such that no single one of these occurs in all of the *ps*. Then the fact that, despite this difference among the *ps*, *w* has the same meaning in each of them will be evidence that no single one of the features ($c_1, c_2, c_3, ...c_n$) distinguishing the *ps* from *p* is such that its presence is necessary for *w* to mean *m*. Hence the absence of any one of them would not warrant the conclusion that *w* is likely to have a meaning other than *m*. In other words, in such a case, no single one of the features distinguishing *ps* from *p* would mark a *relevant* difference between *ps* and *p*. Therefore, an appeal to a difference between *ps* and *p*, in support of the claim that *ps* and *p* are not parallel, is convincing *only if* the distinguishing feature is the same in all of the *ps*; only then would it be justifiable to say that *ps* and *p* are not parallel and consequently that *f* (the fact that *w* means *m* in each of *ps*) is not evidence that *w* means *m* in *p*. But in this case it is clearly not equally justifiable to say that *f is* evidence that *w* means *m* in *p*; for in this case *w* appears to mean *m* only in the presence of some specific contextual feature which is absent in *p*.

Whether the passages *ps* are parallel to *p* and hence whether *f* is or is not evidence that *w* means *m* in *p* depends not only on the characteristics of *ps* and *p*, but also on cer-

Appendix

tain facts about the author. For example, there might be evidence (such as a statement by the author in a letter, essay, or diary) that after having established the usage of a word (w) to mean m, by means of some contextual feature c, the author rarely used c again to make the meaning (m) of w clear because, say, he did not want to repeat himself in any obvious way. Or after a certain number of occurrences of w in the context of c, the author took the usage of w to mean m for granted, or he might have come to associate w with m habitually even in the absence of c. In any of these cases, f (the fact that w means m in each of ps) may very well be evidence that w also means m in p, even if some particular feature c, which is absent in p, occurs in all of the ps.

Hence it is clearly not always possible to dispute that ps and p are parallel; and in the cases in which it is justifiable to do so, it is not equally justifiable to assert that ps and p are parallel. For, as we have seen, whether certain passages are parallel to p depends, not on the meaning of w in p or on a critic's subjective judgment about the meaning of w in p, but on objective characteristics (such as contextual features) of the ps and p and upon certain facts about the author. It follows that it is in principle always possible to determine objectively whether certain passages are parallel to p and hence evidence for its meaning. Consequently, an interpretation of p can be objectively confirmed or disconfirmed by an appeal to other passages.

3.3 *Szondi's Arguments against Beissner's Interpretation of the First Strophe of Hölderlin's "Friedensfeier"*

Szondi cites a specific interpretive dispute in which a critic employs the *Parallelstellenmethode* to support his reading of the following passage from Hölderlin's "Friedensfeier":

Der himmlischen, still wiederklingenden,
Der ruhigwandelnden Töne voll,
Und gelüftet ist der altgebaute,

Appendix

Seeliggewohnte Saal; um grüne Teppiche duftet
Die Freudenwolk' und weithinglänzend stehn,
Gereiftester Früchte voll und goldbekränzter Kelche,
Wohlangeordnet, eine prächtige Reihe,
Zur Seite da und dort aufsteigend über dem
Geebneten Boden die Tische.
Denn ferne kommend haben
Hieher, zur Abendstunde,
Sich liebende Gäste beschieden. (Quoted by Szondi, 15)

With heavenly, quietly echoing,
With calmly modulating music filled,
And aired is the anciently built,
The sweetly familiar hall; upon green carpets wafts
The fragrant cloud of joy and, casting their brightness far,
Full of most mellow fruit and chalices wreathed with gold,
Arranged in seemly order, a splendid row,
Erected here and there on either side above
The levelled floor, stand the tables.
For, come from distant places,
Here, at the evening hour,
Loving guests have forgathered.[9]

Friedrich Beissner has claimed that the hall described here is not meant as a metaphor for the countryside on the grounds that nowhere (else) in Hölderlin's works is there a metaphor in which the metaphorical character of the description is not made explicit:

> If the hall described here were meant to be understood metaphorically, it would be without parallel in Hölderlin's complete works. For such metaphorical images are for the most part detailed comparisons, indeed explicit equations, such as "Brod und Wein," 1. 57 ("der Boden ist Meer! und Tische die Berge" ["the floor is ocean! and tables are mountains"]); but the relation

[9] *Friedrich Hölderlin: Poems and Fragments*, trans. by Michael Hamburger, p. 433.

Appendix

to what is meant by the metaphor always remains clear through the use of a name, as, for example, even in the boldest transformation into images: "Von tausend Tischen duftend" ["Fragrant with a thousand tables"] ("Patmos," later versions, 1. 30), where earlier there is talk of "Gipfel" ["peaks"], for in the next line the use of the name "Asia" makes clear what is meant and earlier the "Länder" ["countries"] are mentioned (1. 24). But here there is no reference to a countryside. . . . (Quoted by Szondi, 16)

In other words, Beissner contends that the disputed passage —call it 'p'—is not, or is not likely to be, metaphorical because there is no clearly metaphorical passage in Hölderlin in which there is not at least one explicitly identifying feature present, that is, "the use of a name" (*Namensnennung*), which is absent in p. Hence—argues Beissner—if Hölderlin had meant p metaphorically, he would have made some explicit, identifying reference to the countryside. Now Szondi gives the following argument to show that Beissner's general claim about metaphors in Hölderlin is untenable:

That the portrayal of the hall cannot be meant metaphorically is inferred from the fact that there is no other metaphor in Hölderlin's complete works in which the relation to what is meant is not made clear through detailed comparisons, explicit equations, or at least through the use of a name. The force of Beissner's argument thus depends, not on specific parallel passages, but on the fact that there are no such parallels. But just as in the positive use of parallel passages, each passage which is adduced as evidence must establish its character as evidence, so in the negative argument it must be clear that no evidence has been found, not because no passage was recognized as evidence, but because there is none. Precisely this condition, however, remains unsatisfied in this case. For in asserting that in Hölderlin's complete works there is no metaphor of the

Appendix

kind as the first strophe of "Friedensfeier" would be, one overlooks that in examining the texts one would not recognize such passages as possible evidence. The metaphorical interpretation of the "Friedensfeier" strophe can be confirmed only by examples which are no more clearly characterized as metaphors than that strophe itself. But if this characterization is regarded as insufficient, then it also will not allow us to separate the related passages from the remaining unmetaphorical material. Consequently, the assertion itself [that in Hölderlin's complete works there is no metaphor of the kind as the first strophe of "Friedensfeier" would be on the metaphorical interpretation] becomes untenable.

(24)

Szondi's argument can be stated as follows:

(a) Only passages which are no more clearly metaphorical than p ("die nicht deutlicher denn sie selbst [p] als Metaphern gekennzeichnet sind") can be parallel to p and hence evidence of what p means.

(b) Beissner does not think that p is metaphorical.

Hence no passage which is or would be evidence of what p means could be recognized by Beissner as metaphorical.

Beissner's claim is untenable, according to Szondi, because it is irrefutable, because, that is, Beissner could not (or would not) recognize any evidence against his interpretation of p and hence against the claim that, in all metaphorical passages in Hölderlin, what is meant by the metaphorical term(s) is indicated at least by the use of a name. It is important to note that if Szondi's conclusion is correct, then Beissner's statement about metaphors in Hölderlin would not be an empirical claim but rather an arbitrary stipulation.

I shall try to show: Szondi's conclusion follows trivially from his premises if we construe (a) in accord with his thesis about parallel passages, but if we construe (a) in

Appendix

accord with what in fact are (or would be) parallel passages, then Szondi's conclusion is a *non sequitur*.

Let us first interpret (a) in accord with Szondi's claim that in order for a passage p_1 to be parallel to p, and hence evidence for the meaning of p, p_1 must have the same meaning as p. On this interpretation, (a) reads as follows:

'Only passages which have the same meaning as p can be parallel to it and hence evidence for its meaning.'

In other words, Szondi's constraint on parallel passages forces us to construe the phrase "no more clearly metaphorical than p" as "having the same meaning as p." Now since Beissner believes that p is not metaphorical, it follows trivially from (a) that only passages which are (in Beissner's view) not metaphorical can be (in Beissner's view) evidence for the meaning of p, or—to put it differently—that Beissner cannot regard any metaphorical passages as evidence for the meaning of p and hence as evidence against his interpretation of p.

The crucial premise in this argument is the assumption that a set of passages (ps) cannot be parallel to p and hence evidence for the meaning of p unless each of ps has the same meaning as p. If this is true, then parallel passages cannot in principle constitute objective evidence for the meaning of p. For whether a particular passage or set of passages is evidence for the meaning of p will then depend on how a critic interprets p. If he construes p metaphorically, only metaphorical passages will be parallel to p and hence evidence for the meaning of p. If another critic holds that p is not metaphorical, then only passages which are not metaphorical can be evidence for the meaning of p. It is obvious that, on Szondi's assumption, there could not be any evidence (from parallel passages) against either interpretation of p. More generally: it follows from Szondi's assumption that there could not be any evidence from parallel passages against *any* interpretation of *any* passage. Hence if this assumption is correct, then it follows trivially

Appendix

that Beissner could not recognize any evidence against his interpretation of p, not because Beissner has made a mistake in his reasoning or has overlooked evidence, but because, on Szondi's assumption about what kinds of passages are parallel to p and hence evidence for its meaning, there *could not be* any evidence (from parallel passages) against Beissner's interpretation of p. Consequently, even if Beissner were unable to recognize any evidence against his interpretation, Szondi could not—if his assumption is correct—infer from this that Beissner's interpretation is invalid.

It is, therefore, strange to find that Szondi *objects* to Beissner's argument on the grounds that he could not recognize any evidence against his interpretation of p, since Szondi's explicit thesis implies that there *could not be* any such evidence. In other words, Szondi's conclusion appears to presuppose what one of his premises denies, namely, that there is some objective, noncircular way (without appealing to the meaning of p) of specifying which passages are parallel to p. In particular, Szondi's statement

> But if this characterization is regarded as insufficient, then it also will not allow us to separate the related passages (*die verwandten Stellen*) from the remaining unmetaphorical material. (24)

would appear to make sense only if we assume that there are (or, at least, can be) passages objectively parallel to p ("die verwandten Stellen") which could disconfirm Beissner's interpretation of p. Otherwise, it simply does not make sense to object that Beissner could not (or would not) recognize such passages.

As we have seen, Szondi's conclusion does follow from the premises *if* his thesis about parallel passages is correct. But since—as I have shown in section 3.2 above—that thesis is false, his conclusion will be unjustified unless it also follows if his premise (a) is construed in accord with what in fact are or would be parallel passages. If we construe (a) and in particular the phrase "no more clearly metaphorical

Appendix

than p" in this way, then Szondi's conclusion that Beissner could not recognize any evidence against his interpretation of p does not follow from his premises, (a) and (b).

What counts in fact as evidence for the meaning of p would be passages in which "the use of a name" (*Namensnennung*) and any other *explicitly* metaphorical features, "detailed comparisons" or "explicit equations" (*ausgeführte Vergleiche* or *ausdrückliche Gleichungen*, 16), for example, are absent, but which do possess elements suggesting the possibility of metaphor (such as, in the first strophe of "Friedensfeier," the cloud of joy which wafts about green carpets and the tables standing upon leveled ground). Suppose there is such a passage or set of passages ps, and critics agree that each of these is metaphorical. Even if Beissner, before being aware of ps, thinks that p is not metaphorical, he may very well, after the ps have been called to his attention, change his mind about the meaning of p and hence about the characteristics (like "the use of a name") which he previously thought to be always associated with metaphors in Hölderlin. From the fact that Beissner initially thinks that p is not metaphorical and that there is no metaphor in Hölderlin's complete works of the kind which the first strophe of "Friedensfeier" would be if it were meant metaphorically, it clearly does not follow that he *could not* recognize the ps as metaphorical and hence as evidence against his interpretation of p.

But even if he continues to hold that p is not metaphorical, it does not follow that he could not recognize any evidence against his interpretation. For Beissner might very well recognize ps as evidence against his view and yet not change it, because he has stronger evidence in favor of his interpretation (a statement of Hölderlin's intention in a diary, notebook, letter, for instance). Or Beissner might persist in his interpretation of p, not because he could not (or would not) recognize any evidence against it, but because in fact there is no such evidence; that is, it is perfectly possible that there are no passages parallel to p in the specified

Appendix

respects which are (generally acknowledged to be) metaphorical.

That Beissner *could not* recognize any evidence against his view follows neither from the fact that he thinks p is not meant metaphorically nor from the fact that he believes there are no metaphors in Hölderlin in which what is meant by the metaphorical term(s) is not indicated at least by the occurrence of a name; the reason is that Beissner may very well have reached these conclusions only *after* examining all the relevant passages. Only if Beissner dogmatically *stipulated* that a passage could not be metaphorical unless it had explicitly metaphorical features (like "the use of a name") would it follow that he could not recognize any evidence against his view and that the latter is consequently irrefutable. In order to show that this is even likely, it would have to be shown that there is a considerable number of passages lacking explicitly metaphorical elements (in particular, "the use of a name") which are (by common consent) metaphorical and that in all of these Beissner categorically denied or would deny that they are metaphorical because they lack explicitly metaphorical elements.

If, as Szondi's conclusion implies, Beissner's claim were just an arbitrary stipulation, it would, construed as an empirical statement, be certainly likely to be false. But Szondi admits that Beissner's claim is very likely true, not because Beissner's 'stipulation' just accidentally happens to fit the facts, but because Beissner, being the leading Hölderlin authority, is likely to have checked all the relevant empirical evidence and hence is likely to know whether there are in fact any metaphorical passages in Hölderlin in which what is meant by the metaphorical term(s) is not indicated at least by the use of a name:

"If the hall described were meant metaphorically," Beissner writes, "it would be without parallel in Hölderlin's complete works." Since this statement is made by the leading authority on Hölderlin's works, it appears

Appendix

idle to want to examine the complete works in search of another example—all the more, since even two cases would not have much force when confronted with the complete works. (20)

As we have seen, the assumption under which Szondi's conclusion (that Beissner could not recognize any evidence against his interpretation of p) does follow from his premises implies that there *could not be* any evidence from parallel passages against an interpretation of the disputed passage p (or indeed of any passage). Hence even *if*—as Szondi contends—Beissner could not recognize any evidence against his interpretation of p (and against his general claim about metaphors in Hölderlin), this could not, on Szondi's assumption, warrant the statement that Beissner's interpretation of p (or his general claim) is "untenable." Furthermore, the assumption in question—namely, Szondi's thesis about parallel passages—is false; for it is entirely possible and proper to specify the kinds of passages which are parallel to p in an objective, noncircular way (without appealing to the meaning of p).

But if Szondi's crucial premise (a) is interpreted in accord with what in fact would count as parallel passages and hence as evidence for the meaning of p, then his conclusion that Beissner could not recognize any evidence against his interpretation no longer follows. Hence Szondi's conclusion (as well as the more general claim which it implies, namely, that parallel passages cannot constitute objective evidence for the meaning of p or of any other passage) is unjustified.

Szondi gives several other arguments against Beissner's interpretation of the disputed passage (p) from "Friedensfeier." These arguments, however, do not only fail to show that there cannot be any objective evidence for an interpretation, but actually imply that there is or can be such evidence.

Szondi's contentions are as follows:

Appendix

(1) Since "Friedensfeier" was written only shortly after the completion of "Brod und Wein," Hölderlin would not, if he meant the first strophe of "Friedensfeier" metaphorically, be likely, for aesthetic reasons, to have repeated himself by making the metaphor explicit.

(2) After the explicitly metaphorical description in "Brod und Wein," Hölderlin could take the metaphorical sense of the relevant words ("Tische," "geebneten Boden," "Saal") for granted.

(3) The fact that in a later version of "Patmos," written after "Friedensfeier," Hölderlin changed "Gipfeln" to "Tischen" in a context in which the metaphorical sense of the latter is made clear by a reference to "Asia" (in the following line) "means . . . not so much that he is still concerned to mark the metaphor as such; rather, it reveals the fact that the use of 'Tisch' in a metaphorical sense has become a matter of course for him." (19)

(4) It would be inappropriate to expect "that in the first strophe of 'Friedensfeier' the countryside, if that is what Hölderlin meant, be referred to by name, since it is virtually the stylistic law of the hymn that (with the one exception of line 42 'unter syrischer Palme' ['beneath the Syrian palm-tree']) it contains neither substantival nor adjectival proper names." (19)

If (1) is true, as Szondi maintains (18), then it is difficult to see why this should not be objective evidence against Beissner's claim that if Hölderlin meant p metaphorically, he would be likely to have indicated this by an explicit reference to the countryside. In other words, under the assumption that (1) is true, we should expect that if Hölderlin meant p metaphorically, he would subtly suggest this rather than indicate it explicitly. And the assertion that (1) is true —that Hölderlin would not have repeated himself within such a short time and in the way that Beissner's argument would require—is clearly an empirical claim which can certainly be in principle objectively confirmed or disconfirmed.

Appendix

The same holds true for (2). And if (2) is correct, would this not be objective evidence that Hölderlin might very well have meant p metaphorically even though there are no explicitly metaphorical elements present in p? As for (3), if it is true that Hölderlin had, by the time he changed "Gipfeln" to "Tischen" in "Patmos," habitually or almost instinctively associated the word "Tisch" with the metaphorical sense in which he used it in "Brod und Wein," then this would be objective evidence against the view that without an explicit reference, in this case to "Asia," Hölderlin would not be likely to have used "Tische" in a metaphorical sense. Finally, if indeed Hölderlin intentionally avoided proper names in "Friedensfeier" for stylistic reasons, then this would (objectively) weaken the force of Beissner's argument that Hölderlin would at least have used a proper name if he had meant the first strophe metaphorically.

None of Szondi's four arguments can properly be called 'subjective' in any relevant sense. The assumptions upon which they rest are clearly factual statements about Hölderlin, which—like any other empirical claim—can always be in principle objectively confirmed or disconfirmed. And as we have seen, if these statements are true, then they will be (objective) evidence for the respective interpretive claims in support of which Szondi adduces them. What Szondi's arguments show is that the validity of an argument from parallel passages (or from their absence) depends on a number of assumptions about the author—whether or not he would be reluctant to repeat himself in certain ways, whether or not he would be likely to take a certain somewhat unusual usage of a word for granted after a certain time, whether he habitually associates a certain word with a particular meaning, whether he does so irrespective of the contextual features, and so on. This confirms the conclusion of section 3.2.

To summarize what emerges from the examination of Szondi's examples: The claim that in order to establish that a fact (f) is evidence for an interpretation (J) we need to

Appendix

establish J is false, if Szondi means by it (i) that the truth of J is either a necessary or a sufficient condition (or both) for f to be evidence for J, or if he means (ii) that f is evidence for J only if f entails J. In the first case, Szondi would be misconstruing the nature of evidence in general, in the second case, of evidence for empirical claims, not merely in literary criticism but in the natural sciences as well. From the fact that the empirical evidence (e) for a claim (J) about the meaning of a literary work (or for any empirical claim) cannot entail the latter (J), it does not follow that e is not (or cannot be) genuine evidence for J. We can, as I have shown, establish objectively (without circularity) whether a fact is or is not evidence for an interpretation; hence it is possible to confirm or disconfirm (objectively) an interpretive claim. To maintain, for example, that certain passages (ps), all of which mean m, cannot be evidence that another passage, p, means m, unless p actually means m or unless the fact that all the passages ps mean m logically entails that p means m, would be to trade the possibility of reasonable assurance for total scepticism in a misguided search for intuitive certainty.

4. The Conceptual Relation between the Meaning of a Work and the Author's Intention

I have so far examined Szondi's arguments for the thesis that an interpretation (J) of a literary work or passage cannot be objectively confirmed because in order to appeal to any fact (f) in support of J we need to establish (or presuppose) that J is true. Now Szondi's "variant readings" (*Lesarten*) example (26), his detailed arguments against Beissner (18-19), and especially his claim that the appropriate task of the interpreter is to study the genesis of the literary work he is attempting to interpret (18, 21-22, 27) suggest that there is a general criterion for determining whether a particular passage (or work) p means m, namely, whether the author meant m by p. Szondi has not then so far denied that *if* some

Appendix

fact *f* is evidence of what the author intended to convey by a word or passage *p*, about the meaning of which we are in doubt, then *f* will be evidence of what *p* means; rather, he has argued that we cannot objectively establish that *f* is evidence for the claim that the author intended to convey *m* (and not *n*) by *p*.

In the last part of his essay, however, Szondi rejects as well the thesis that the meaning of a work is determined by what the author intended to convey:

> The philological postulate that an ambiguity is to be recognized as such only if the author intended it seems to do full justice neither to the distinctive character of the poetic process nor to the distinctive character of the literary work of art. For it presupposes that a poetic text is the representation of thoughts or mental images. If the word is a vehicle, as it were, in the service of thoughts or mental images, then in the case of ambiguity only *that* meaning or *those* meanings are to be considered which correspond to the thought or to the mental image. . . . But as soon as the word is no longer seen as a mere means of expression, it acquires an autonomy which prohibits making its interpretation depend solely on the author's intention. Even if the work thereby threatens to slip out of the author's hands, he is nevertheless not the loser, and it should not be the task of philology to draw literary works *against the will* and against the insight of the poets into the imaginary net of intention. (30-31, last italics added)

Only if it is the author's (or authors') will that his (their) intention should not count is the latter irrelevant to determining the meaning of a work. Szondi seems to be returning with his left hand what he takes away with his right. Thus also his word of caution: "nevertheless, this idea [that an author's intention does not (entirely) determine the meaning of a work] should not be applied unhistorically to the earlier epochs." (33)

Appendix

In accordance with his assertion that an author's intention is of only limited relevance, Szondi maintains that it cannot be the task of the interpreter to remove an "ambiguity which belongs to the text itself" (30). I want to consider Szondi's example of such an ambiguity, in order to shed some light on the notion of what belongs to the text itself.

In Kleist's *Amphitryon* Sosias answers his master's question "Auf den Befehl, den ich dir gab—?" as follows: "Ging ich/ Durch eine Höllenfinsternis, als wäre/ Der Tag zehntausend Klaftern tief versunken,/ Euch allen Teufeln, und den Auftrag, gebend,/ Den Weg nach Theben, und die Königsburg." Critics have spoken here of a grammatical case error, since—or so they have claimed—the passage should read ". . . den Weg nach Theben und *der* Königsburg"; and they have sought the reason for this in the French model which lacks inflection. One might reply that perhaps the last phrase, "und die Königsburg," does not belong to "ging ich den Weg nach. . . ," but to the participial clause "Euch allen Teufeln, und den Auftrag, gebend. . . ." Sosias curses both his master and the task he has given him as well as the place to which it is to lead him. But the question is not only what is more likely: the grammatical error or the bold syntactic construction (one can find examples of both in Kleist and even something which would be unique is not thereby already refuted). The question is, rather, whether it is appropriate at all to make a choice here, whether the alternative is not inherent in the matter itself [that is, whether the ambiguity is not an inherent part of the text itself]. Just as the insertion of "und den Auftrag" between "Euch allen Teufeln" and "gebend" seems to count on the confusing association "den Auftrag gebend," so the third object of the curse, "die Königsburg," could be joined to the phrase "den Weg nach Theben" in order to lead us on the wrong track of the indication of direction. (29-30)

Appendix

Now Szondi's claim that "the question is *not only* what is more probable: the grammatical error or the bold syntactic construction" is clearly in logical conflict with his assertion that "The question is, rather, whether it is appropriate at all to make a choice here...." For if a decisive interpretive question here is whether one is more probable than the other, then it must be appropriate to decide the matter; but if, as Szondi implies, it is not appropriate to decide between the two possibilities (the grammatical error or the "kühne Fernstellung"), then the relevant question cannot be *at all* (and not merely "nicht nur") whether one is more probable than the other.[10] I mention this inconsistency not to point out a logical difficulty in Szondi's argument (which can easily be corrected), but rather to suggest that he has implicit qualms about dismissing Kleist's intention (that is, about saying 'the question *is not* . . .' instead of 'the question is *not only*. . .'); and I wish to suggest that he does because his implicit conception of the meaning of a literary work is such that the author's intention is indeed decisive in determining what the work means.

This conception comes out quite clearly in his attempt to justify taking the phrase "und die Königsburg" as belonging, not to "ging ich den Weg nach . . . ," but to the participial clause "Euch allen Teufeln, und den Auftrag, gebend. . . ." For if "die Königsburg" is one of the objects of Sosias' curse, then we would want an explanation of its unusual position after "Den Weg nach Theben." Szondi accounts for this in

[10] Indeed, this decision is not only appropriate but necessary, since Kleist could not have made the mistake attributed to him by some critics (in the grammatical case of the article in the phrase "und die Königsburg") if, as Szondi suggests, "die Königsburg" is the third object of Sosias' curse and is placed after the phrase "Den Weg nach Theben," "um auf den Irrweg der Richtungsangabe zu locken." But perhaps Szondi means that Kleist may well have intended "die Königsburg" to be taken as the third object of Sosias' curse *and* have wanted to suggest as well the interpretation according to which 'die' would be a mistake. And *this* is, of course, very possible. But if it is true, then Kleist did not make a mistake.

Appendix

terms of the assumption that "die Königsburg" "could be joined to the phrase 'den Weg nach Theben' in order to lead us on the wrong track of the indication of direction." This is certainly a plausible and ingenious explanation. I do not wish to argue for or against it; the point I want to make, rather, is that Szondi's explanation implies that it is Kleist's intention which determines what the text means.

It is surely undeniable that the interpretation of "die Königsburg" as one of the objects of Sosias' curse is significantly more plausible if we can give a convincing explanation (like Szondi's) of the position of "und die Königsburg." It follows that the interpretation of "die Königsburg" as an object of Sosias' curse logically implies that Kleist intended the phrase "die Königsburg" to be taken in that way. For *only if* the interpretation implies this does it make sense to give an explanation (of the sort offered by Szondi) of the position of the phrase "und die Königsburg." I shall briefly indicate why this is so.

The explanation called for by the interpretation which Szondi suggests is clearly an explanation in terms of Kleist's reason(s) or purpose. What we want to know is: Why, for what reason or purpose, did Kleist place the phrase "und die Königsburg" after "Den Weg nach Theben" if "die Königsburg" is one of the objects of Sosias' curse? In other words, we would want an explanation, since the interpretation suggested by Szondi (taking "die Königsburg" as an object of Sosias' curse) would appear to conflict with Kleist's placing the phrase "und die Königsburg" after "Den Weg nach Theben." But why does that interpretation conflict with Kleist's action? It does so because normally, if an author had placed the phrase "und die Königsburg" after "Den Weg nach Theben," the likely reason would be that he *intended* it to be taken as belonging to the latter.

And now it is obvious that the need for an explanation of Kleist's action (in terms of his reason or purpose) arises because the possibility that Kleist intended "die Königsburg" to be taken (only) in the way which its position suggests

Appendix

conflicts with the interpretation of "die Königsburg" as an object of Sosias' curse. This shows clearly that the latter interpretation implies that Kleist intended it,[11] for otherwise it could not come into conflict with the intention which we might (normally) expect Kleist to have had, on the basis of the position of the phrase "und die Königsburg," and consequently the question of explaining the position of the latter phrase in terms of Kleist's intention would not arise. But since such an explanation would clearly be called for, if we believe that "die Königsburg" is an object of Sosias' curse, the latter interpretation must imply that Kleist intended it (and hence cannot be correct unless Kleist had the intention in question).

If the interpretation were not a statement about Kleist's intention, then it would not make sense to ask, 'If that interpretation is correct, then why did Kleist place the phrase "und die Königsburg" after "Den Weg nach Theben"?' In other words, if that interpretation were a statement about the meaning of the word sequence taken *in abstracto*, not a statement about Kleist's intention in producing that word sequence, then the answer to the question 'Why did Kleist place the phrase "und die Königsburg" after "Den Weg nach Theben"?' could have no conceivable bearing on the interpretation of the speaker's utterance.

One might object to my conclusion that it follows only if what needs to be explained (on the interpretation of "die Königsburg" as an object of Sosias' curse) is a human action—in this case, Kleist's placing the phrase where he has. The answer to this objection is that it does not make sense to ask, for example, 'If, on *P*'s interpretation of the line "Von tausend Tischen duftend" ("Patmos," later versions, line 30), the word 'Tisch' has its literal sense, then how does *P* explain that it is "Asia" which the phrase "Von tausend

[11] It is obviously not (or not merely) Sosias who must be taken to mean this, for to ask why the phrase "und die Königsburg" comes after "Den Weg nach Theben" is clearly not, or at least not merely, to ask why Sosias placed it there, but why Kleist did.

Appendix

Tischen duftend" modifies?' unless the latter locution is understood as 'then how does P explain the fact that *Hölderlin uses* (or has the speaker use) "Von tausend Tischen duftend" to modify "Asia"?' In general: it does not make sense to ask 'If this word (w) means m, then why does that word (w_1) with such obvious associations of such-and-such occur in the immediate context?' or 'Why does w, if it means m, have such a curious position in the sentence?' unless the latter locutions are understood as 'Why did the *author use* w_1 ... ?' and 'Why did *the author place* w ... ?'

To put the point in a slightly different way, questions of the kind 'Why, if w means m, does w_1 occur in the immediate context?' or 'Why, if w means m, is w placed in such-and-such a position in the sentence?' are essentially requests for an explanation of *human actions* (or acts) in terms of the agent's reason(s), motive(s), purpose(s), or intention(s). (An explanation in terms of physical causes, such as the movements of a hand, would clearly be irrelevant.) And—as I have suggested above—it does not make sense to ask 'If w means m, then why did the author use w_1 in the immediate context?' or 'If w means m, then why did the author place w in that curious position?' unless the interpretation in question, that w means m, is a claim about the author's intention—or, to put it differently, unless the locution 'if w means m' is construed as 'if the author meant (or intended the speaker to mean) m by w.' If such questions can legitimately be asked and are relevant to a given interpretation, then it must be a claim about the author's intention.

Furthermore, could we maintain that the phrase "und die Königsburg" belongs to the participial clause "Euch allen Teufeln, und den Auftrag, gebend" if we knew that Kleist had really made a mistake and, having forgotten to correct it in a later edition, added a note to the effect that he had erroneously written "die Königsburg" instead of "der Königsburg"? Or suppose that there was no doubt that Kleist had *not* in fact made a mistake (we might know this from,

285

Appendix

say, a letter or from a note to the play) but consciously wrote "die Königsburg" and placed it after the phrase "Den Weg nach Theben" for precisely the reason Szondi suggests; could we still maintain that "die Königsburg" is not an object of Sosias' curse since the phrase should read "und der Königsburg"?

In view of his insistence that an author's intention does not determine the meaning of a work, Szondi is concerned to deny that it follows

> that now *all* interpretations are justified. Rather, it is only after rejecting this false alternative that we can appreciate the real difficulty as well as the task of understanding a text: namely, to distinguish between correct and incorrect, plausible and implausible (*sinnbezogen* and *sinnfremd*) without refusing to recognize the sometimes objectively ambiguous word and the rarely unambiguous motif for the sake of the alleged unambiguously intended meaning. (32)

The problem is that the terms "correct" (*richtig*) and "incorrect" (*falsch*) lose their (objective) meaning if, as Szondi claims, interpretive statements are irreducibly subjective—if, that is, such statements can only be, and are properly, verified by an appeal to their self-evidence; for the same interpretation may clearly be self-evident to one critic but not to another, and hence it may be both correct and incorrect. The same is true for "plausible" (*sinnbezogen*) and "implausible" (*sinnfremd*); what one critic, on the basis of his intuitive understanding, is justified in calling "plausible," another, on the basis of his intuitive understanding, is equally justified in regarding as "implausible." On Szondi's premises, it makes no sense to call a particular interpretation "correct" or "incorrect," "plausible" or "implausible." For if an interpretation is correct if and only if it is self-evident or intuitively obvious, and incorrect if and only if it is not self-evident or intuitively obvious, or self-

Appendix

evidently false, then the most we can say is that an interpretation is true (or false) for a particular critic (or group of critics); and there may in principle be as many correct interpretations as there are critics.

5. THE INTERPRETATION OF FACTS AS EVIDENCE FOR AN INTERPRETATION OF A LITERARY WORK

I want to turn now to that one of Szondi's premises which I think is true and important. It is the claim that before facts can be adduced for or against an interpretation of a literary work, they must themselves be interpreted (understood) in a way in which facts in the natural sciences are properly left uninterpreted. The need for such an interpretation of facts in literary criticism is due to the difference between human actions and physical events. What distinguishes a physical event like someone's arm rising from an action like someone's raising his arm is the 'meaning' which the physical event has in the latter but not in the former case.[12] We understand (explain) a physical event by subsuming it under a general law which (together with appropriate additional premises) allows us to deduce (or predict) the occurrence of the event.[13] Understanding an action, on the other hand, such as determining whether certain intentional movements of a person's arm are a warning, a greeting, a threat, or a prayer, and so on, involves grasping the point or significance of the action in terms of the agent's beliefs, motives, reasons, or intentions.[14] Thus we could, for example, formulate statistical laws correctly specifying the conditions

[12] For a detailed discussion, see May Brodbeck, "Meaning and Action"; von Wright, *Explanation and Understanding*, pp. 86ff; and Winch, *The Idea of a Social Science*, pp. 45ff.

[13] But see Waismann, "Verifiability," in Flew (ed.), *Logic and Language*, pp. 131ff. Waismann gives persuasive arguments to show that statements about specific physical events are not strictly deducible in this way.

[14] See Winch, *The Idea of a Social Science*, p. 115.

Appendix

under which people in a particular society move their arms in a certain way without, in any relevant sense, understanding what they are doing.[15]

Szondi emphasizes repeatedly that in interpreting a work we have to examine its genesis, the concrete process of *composition* (18, 21, 27) of which the work is the result. In doing so, he is rightly calling attention to the fact that a literary work is not, so to speak, a product of nature, like marks imprinted on the sand or upon rocks by wind and water, but rather the result or record of a human act of saying something. This would not in itself be very significant if it were not for the fact that it is *part of our concept* of a literary work that it is (the record of) a speech act, the understanding of which, therefore, logically involves grasping certain of the agent's beliefs, motives, reasons, or intentions. In the sense in which we use the term 'interpret' when we speak of interpreting words or sentences, it would be meaningless to speak of interpreting a natural object or an aggregate of physical marks not the result or creation of a human agent, except insofar as we were interpreting what a human agent *could* mean by it had he produced it or were he to do so.[16]

The thesis that an author's intention is logically irrelevant to what a work means implies that the latter is, in regard to its logical status, not a speech act, or record thereof, but an aggregate of words (taken *in abstracto*) which a member of the speech community *could* use to perform one of a certain number of possible speech acts; hence it is, on this view,

[15] *Ibid.*

[16] As John Searle has pointed out: "It is a logical presupposition, for example, of current attempts to decipher the Mayan hieroglyphs that we at least hypothesize that the marks we see on the stones were produced by beings more or less like ourselves and produced with certain kinds of intentions. If we were certain the marks were a consequence of, say, water erosion, then the question of deciphering them or even calling them hieroglyphs could not arise. To construe them under the category of linguistic communication necessarily involves construing their production as speech acts." ("What is a Speech Act?" in Searle [ed.], *The Philosophy of Language*, p. 40.)

Appendix

rather like a series of physical movements which, if they had been performed by a human agent, could have one of a certain number of possible meanings. But if a literary work is *essentially* a speech act, as Szondi rightly suggests (18, 21-22, 27, 34,), then its meaning is logically tied to the author's intention—that is, to what he meant. And, as I have argued briefly in the last section and more fully in Chapters III to VI, this is indeed the case. It follows that a fact will be evidence for or against an interpretation of a work if and only if it is evidence of what the author meant. It is in this sense that facts need themselves to be interpreted before they can become evidence for the meaning of a work or a passage from it.[17] To be more precise: in order to be able to adduce some fact f for or against an interpretation of a passage (or a work) p, we must establish, or be justified in assuming, that f is evidence of what the author is likely to have meant by p.

Suppose, for example, we are puzzled about the meaning of word w in a passage p of a work by author A. We discover a number of other passages (ps) in which w occurs. Now in order to adduce ps as evidence for the meaning of w in p, we need to show, or be able to assume, that ps are evidence of what A is likely to have intended to convey by w in p. Frequently this presents no problem; but it might be, for example, that the ps were not written by A. Hence it is important to establish authorship. Or it is possible that the ps were written much earlier than p and by that time A's style and general views may have changed in such a way that w may have taken on a very different meaning for him than the one it had when he wrote the other passages (ps). Hence later passages in which w occurs—written at approximately the same time as p—would be significantly stronger

[17] In addition to the more obvious sense—which Szondi also sometimes has in mind—that individual words or passages from a work need to be interpreted before the fact that they have a certain meaning can be construed as evidence for or against an interpretation of the work or of a particular passage from it.

Appendix

evidence for the meaning of w in p than the earlier passages (ps). The reason is that what A meant by w in the passages he wrote at approximately the same time as p is (generally) better evidence of what he is likely to have meant by w in p than his use of w in the earlier passages (ps). On the basis of considerations such as these, as well as those mentioned above (section 3.2)—authorship, time of composition, style, similarity in contextual features of w, and so on—we determine whether certain passages in which w occurs are parallel to p and hence evidence of what w in p means and, if they are parallel, the approximate strength of such evidence. This is how we establish an interpretation of the fact that w is used in a certain way in passages other than p as evidence that w is used in the same way in p.

In order now to determine which particular hypothesis about the meaning of w in p (of the work by A) the evidence confirms, we clearly need to interpret the relevant passages. Let us assume that there are a number of passages, in which w occurs, written at approximately the same time as p. If in all of these w means, say, m, then it is likely that w means m in p as well. What justifies this inference is that, at the time he wrote p, A consistently used w to mean m and hence appears to have habitually (or in virtue of some implicit rule) associated w with m; for this makes it likely that he meant m by w in p as well. Of course, it does not guarantee this; A *may* on this occasion, for whatever reason, have used w differently.[18] But, in the absence of appropriate evi-

---

[18] As I have suggested earlier (3.2), it is in principle impossible to verify an interpretive statement conclusively. It should be remembered, however, that no empirical claim can be conclusively verified (see Waismann, "Verifiability"). But the reasons why an empirical claim about what A meant by a certain word (w) in a certain passage (p) cannot be conclusively verified are not exactly the same as the reasons why an empirical claim about physical objects or events cannot be so verified. For the behavior of human beings, unlike that of physical objects or particles, may be influenced by decisions; and A's decision, say, to use w in one way rather than in another in p, may not be predictable even if we could have complete knowledge of the con-

Appendix

dence for such a claim, we are clearly justified in inferring, on the basis of A's established, habitual usage of w, that he is likely to mean m by w in p as well.

Furthermore, even when the evidence for the meaning of a particular passage p is conflicting, the question what p means does not reduce to the question which interpretation of p is self-evident or intuitively obvious. The reason is that the reliability of my intuitive assurance ('knowledge') that A meant m by p depends on the factual assumption that A is likely to have viewed or evaluated his situation in exactly the same way as I would, that he is likely to have had the same beliefs, reasons, motives, and hence intention(s) as I imagine I would have in his position. My intuitive assurance *per se* shows at most that the interpretation in question is *possible* (given the possibility that A meant what I would have meant by p), but constitutes no evidence that in fact it is correct. If we have reasonably good evidence of how A viewed the situation, of A's likely beliefs, reasons, motives, and hence intention(s) under the circumstances or under similar circumstances (and this is clearly necessary for my 'understanding' to be at all reliable), then the fact that it seems intuitively obvious to me that A should have the intention(s) in question would appear to be superfluous, inasmuch as it would add nothing to the evidence that A in fact had the intention(s) in question and therefore meant m by p.

But suppose the relevant objective evidence is conflicting, such that it is not possible to say (objectively) of any one of a set of possible intentions (i_1, i_2, i_3) that it is the intention which A is most likely to have had under the circumstances; that is, we cannot tell (objectively) how A viewed

---

text in which A's decision is made—A's beliefs, the factors he takes into consideration in deciding how to use w, the motives, reasons, purposes, and so on, which have led him to use w in a certain way in the past. But it is clear that facts about A's previous or general use of w do constitute (objective) *evidence* for A's likely use of w in p; and on the basis of such evidence we can be reasonably sure of what A is likely to have meant by w in p.

Appendix

the situation, what beliefs, reasons, or motives he is likely to have had under the circumstances in question or under similar ones. Then it would be clearly arbitrary and unwarranted for me to assert that A had, say, intention i_2 on the grounds that this is intuitively obvious or self-evident to me, since the reliability of my intuitive 'understanding' depends on the very facts which in this case (*ex hypothesi*) we do not possess.

Szondi's insistence that the factual 'evidence' in support of an interpretation must itself be (first) interpreted brings out two further points.

(1) Although there is a fairly simple general test for determining whether a fact (f) is evidence that a work or passage (p) means, say, m, namely, whether f is evidence that the author intended to convey m by p, it is in practice not always easy to determine whether f is evidence that the author meant m by p. The claim that a particular fact is evidence for an interpretation frequently involves a number of tacit assumptions about the author which may themselves require justification. (Szondi's substantive arguments against Beissner are a good illustration; see section 3.3 above.) It may turn out that the evidence for these assumptions is inconclusive (an author's statement about his general stylistic aims or principles, for instance[19]), or is itself open to different interpretations. Although this does not show that it is in principle impossible to confirm an interpretation objectively, it does indicate that interpretive issues are frequently considerably more complex than appears at first sight. This complexity may help to explain why it is in practice often extremely difficult to resolve an interpretive controversy and why it may sometimes seem that interpretive statements are not in principle susceptible to objective confirmation or disconfirmation.

(2) The further we carry the process of justifying a particular interpretive claim (because the immediate context of the passage in question is itself ambiguous, or because

[19] See Wellek and Warren, *Theory of Literature*, pp. 148-49.

Appendix

there are no unproblematical parallel passages or specific statements by the author, for example), the more explicit becomes the general knowledge or assumptions about an author and his time upon which we rely in interpreting a text. These are, typically, facts or assumptions about the conceptual framework within which an age or an author views the world, aesthetic and moral ideals, literary and social conventions, socio-political conditions, the language of the time, and so on—in short, about the whole social and cultural background of a work. But it is not just in *interpreting* a text that we need to rely on such knowledge or assumptions; we cannot even *describe* the relevant aspects (facts) of a text without it.[20] As Wolfgang Stegmüller has recently put it, we cannot draw a sharp distinction between the facts in a particular case, " 'what the text says' " (*was da auf dem Papier steht*),[21] and the background knowledge, since the latter determines in large measure what those 'facts' are.[22] In other words, we cannot sharply distinguish between what is 'in a text' and what we bring to it.[23] This, as Stegmüller has suggested, is probably the reason why the attempt to justify an interpretation of a literary work (or historical document) may appear to be necessarily circular. In his words, "Already in the description of the facts, 'the critic gets the background knowledge which he used for their interpretation back out of that description.' "[24] This increases considerably the difficulties mentioned under (1) above in resolving an interpretive controversy, since we need to agree about the background facts before we can agree what the facts (the relevant 'observational' data) are in the case of a particular text and hence which interpretation of the work they confirm or disconfirm.[25]

[20] See Juhl, "Intention and Literary Interpretation," p. 23.
[21] Stegmüller, "Der sogenannte Zirkel des Verstehens," p. 44.
[22] *Ibid.*, p. 43.
[23] See Cioffi, "Intention and Interpretation in Criticism," in Barrett (ed.), *Collected Papers on Aesthetics*, pp. 171-72.
[24] Stegmüller, "Der sogenannte Zirkel des Verstehens," p. 43.
[25] See Hirsch, *Validity in Interpretation*, pp. 165-67.

Appendix

What a reader or critic takes to be the facts in the case of a particular text depends on his background knowledge—that is, on how he interprets the background; and how he interprets the background depends on what he takes to be the facts in this as well as other cases of works and documents which are part of the background. Hence it might be tempting to think: 'If several critics disagree about the meaning of a work (or passage), then they will, and *can always legitimately*, also disagree in the interpretation of the facts (background) relevant to an understanding of the work in question, since how a critic interprets those facts (the background) depends on how he interprets the work (or other works and documents which are part of the background).' If this argument were valid, then any interpretation of a work or passage would be as 'legitimate' as any other.

Gadamer apparently believes that this does not follow from the hermeneutic circle.[26] He maintains that an incorrect interpretation will not be able to make sense of the relevant facts.[27] The doctrine of the hermeneutic circle implies, however, that any interpretation of a work or passage will be able to make sense of the relevant facts. For if—as the doctrine of the hermeneutic circle has it—the only constraint on the interpretation of the background facts (B) relevant to the interpretation of a work (w) is a critic's interpretation of w (or his interpretation of any other work, document, or

---

[26] Gadamer, *Wahrheit und Methode*, pp. 250-54 (*Truth and Method*, pp. 235-40).

[27] "Was kennzeichnet die Beliebigkeit sachunangemessener Vormeinungen anders, als daß sie in der Durchführung zunichte werden? . . . Nun sind zwar Meinungen eine bewegliche Vielfalt von Möglichkeiten (im Vergleich zu der Übereinstimmung, die eine Sprache und ein Vokabular darstellen), aber innerhalb dieser Vielfalt des Meinbaren, d.h. dessen, was ein Leser sinnvoll finden und insofern erwarten kann, ist doch nicht alles möglich, und wer an dem vorbeihört, was der andere wirklich sagt, wird das Mißverstandene am Ende auch der eigenen vielfältigen Sinnerwartung nicht einordnen können. So gibt es auch hier einen Maßstab." *Ibid*, pp. 252 and 253 respectively; see also p. 275 (*Truth and Method*, pp. 237, 238, 259).

Appendix

fact relevant to the interpretation of B), then clearly we cannot in principle objectively confirm or disconfirm an interpretation of w. For given any interpretation (I) of w, we can always find an interpretation (J) of B, such that, under J (if J were 'correct'), I would be highly likely; it follows that any interpretation of w will be able to make sense of the relevant facts. Consequently, Gadamer's acceptance of the doctrine of the hermeneutic circle[28] would appear to commit him to the view that we cannot even in principle (objectively) disconfirm, let alone rule out, any interpretation of a work.

Hence Gadamer is hard pressed to make sense of the notion of misunderstanding. For if the doctrine of the hermeneutic circle provides a correct statement about the constraints on the interpretation of a literary work, then a critic or reader could 'misunderstand' a work (or an author) only in the sense that his interpretation of the latter is inconsistent with his interpretation of the relevant facts (the context or background). As Gadamer puts it, ". . . he who fails to hear what another person is really saying will in the end be unable to fit what he has incorrectly taken the other one to mean into his own various expectations of meaning."[29] This is inadequate for two reasons: (a) in any ordinary sense of 'misunderstand,' it is clearly possible for a critic or reader to misunderstand a work (w) even if his interpretation of w is perfectly consistent with, or highly likely on the basis of, his interpretation of the relevant facts (B); (b) even if, for lack of ingenuity, a particular reader were not able to find an interpretation of B under which his interpretation (I) of w would be highly likely, Gadamer could not say that to hold I would be to misunderstand w (in Gadamer's sense of 'misunderstand'), since another reader or critic might very well find the required interpretation of B.[30] Whatever plausi-

[28] See *ibid.*, pp. 250, 254, 277 (*Truth and Method*, pp. 235-36, 239, 261).

[29] *Ibid.*, p. 253 (*Truth and Method*, p. 238).

[30] That there are no objective constraints on an interpretation of a

Appendix

bility Gadamer's claim has is derived from our implicit assumption that a critic's interpretation of w (or of other relevant facts or documents) is not the only constraint on the interpretation of B (that is, on how he can legitimately interpret B).

But it is clear, I think, that the doctrine of the hermeneutic circle misrepresents the relation between a critic's (or reader's) interpretation of a particular work and the interpretation of the larger context relevant to its understanding. How we interpret the background does not generally depend on our interpretation of one particular work of a period. It usually depends on our interpretation of a fairly large number of other literary works, upon treatises, essays, letters, diaries, or notes of the various authors of a period, upon explicit information about the language (dictionaries, grammars), upon social and political conditions, historical events, and so on. Surely, it is not true that *all* the elements which constitute the relevant background of a particular work are equally ambiguous. Surely, the interpretation of *some* of them is (by common consent) unproblematical and would thus rule out at least some of all the interpretations of a work that might conceivably be proposed. But even if in a particular case the background of a work can plausibly be construed in several different ways (on the basis of all the

---

work or of what an author is saying would appear to follow also from Gadamer's following statements: "So scheint die Bezugnahme auf den ursprünglichen Leser ebenso wie die auf den Sinn des Verfassers nur einen sehr rohen historisch-hermeneutischen Kanon darzustellen, der den Sinnhorizont von Texten nicht wirklich begrenzen darf. Was schriftlich fixiert ist, hat sich von der Kontingenz seines Ursprungs und seines Urhebers abgelöst und für neuen Bezug positiv freigegeben. Normbegriffe wie die Meinung des Verfassers oder das Verständnis des ursprünglichen Lesers repräsentieren in Wahrheit nur eine leere Stelle, die sich von Gelegenheit zu Gelegenheit des Verstehens ausfüllt." *Ibid.*, p. 373 (*Truth and Method*, p. 357). This is what Gadamer's 'liberation' of hermeneutics "von den ontologischen Hemmungen des Objektivitätsbegriffs der Wissenschaft" clearly entails. *Ibid.*, p. 250 (*Truth and Method*, p. 235).

Appendix

available evidence), in a case, for example, in which there are only a few fragmentary works and documents of a period, it would not follow that we could not in principle objectively decide between the different interpretations, since it is clearly possible that the discovery of further texts or facts will confirm one of the interpretive hypotheses and eliminate some or all of the others.[31]

If, as I have tried to show, an interpretation of a literary work is a statement about what the author intended to convey, then it would certainly appear to be always possible that a note, a letter, an essay, or other document or work by author A objectively confirm or disconfirm an interpretation of a given work(w) by A. Surely, it is not always possible to give a plausible interpretation of a relevant note or of an essay, letter, or other relevant work by A, for each of the interpretations of w that might conceivably be held by someone, such that none of the latter interpretations is, on the basis of the note (or other document), any more likely to be correct than any other of those interpretations. That is to say, the question whether a particular interpretation (J) of the note (or other document) is plausible surely does not depend merely on whether someone might conceivably hold an interpretation (I) of w such that I would not be likely to be correct unless J were correct.[32]

It might nevertheless, for another reason, be tempting to say that any attempt to justify an interpretive claim objectively is ultimately circular. For any such justification relies

[31] See Hirsch, *Validity in Interpretation*, p. 165.

[32] One might object that when one or more elements of the relevant background (a note, letter, or other works) make only one particular interpretation of a given work likely to be correct, no competent critic would persist in a different interpretation. And this is, of course, true, but beside the point. What is at issue is not whether we can always (or even generally) *in fact* objectively decide between different interpretations, but wether it makes sense to suppose that an interpretation is objectively incorrect or, to put it differently, whether it is logically possible for the background of a work or passage to be such that a given interpretation would be objectively false.

Appendix

on an interpretation of some other document(s) or fact(s); and the same is true of a justification of that interpretation. Hence if we wanted to provide a 'complete' justification—that is, a justification of every interpretive assumption involved in our attempt to justify a particular interpretation—then, given a finite number of relevant documents and facts, we would eventually have to rely on the very interpretation (or one along the line of interpretations) which we set out to justify. Consequently, our justification would ultimately be circular. But in this sense it is trivially true that any 'complete' justification of an interpretation would be circular; for it is obvious that, given a finite set of propositions, we cannot without circularity justify each one of them by appealing to other propositions of the same set. This would, however, warrant the conclusion that a justification of an interpretation of a work is (ultimately) necessarily circular only if *any* interpretation of *any* element of the background —in particular, any interpretation of any piece of information relevant to what the author is likely to have intended to convey by the work in question—were necessarily just as much in need of justification as the original interpretation itself. And this, I think, is clearly not so.[33]

Szondi's thesis that facts need to be interpreted before they can become evidence for an interpretation, then, is correct and throws light on the nature of interpretive statements. But the claim that such statements cannot in principle be objectively confirmed or disconfirmed is false. For (1) what a work means is logically tied to what the author meant; and (2) we can in principle always establish objectively what an author meant by a particular work or passage (p), since it is always in principle possible to determine objectively whether a particular fact confirms, disconfirms, or is irrelevant to the truth or falsity of a claim about what the author intended to convey by p.

[33] For a detailed discussion of various related issues concerning the hermeneutic circle, see Göttner, *Logik der Interpretation*, pp. 131-78.

Appendix

6. Concluding Remarks

The thesis I have examined has been that a critic's subjective *Verstehen* is the proper criterion for verifying an interpretation of a literary work. It follows that statements about the meaning of a work cannot be objectively confirmed or disconfirmed. Szondi has tried to support this thesis by maintaining (a) that facts do not speak for themselves but must be 'understood' before they can become evidence for an interpretation, and (b) that we cannot establish that a fact is evidence for an interpretation independently of establishing that interpretation; that is, in order for facts to be evidence for an interpretation, the latter must be correct or the facts must logically entail it. This is the "interdependence of evidence and understanding" (*Interdependenz von Beweis und Erkenntnis*, 26). But since no fact or set of facts can entail the truth of an interpretive claim, Szondi concludes that facts cannot constitute (objective) evidence for an interpretation. The only constraint on how a critic can legitimately interpret the facts relevant to the meaning of a work (w) is his intuitive understanding of w. On Szondi's view, there is no way out of the 'hermeneutic circle.'

I have indicated that Szondi's conclusion is unwarranted because no empirical claim in the social or natural sciences is ever logically entailed by the evidence for it. I have argued further that Szondi's thesis (a) is correct both (i) in the sense that we need to establish (or be able to assume) that a fact f is evidence that an author meant, say, m by a work (w) in order to adduce f as evidence for the claim that w means m, and (ii) in the sense that what the facts, even the 'observational data' of a text, are is not somehow immediately given but is the result of an interpretation. What is more, we cannot sharply distinguish between the 'observational data' of a text and our knowledge or assumptions about the background. I have tried to show, however, that we can in principle always determine objectively whether a 'fact' which a critic adduces in support of an interpretation

Appendix

(*J*) of a work is or is not a fact and, if it is, whether it confirms, disconfirms, or is irrelevant to the truth or falsity of *J*. What enables us (in principle) to do this is, on the one hand, an accepted background knowledge—that is, facts the interpretation of which is not in question—and, on the other, a criterion which specifies the (objective) conditions under which a fact is evidence for an interpretation of a work (this criterion being entailed by the logical relation between the meaning of a work and the author's intention).

If Szondi's basic premise, the "interdependence of evidence and understanding," were correct, then we could be certain of an interpretation for which we have 'evidence'; for having such evidence presupposes knowing what the work means. It is this desire for certainty which, I have suggested, lies at the root of Szondi's central thesis from which the conclusion that interpretive claims are irreducibly subjective necessarily follows.

BIBLIOGRAPHY

The following list contains only those works from which I have quoted or to which I have referred in the footnotes.

Abel, Theodore. "The Operation Called *Verstehen.*" *American Journal of Sociology*, Vol. 54, 1948. Reprinted in *Readings in the Philosophy of Science*. Ed. Herbert Feigl and May Brodbeck. Appleton Century-Crofts, New York, 1953.

Abrams, M. H. "What's the Use of Theorizing about the Arts?" In *In Search of Literary Theory*. Ed. Morton W. Bloomfield. Cornell University Press, Ithaca, N. Y., 1972.

Adorno, Theodor W. "Zum Klassizismus von Goethes Iphigenie." *Noten zur Literatur IV*. Suhrkamp Verlag, Frankfurt a. M., 1974.

Aiken, Henry David. "The Aesthetic Relevance of Artists' Intentions." *Journal of Philosophy*, Vol. 52, 1955.

Aldrich, Virgil C. *Philosophy of Art*. Prentice-Hall, Englewood Cliffs, N. J., 1963.

Anderegg, Johannes. *Fiktion und Kommunikation: Ein Beitrag zur Theorie der Prosa*. Vandenhoeck & Ruprecht, Göttingen, 1973.

Anscombe, G.E.M. *Intention*. Cornell University Press, Ithaca, N. Y., 1957.

Aschenbrenner, Karl. "Intention and Understanding." *University of California Publications in Philosophy*, Vol. 25, Berkeley, 1950.

Austin, J. L. *How to Do Things with Words*. Harvard University Press, Cambridge, Mass., 1962.

Ayer, A. J. "Can There Be a Private Language?" *Proceedings of the Aristotelian Society*, Suppl. Vol. 28, 1954. Reprinted in *Wittgenstein, The Philosophical Investigations: A Collection of Critical Essays*. Ed. George Pitcher. Doubleday, Garden City, N. Y., 1966.

Baker, John Ross. "From Imitation to Rhetoric: The Chicago Critics, Wayne C. Booth, and *Tom Jones*." In *Towards a Poetics of Fiction*. Ed. Mark Spilka. Indiana University Press, Bloomington, 1977.

Bibliography

Barnes, Annette. "Half an Hour Before Breakfast." *Journal of Aesthetics and Art Criticism*, Vol. 34, 1975.

Barrett, Cyril, S.J., ed. *Collected Papers on Aesthetics*. Basil Blackwell, Oxford, 1965.

Bateson, F. W. *English Poetry: A Critical Introduction*. Longmans Green & Co., London, 2nd edn., 1966.

———. "Linguistics and Literary Criticism." In *The Disciplines of Criticism: Essays in Literary Theory, Interpretation, and History*. Ed. Peter Demetz et al. Yale University Press, New Haven, Conn., 1968.

Beardsley, Monroe C., and Herbert M. Schueller, eds. *Aesthetic Inquiry: Essays on Art Criticism and the Philosophy of Art*. Dickenson Publishing Co., Belmont, Calif., 1967.

Beardsley, Monroe C. *Aesthetics: Problems in the Philosophy of Criticism*. Harcourt, Brace & World, New York, 1958.

———. "The Concept of Literature." In *Literary Theory and Structure: Essays in Honor of William K. Wimsatt*. Ed. Frank Brady et al. Yale University Press, New Haven, Conn., 1973.

———. "The Limits of Critical Interpretation." In *Art and Philosophy: A Symposium*. Ed. Sidney Hook. New York University Press, New York, 1966.

———. "The Philosophy of Literature." In *Aesthetics: A Critical Anthology*. Eds. George Dickie and Richard J. Sclafani. St. Martin's Press, New York, 1977.

———. *The Possibility of Criticism*. Wayne State University Press, Detroit, Mich., 1970.

———. Review of Cyril Barrett, S.J., ed., *Collected Papers on Aesthetics*. In *Journal of Aesthetics and Art Criticism*, Vol. 26, 1967.

Beckett, Samuel. *Watt*. Grove Press, New York, 1959.

Bennett, Jonathan. *Linguistic Behavior*. Cambridge University Press, Cambridge, 1976.

Betti, Emilio. *Die Hermeneutik als Allgemeine Methodik der Geisteswissenschaften*. J.C.B. Mohr, Tübingen, 1962.

Bierwisch, Manfred. "Poetik und Linguistik." In *Mathematik und Dichtung*. Ed. Rul Gunzenhäuser and Helmut Kreuzer. Nymphenburger Verlagshandlung, München, 1965. Reprinted in *Methoden der deutschen Literaturwissenschaft: Eine Dokumentation*. Ed. Viktor Žmegač. Athenäum Verlag, Frankfurt a. M., 1971.

Bibliography

Black, Max, ed. *Philosophical Analysis*. Cornell University Press, Ithaca, N. Y., 1950.

Bloom, Harold. *The Visionary Company: A Reading of English Romantic Poetry*. Cornell University Press, Ithaca, N. Y., rev. edn., 1971.

Bloomfield, Morton W., ed. *In Search of Literary Theory*. Cornell University Press, Ithaca, N. Y., 1972.

Booth, Wayne C. *The Rhetoric of Fiction*. University of Chicago Press, Chicago, Ill., 1961.

———. "The Rhetoric of Fiction and the Poetics of Fictions." In *Towards a Poetics of Fiction*. Ed. Mark Spilka. Indiana University Press, Bloomington, 1977.

———. *A Rhetoric of Irony*. University of Chicago Press, Chicago, Ill., 1974.

Boswell, James. *Life of Johnson*. Oxford University Press, London, 1965 (1904).

Brady, Frank, John Palmer, and Martin Price, eds. *Literary Theory and Structure: Essays in Honor of William K. Wimsatt*. Yale University Press, New Haven, Conn., 1973.

Brecht, Bertolt, *Leben des Galilei*. Suhrkamp Verlag, Frankfurt a. M., 1962.

Brodbeck, May. "Meaning and Action." *Philosophy of Science*, Vol. 30, 1963.

Brooke-Rose, Christine. "The Squirm of the True: A Structural Analysis of Henry James's *The Turn of the Screw*." *PTL: A Journal for Descriptive Poetics and Theory of Literature*, Vol. 1, 1976.

Brooks, Cleanth. "Irony as a Principle of Structure." In *Literary Opinion in America*. Ed. Morton D. Zabel. Harper & Brothers, New York, 2nd edn., 1951.

Burke, Kenneth. *The Philosophy of Literary Form: Studies in Symbolic Action*. Louisiana State University Press, Baton Rouge, 1941.

———. "Symbolic Action in a Poem by Keats." *A Grammar of Motives*. Prentice-Hall, New York, 1945. Reprinted in *The Critical Performance*. Ed. Stanley Edgar Hyman. Random House, New York, 1956.

Callaghan, William, et al., eds. *Aesthetics and the Theory of Criticism: Selected Essays of Arnold Isenberg*. University of Chicago Press, Chicago, Ill., 1973.

Cargill, Oscar. "Viable Meaning in Literary Art." In *Art and*

Bibliography

Philosophy: A Symposium. Ed. Sidney Hook. New York University Press, New York, 1966.

Casey, John. *The Language of Criticism.* Methuen & Co., London, 1966.

Cavell, Stanley. "Aesthetic Problems of Modern Philosophy." *Must We Mean What We Say? A Book of Essays.* Charles Scribner's Sons, New York, 1969.

———. "A Matter of Meaning It." *Must We Mean What We Say? A Book of Essays.*

Child, Arthur. *Interpretation: A General Theory.* University of California Press, Berkeley, 1965.

Chomsky, Noam. *Aspects of the Theory of Syntax.* MIT Press, Cambridge, Mass., 1965.

———. "Degrees of Grammaticalness." In *The Structure of Language.* Ed. Jerry A. Fodor and Jerrold J. Katz. Prentice-Hall, Englewood Cliffs, N. J., 1964.

———. *Reflections on Language.* Random House, New York, 1975.

Cioffi, F. "Intention and Interpretation in Criticism," *Proceedings of the Aristotelian Society,* Vol. 64, 1964. Reprinted in *Collected Papers on Aesthetics.* Ed. Cyril Barrett, S.J. Basil Blackwell, Oxford, 1965.

Close, A. J. "*Don Quixote* and the 'Intentionalist Fallacy'." *British Journal of Aesthetics,* Vol. 12, 1972. Reprinted in *On Literary Intention: Critical Essays.* Ed. David Newton-de Molina. Edinburgh University Press, Edinburgh, 1976.

Cohen, L. Jonathan. *The Diversity of Meaning.* Herder & Herder, New York, 1963.

———, and Avishai Margalit. "The Role of Inductive Reasoning in the Interpretation of Metaphor." In *Semantics of Natural Language.* Ed. Donald Davidson and Gilbert Harman. Reidel Co., Dordrecht, Holland, 1972.

Coleman, Francis X. J., ed. *Contemporary Studies in Aesthetics.* McGraw-Hill, New York, 1968.

———. "A Few Observations on Fictional Discourse." In *Language and Aesthetics.* Ed. Benjamin R. Tilghman. University Press of Kansas, Lawrence, 1973.

Crane, R. S. "The Houyhnhnms, the Yahoos, and the History of Ideas." In *Reason and the Imagination: Studies in the History of Ideas 1600-1800.* Ed. J. A. Mazzeo. Columbia University Press, New York, 1962.

Bibliography

Crittenden, Charles. "Fictional Existence." *American Philosophical Quarterly*, Vol. 3, 1966.

Cruttwell, Patrick. "Makers and Persons." *Hudson Review*, Vol. 12, 1959-60.

Culler, Jonathan. *Structuralist Poetics: Structuralism, Linguistics and the Study of Literature*. Cornell University Press, Ithaca, N. Y., 1975.

Damon, Phillip, ed. *Literary Criticism and Historical Understanding*. Columbia University Press, New York, 1967.

Davidson, Donald, and Gilbert Harman, eds. *Semantics of Natural Language*. Reidel Co., Dordrecht, Holland, 1972.

Davis, Walter A. *The Act of Interpretation: A Critique of Literary Reason*. University of Chicago Press, Chicago, Ill., 1978.

Demetz, Peter, Theodore M. Greene, and Lowry Nelson, eds. *The Disciplines of Criticism: Essays in Literary Theory, Interpretation, and History*. Yale University Press, New Haven, Conn., 1968.

Dickie, George. *Aesthetics: An Introduction*. Pegasus, Indianapolis, Ind., 1971.

———. *Art and the Aesthetic: An Institutional Analysis*. Cornell University Press, Ithaca, N. Y., 1974.

———. "Meaning and Intention." *Genre*, Vol. I, 1968.

Donagan, Alan. "Wittgenstein on Sensations." In *Wittgenstein, The Philosophical Investigations: A Collection of Critical Essays*. Ed. George Pitcher. Doubleday, Garden City, N. Y., 1966.

Eaton, Marcia M. "Good and Correct Interpretations of Literature." *Journal of Aesthetics and Art Criticism*, Vol. 29, 1970-71.

———. "Liars, Ranters, and Dramatic Speakers." In *Language and Aesthetics*. Ed. Benjamin R. Tilghman. University Press of Kansas, Lawrence, 1973.

———. "The Truth Value of Literary Statements." *British Journal of Aesthetics*, Vol. 12, 1972.

Eco, Umberto. *Das offene Kunstwerk*. Trans. Günter Memmert. Suhrkamp, Frankfurt a. M., 1973. (Translation of *Opera aperta*. Bompiani, Milano, 1962.)

Eliot, T. S. "The Frontiers of Criticism." *On Poetry and Poets*. Faber & Faber, London, 1957.

———. "Rudyard Kipling." *On Poetry and Poets*. Faber & Faber, London, 1957.

Bibliography

———. "Tradition and the Individual Talent." *Selected Essays: 1917-1932.* Harcourt, Brace & Co., New York, 1932.
Ellis, John M. *The Theory of Literary Criticism: A Logical Analysis.* University of California Press, Berkeley, 1974.
Empson, William. *Seven Types of Ambiguity.* New Directions, New York, 1949.
———. *The Structure of Complex Words.* Chatto & Windus, London, 1952.
Farrell, B. A. "The Criteria for a Psycho-Analytic Interpretation." In *The Philosophy of Mind.* Ed. Jonathan Grover. Oxford University Press, Oxford, 1976.
Fiedler, Leslie. "Archetype and Signature: A Study of the Relationship between Biography and Poetry." *Sewanee Review*, Vol. 60, 1952.
Fodor, Jerry A., and Jerrold J. Katz, eds. *The Structure of Language: Readings in the Philosophy of Language.* Prentice-Hall, Englewood Cliffs, N. J., 1964.
———. "The Structure of a Semantic Theory." In *The Structure of Language: Readings in the Philosophy of Language.* Ed. Jerry A. Fodor and Jerrold J. Katz. Prentice-Hall, Englewood Cliffs, N. J., 1964.
Foulkes, A. P. "On Wings of Fictionality: Some Thoughts on Literature's Relationship to Reality." In *The Uses of Criticism.* Ed. A. P. Foulkes. Herbert Lang Verlag, Bern, 1976.
———. *The Search for Literary Meaning: A Semiotic Approach to the Problem of Interpretation in Education.* Herbert Lang Verlag, Bern, 1975.
———, ed. *The Uses of Criticism.* Herbert Lang Verlag, Bern, 1976.
Fowler, Alastair. "Intention Floreat." In *On Literary Intention: Critical Essays.* Ed. David Newton-de Molina. Edinburgh University Press, Edinburgh, 1976.
Freedman, Ralph. "Intentionality and the Literary Object." *Contemporary Literature,* Summer 1976. Reprinted in *Directions for Criticism: Structuralism and its Alternatives.* Ed. Murray Krieger and L. S. Dembo. University of Wisconsin Press, Madison, 1976.
Frege, Gottlob. "Über Sinn und Bedeutung." *Zeitschrift für Philosophie und philosophische Kritik,* N.F. 100, 1892. Reprinted in *Funktion, Begriff, Bedeutung.* Ed. G. Patzig. Vandenhoeck & Ruprecht, Göttingen, 1966. English translation: "On Sense and Reference." *Philosophical Writings*

Bibliography

of Gottlob Frege. Trans. P. T. Geach and Max Black. Basil Blackwell, Oxford, 1952.

Frye, Northrop. *Anatomy of Criticism: Four Essays.* Princeton University Press, Princeton, N. J., 1957.

―――. "The Critical Path: An Essay on the Social Context of Literary Criticism." In *In Search of Literary Theory.* Ed. Morton W. Bloomfield, Cornell University Press, Ithaca, N. Y., 1972.

―――. *The Educated Imagination.* Indiana University Press, Bloomington, 1964.

―――. *Fearful Symmetry: A Study of William Blake.* Princeton University Press, Princeton, N. J., 1947.

Gabriel, Gottfried. *Fiktion und Wahrheit: Eine semantische Theorie der Literatur.* Frommann Verlag, Stuttgart, 1975.

Gadamer, Hans-Georg. *Wahrheit und Methode: Grundzüge einer philosophischen Hermeneutik.* J.C.B. Mohr, Tübingen, 1965. English translation: *Truth and Method.* Ed. Garrett Barden and John Cumming (no translator given). The Seabury Press, New York, 1975.

Gale, Richard. "The Fictive Use of Language." *Philosophy,* Vol. 46, 1971.

Gang, T. M. "Intention." *Essays in Criticism,* Vol. 7, 1957. Reprinted in *Aesthetics and the Philosophy of Criticism.* Ed. Marvin Levich. Random House, New York, 1963.

Gardiner, Patrick. *The Nature of Historical Explanation.* Oxford University Press, Oxford, 1961.

Gardner, Helen. *The Business of Criticism.* Oxford University Press, London, 1959.

Glinz, Hans. "Methoden zur Objektivierung des Verstehens von Texten, gezeigt an Kafka, 'Kinder auf der Landstrasse'." *Jahrbuch für Internationale Germanistik* I, 1969.

―――. *Sprachwissenschaft heute: Aufgaben und Möglichkeiten.* J. B. Metzlersche Verlagsbuchhandlung, Stuttgart, 1970.

Glover, Jonathan. "Introduction." In *The Philosophy of Mind.* Ed. Jonathan Glover. Oxford University Press, Oxford, 1976.

Göttner, Heide. *Logik der Interpretation: Analyse einer literaturwissenschaftlichen Methode unter kritischer Betrachtung der Hermeneutik.* Wilhelm Fink Verlag, München, 1973.

Bibliography

Gräf, Hans Gerhard. *Goethe über seine Dichtungen, Zweiter Teil: Die dramatischen Dichtungen*, Bd. 3. Wissenschaftliche Buchgesellschaft, Darmstadt, 1968 (1902).

Graham, Ilse. *Schiller's Drama: Talent and Integrity*. Methuen, London, 1974.

Greene, Theodore Meyer, ed. *The Meaning of the Humanities*. Princeton University Press, Princeton, N. J., 1938.

Grewendorf, Günter. *Argumentation und Interpretation: Wissenschaftstheoretische Untersuchungen am Beispiel germanistischer Lyrikinterpretationen*. Scriptor, Kronberg/ Taunus, 1975.

Grice, H. P. "Meaning." *Philosophical Review*, Vol. 66, 1957. Reprinted in *Problems in the Philosophy of Language*. Ed. Thomas M. Olshewsky. Holt, Rinehart, & Winston, New York, 1969.

―――. "Utterer's Meaning and Intentions." *Philosophical Review*, Vol. 78, 1969.

―――. "Utterer's Meaning, Sentence-Meaning, and Word-Meaning." *Foundations of Language*, Vol. 4, 1968. Reprinted in *The Philosophy of Language*. Ed. John R. Searle. Oxford University Press, London, 1971.

Grimm, Reinhold, and Jost Hermand, eds. *Methodenfragen der deutschen Literaturwissenschaft*. Wissenschaftliche Buchgesellschaft, Darmstadt, 1973.

Gunzenhäuser, Rul, and Helmut Kreuzer, eds. *Mathematik und Dichtung*. Nymphenburger Verlagshandlung, München, 1965.

Hamburger, Käte. *Die Logik der Dichtung*. Klett, Stuttgart, 2nd edn., 1968. English translation: *The Logic of Literature*. Trans. Marilynn J. Rose. Indiana University Press, Bloomington, 1973.

―――. *Wahrheit und ästhetische Wahrheit*. Klett-Cotta, Stuttgart, 1979.

Hamburger, Michael, trans. *Friedrich Hölderlin: Poems and Fragments*. Routledge & Kegan Paul, London, 1966.

Hamlyn, D. W. "Unconscious Intentions." *Philosophy*, Vol. 46, 1971.

Hampshire, Stuart. "On Referring and Intending." *Freedom of Mind and Other Essays*. Princeton University Press, Princeton, N. J., 1971.

―――. *Thought and Action*. Chatto & Windus, London, 1959.

Bibliography

———. "Types of Interpretation." In *Art and Philosophy: A Symposium.* Ed. Sidney Hook. New York University Press, New York, 1966.

Hancher, Michael. "Beyond a Speech Act Theory of Literary Discourse." *Modern Language Notes,* Vol. 92, 1977.

———. "Describing and Interpreting Speech Acts." *Journal of Aesthetics and Art Criticism,* Vol. 36, 1978.

———. "Three Kinds of Intention." *Modern Language Notes,* Vol. 87, 1972.

Harris, Frank. *Latest Contemporary Portraits.* The Macaulay Co., New York, 1927.

Hass, H. E. *Das Problem der literarischen Wertung.* Wissenschaftliche Buchgesellschaft, Darmstadt, 1970.

Hawthorn, Jeremy M. *Identity and Relationship: A Contribution to Marxist Theory of Literary Criticism.* Lawrence & Wishart, London, 1973.

Hempel, Carl G., and Paul Oppenheim. "The Logic of Explanation." *Philosophy of Science,* Vol. 15, 1948. Reprinted in *Readings in the Philosophy of Science.* Ed. Herbert Feigl and May Brodbeck. Appleton Century-Crofts, New York, 1953.

Hepburn, Ronald. "Poetry and 'Concrete Imagination': Problems of Truth and Illusion." *British Journal of Aesthetics,* Vol. 12, 1972.

Hermand, Jost. *Synthetisches Interpretieren: Zur Methodik der Literaturwissenschaft.* Nymphenburger Verlagshandlung, München, 1968.

Hermerén, Göran. "Intention and Interpretation in Literary Criticism." *New Literary History,* Vol. 7, 1975.

Hirsch, E. D. *The Aims of Interpretation.* University of Chicago Press, Chicago, Ill., 1976.

———. "Gadamer's Theory of Interpretation." *The Review of Metaphysics,* Vol. 18, 1965. Reprinted in *Validity in Interpretation.*

———. *Innocence and Experience: An Introduction to Blake.* Yale University Press, New Haven, Conn., 1964.

———. "The Norms of Interpretation—A Brief Response." *Genre,* Vol. II, 1969.

———. "Objective Interpretation." *Publications of the Modern Language Association of America,* Vol. 75, 1960. Reprinted in *Validity in Interpretation.*

Bibliography

Hirsch, E. D. "Some Aims of Criticism." In *Literary Theory and Structure: Essays in Honor of William K. Wimsatt.* Ed. Frank Brady et al. Yale University Press, New Haven, Conn., 1973. Reprinted in *The Aims of Interpretation.*

———. "Three Dimensions of Hermeneutics." *New Literary History,* Vol. 3, 1971-72. Reprinted in *The Aims of Interpretation.*

———. *Validity in Interpretation.* Yale University Press, New Haven, Conn., 1967.

———. "Value and Knowledge in the Humanities." In *In Search of Literary Theory.* Ed. Morton W. Bloomfield. Cornell University Press, Ithaca, N. Y., 1972.

Hogan, Homer. "Hermeneutics and Folk Songs." *Journal of Aesthetics and Art Criticism,* Vol. 28, 1969.

Hook, Sidney, ed. *Art and Philosophy: A Symposium.* New York University Press, New York, 1966.

Horn, András. *Das Literarische: Formalistische Versuche zu seiner Bestimmung.* Walter de Gruyter, Berlin, 1978.

Hospers, John. "Implied Truths in Literature." *Journal of Aesthetics and Art Criticism,* Vol. 19, 1960. Reprinted in *Art and Philosophy.* Ed. William E. Kennick. St. Martin's Press, New York, 1964.

———, ed. *Introductory Readings in Aesthetics.* The Free Press, New York, 1969.

Hough, Graham. "An Eighth Type of Ambiguity." In *William Empson: the Man and his Work.* Ed. Roma Gill. Routledge & Kegan Paul, London, 1974. Reprinted in *On Literary Intention: Critical Essays.* Ed. David Newton-de Molina. Edinburgh University Press, Edinburgh, 1976.

Hoy, David Couzens. *The Critical Circle: Literature, History, and Philosophical Hermeneutics.* University of California Press, Berkeley, 1978.

Hübner, Kurt, and Albert Menne, eds. *Natur und Geschichte: X. Deutscher Kongress für Philosophie.* Felix Meiner Verlag, Hamburg, 1973.

Hungerland, I. C. "The Concept of Intention in Art Criticism." *Journal of Philosophy,* Vol. 52, 1955.

———. "Contextual Implication." *Inquiry,* Vol. 3, 1960.

———. "The Interpretation of Poetry." *Journal of Aesthetics and Art Criticism,* Vol. 13, 1955. Reprinted in *Aesthetic Inquiry: Essays on Art Criticism and the Philosophy of Art.*

Bibliography

Ed. Monroe C. Beardsley and Herbert M. Schueller. Dickenson Publishing Co., Belmont, Calif., 1967.

———. *Poetic Discourse*. University of California Press, Berkeley, 1958.

Hyman, Stanley E., ed. *The Critical Performance: An Anthology of American and British Literary Criticism of Our Century*. Vintage Books, New York, 1956.

Ingarden, Roman. *Das literarische Kunstwerk*. Max Niemeyer Verlag, Tübingen, 3rd edn., 1965. English translation: *The Literary Work of Art: An Investigation on the Borderlines of Ontology, Logic, and Theory of Literature*. Trans. George Grabowicz. Northwestern University Press, Evanston, Ill., 1973.

Isenberg, Arnold. "Some Problems of Interpretation." In *Studies in Chinese Thought*. Ed. Arthur F. Wright. University of Chicago Press, Chicago, Ill., 1953. Reprinted in *Aesthetics and the Theory of Criticism: Selected Essays of Arnold Isenberg*. Ed. William Callaghan et al. University of Chicago Press, Chicago, Ill., 1973.

Iser, Wolfgang. "Die Appellstruktur der Texte." In *Rezeptionsästhetik: Theorie und Praxis*. Ed. Rainer Warning. Fink Verlag, München, 1975.

———. *The Implied Reader*. The Johns Hopkins University Press, Baltimore, Md., 1974.

———. "The Reality of Fiction: A Functionalist Approach to Literature." *New Literary History*, Vol. 6, 1975.

Jakobson, Roman, and Claude Lévi-Strauss. "'Les Chats' de Charles Baudelaire." *L'Homme*, Vol. 2, 1962. English translation: "Charles Baudelaire's 'Les Chats'." In *The Structuralists: From Marx to Lévi-Strauss*. Ed. Richard T. and Fernande M. de George. Doubleday, New York, 1972.

Japp, Uwe. *Hermeneutik: Der theoretische Diskurs, die Literatur und die Konstruktion ihres Zusammenhanges in den philologischen Wissenschaften*. Fink Verlag, München, 1977.

Jauss, Hans Robert. "Racines und Goethes Iphigenie; Mit einem Nachwort über die Partialität der rezeptionsästhetischen Methode." *Neue Hefte für Philosophie*, Heft 4, 1973.

Jones, Alexander E. "Point of View in *The Turn of the Screw*." *Publications of the Modern Language Association*, Vol. 74,

Bibliography

1959. Reprinted in *A Casebook on Henry James's* The Turn of the Screw. Ed. Gerald Willen. Crowell, New York, 1960.

Jones, Peter. *Philosophy and the Novel: Philosophical Aspects of* Middlemarch, Anna Karenina, The Brothers Karamazov, A la recherche du temps perdu *and of the Methods of Criticism*. Oxford University Press, Oxford, 1975.

Juhl, P. D. "Can the Meaning of a Literary Work Change?" In *The Uses of Criticism*. Ed. A. P. Foulkes. Herbert Lang Verlag, Bern, 1976.

———. "The Doctrine of 'Verstehen' and the Objectivity of Literary Interpretations." *Deutsche Vierteljahrsschrift für Literaturwissenschaft und Geistesgeschichte*, Jg. 49, 1975.

———. "Intention and Literary Interpretation." *Deutsche Vierteljahrsschrift für Literaturwissenschaft und Geistesgeschichte*, Jg. 45, 1971.

Kahn, S. J. "What does a Critic Analyze?" *Philosophy and Phenomenological Research*, Vol. 13, 1952-53.

Kaufmann, Walter. "Literature and Reality." In *Art and Philosophy: A Symposium*. Ed. Sidney Hook. New York University Press, New York, 1966.

Kayser, Wolfgang. *Entstehung und Krise des modernen Romans*. J. B. Metzler, Stuttgart, 5th edn., 1968.

———. "Wer Erzählt den Roman?" *Die Vortragsreise: Studien zur Literatur*. Francke Verlag, Bern, 1958.

Kelkar, Ashok R. "The Being of a Poem." *Foundations of Language*, Vol. 5, 1969.

Kemp, John. "The Work of Art and the Artist's Intentions." *British Journal of Aesthetics*, Vol. 4, 1964.

Kennick, William E., ed. *Art and Philosophy: Readings in Aesthetics*. St. Martin's Press, New York, 1964.

Kenny, Anthony. *Action, Emotion and Will*. Routledge & Kegan Paul, London, 1963.

Kermode, Frank. "Can We Say Absolutely Anything We Like?" In *Art, Politics, and Will: Essays in Honor of Lionel Trilling*. Ed. Quentin Anderson et al. Basic Books, New York, 1977.

Klotz, Volker, ed. *Zur Poetik des Romans*. Wissenschaftliche Buchgesellschaft, Darmstadt, 1965.

Knight, G. Wilson. *The Wheel of Fire: Interpretations of Shakespearian Tragedy with Three New Essays*. Methuen & Co., London, 1949.

Krieger, Murray. *Theory of Criticism: A Tradition and its Sys-*

Bibliography

tem. The Johns Hopkins University Press, Baltimore, Md., 1976.

Kris, Ernest, and Abraham Kaplan. "Aesthetic Ambiguity." *Psychoanalytic Explorations in Art.* International Universities Press, New York, 1952. Reprinted in *Art and Philosophy.* Ed. William E. Kennick. St. Martin's Press, New York, 1964.

Kuhn, Thomas S. *The Structure of Scientific Revolutions.* University of Chicago Press, Chicago, Ill., 2nd edn., 1970.

Kuhns, Richard. "Criticism and the Problem of Intention." *Journal of Philosophy,* Vol. 57, 1960.

———. "Semantics for Literary Languages." *New Literary History,* Vol. 4, 1972.

Kunze, Michael. "Probleme der rezeptionsästhetischen Interpretation. Überlegungen zu Hans Robert Jauss: 'Racines und Goethes Iphigenie'." In *Interpretationsanalysen: Argumentationsstrukturen in literaturwissenschaftlichen Interpretationen.* Ed. Walter Kindt and Siegfried J. Schmidt. Fink Verlag, München, 1976.

Lamprecht, Helmut, ed. *Deutschland, Deutschland: Politische Gedichte vom Vormärz bis zur Gegenwart.* Schünemann, Bremen, 1969.

Lange, Victor. "Erzählformen im Roman des achtzehnten Jahrhunderts." *Anglia. Zeitschrift für englische Philologie,* 1958. Reprinted in *Zur Poetik des Romans.* Ed. Volker Klotz. Wissenschaftliche Buchgesellschaft, Darmstadt, 1965.

Lees, Francis Noel. "The Keys are at the Palace: A Note on Criticism and Biography." In *Literary Criticism and Historical Understanding.* Ed. Phillip Damon. Columbia University Press, New York, 1967.

Leibfried, Erwin. *Kritische Wissenschaft vom Text: Manipulation, Reflexion, Transparente Poetologie.* J. B. Metzlersche Verlagsbuchhandlung, Stuttgart, 1970.

Levich, Marvin, ed. *Aesthetics and the Philosophy of Criticism.* Random House, New York, 1963.

Lewis, David. "Truth in Fiction." *American Philosophical Quarterly,* Vol. 15, 1978.

Linsky, Leonard. "Reference and Referents." In *Philosophy and Ordinary Language.* Ed. Charles Caton. University of Illinois Press, Urbana, 1963. Reprinted in *Problems in the Philosophy of Language.* Ed. Thomas M. Olshewsky. Holt, Rinehart, & Winston, New York, 1969.

Bibliography

Lohner, Edgar. "The Intrinsic Method: Some Reconsiderations." In *The Disciplines of Criticism*. Ed. Peter Demetz et al. Yale University Press, New Haven, Conn., 1968.

Lyas, Colin. "Personal Qualities and the Intentional Fallacy." In *Philosophy and the Arts: Royal Institute of Philosophy Lectures*, Vol. 6, St. Martin's Press, New York, 1973.

Macdonald, Margaret. "The Language of Fiction." *Proceedings of the Aristotelian Society*, Suppl. Vol. 28, 1954. Reprinted in *Contemporary Studies in Aesthetics*. Ed. Francis X. J. Coleman. McGraw-Hill, New York, 1968.

Mace, C. A., ed. *British Philosophy in the Mid-Century*. Allen & Unwin, London, 1957.

MacIntyre, Alasdair C. *The Unconscious: A Conceptual Analysis*. Routledge & Kegan Paul, London, 1958.

Mackie, J. L. *Ethics: Inventing Right and Wrong*. Penguin Books, Harmondsworth, 1977.

Malcolm, Norman. "Wittgenstein's *Philosophical Investigations*." *Knowledge and Certainty: Essays and Lectures*. Prentice-Hall, Englewood Cliffs, N. J., 1963. Reprinted in *Wittgenstein, The Philosophical Investigations: A Collection of Critical Essays*. Ed. George Pitcher. Doubleday, Garden City, N. Y., 1966.

Man, Paul de. *Blindness and Insight: Essays in the Rhetoric of Contemporary Criticism*. Oxford University Press, New York, 1971.

Margolis, Joseph. "Critics and Literature." *British Journal of Aesthetics*, Vol. 11, 1971.

―――. *The Language of Art and Art Criticism*. Wayne State University Press, Detroit, Mich., 1965.

―――. "Three Problems in Aesthetics." In *Art and Philosophy: A Symposium*. Ed. Sidney Hook. New York University Press, New York, 1966.

―――. "Works of Art Are Physically Embodied and Culturally Emergent Entities." *British Journal of Aesthetics*, Vol. 14, 1974. Reprinted in *Culture and Art: An Anthology*. Ed. Lars Aagaard-Mogensen. Humanities Press, Atlantic Highlands, N. J., 1976.

Marsh, Robert. "Historical Interpretation and the History of Criticism." In *Literary Criticism and Historical Understanding*. Ed. Phillip Damon. Columbia University Press, New York, 1967.

Bibliography

Martinez-Bonati, Felix. "Die logische Struktur der Dichtung: Ein Vortrag." *Deutsche Vierteljahrsschrift für Literaturwissenschaft und Geistesgeschichte*, Vol. 47, 1973.

Matthews, Robert J. "Describing and Interpreting a Work of Art." *Journal of Aesthetics and Art Criticism*, Vol. 36, 1977.

Meggle, Georg, and Manfred Beetz. *Interpretationstheorie und Interpretationspraxis*. Scriptor, Kronberg/Taunus, 1976.

Meiland, Jack W. "Interpretation as a Cognitive Discipline." *Philosophy and Literature*, Vol. 2, 1978.

———. *The Nature of Intention*. Methuen & Co., London, 1970.

Melden, A. I. *Free Action*. Routledge & Kegan Paul, London, 1961.

Mew, Peter. "Facts in Fiction." *Journal of Aesthetics and Art Criticism*, Vol. 31, 1973.

Mink, Louis O. "History and Fiction as Modes of Comprehension." In *New Directions for Literary History*. Ed. Ralph Cohen. The Johns Hopkins University Press, Baltimore, Md., 1974.

Nagel, Ernest. *The Structure of Science: Problems in the Logic of Scientific Explanation*. Harcourt, Brace & World, New York, 1961.

Nathan, Daniel O. "Categories and Intentions." *Journal of Aesthetics and Art Criticism*, Vol. 31, 1973.

Newton-de Molina, David, ed. *On Literary Intention: Critical Essays*. Edinburgh University Press, Edinburgh, 1976.

Ohmann, Richard. "Speech, Action, and Style." In *Literary Style: A Symposium*. Ed. Seymour Chatman. Oxford University Press, London, 1971.

———. "Speech Acts and the Definition of Literature." *Philosophy and Rhetoric*, Vol. 4, 1971.

Olshewsky, Thomas M., ed. *Problems in the Philosophy of Language*. Holt, Rinehart & Winston, New York, 1969.

Orwell, George. "Rudyard Kipling." *Critical Essays*. Martin Secker & Warburg, London, 1946. Reprinted in *Kipling's Mind and Art*. Ed. Andrew Rutherford. Stanford University Press, Stanford, Calif., 1964.

Osborne, Harold, ed. *Aesthetics*. Oxford University Press, London, 1972.

Palmer, Richard E. *Hermeneutics: Interpretation Theory in Schleiermacher, Dilthey, Heidegger, and Gadamer*. Northwestern University Press, Evanston, Ill., 1969.

Bibliography

Panofsky, Erwin. "The History of Art as a Humanistic Discipline." In *The Meaning of the Humanities*. Ed. T. M. Greene. Princeton University Press, Princeton, N. J., 1938.

Pap, Arthur. "Theory of Definition." *Philosophy of Science*, Vol. 31, 1964. Reprinted in *Problems in the Philosophy of Language*. Ed. Thomas M. Olshewsky. Holt, Rinehart & Winston, New York, 1969.

Patton, T. E., and D. W. Stampe. "The Rudiments of Meaning: On Ziff on Grice." *Foundations of Language*, Vol. 5, 1969.

Pitcher, George, ed. *Wittgenstein, The Philosophical Investigations: A Collection of Critical Essays*. Doubleday, Garden City, N. Y., 1966.

Pleydell-Pearce, A. G. "Sense, Reference and Fiction." *British Journal of Aesthetics*, Vol. 7, 1967.

Politzer, Heinz. "Das Handwerk der Interpretation." *Das Schweigen der Sirenen: Studien zur deutschen und österreichischen Literatur*. J. B. Metzler, Stuttgart, 1968.

Pollard, D.E.B. "M. J. Sirridge, Fiction, and Truth." *Philosophy and Phenomenological Research*, Vol. 38, 1977.

Pratt, Mary Louise. *Toward a Speech Act Theory of Literary Discourse*. Indiana University Press, Bloomington, 1977.

Price, Kingsley B. "Is a Work of Art a Symbol?" *Journal of Philosophy*. Vol. 50, 1953. Reprinted in *Contemporary Studies in Aesthetics*. Ed. Francis X. J. Coleman. McGraw-Hill, New York, 1968.

Quine, Willard Van Orman. "Two Dogmas of Empiricism." *Philosophical Review*, Vol. 60, 1951. Reprinted in *Problems in the Philosophy of Language*. Ed. Thomas M. Olshewsky. Holt, Rinehart & Winston, New York, 1969.

Rader, Melvin. *Wordsworth: A Philosophical Approach*. Oxford University Press, London, 1967.

Redpath, Theodore. "The Meaning of a Poem." In *British Philosophy in the Mid-Century*. Ed. C. A. Mace. Allen & Unwin, London, 1957. Reprinted in *Problems in Aesthetics*. Ed. Morris Weitz. Macmillan, New York, 1970.

Reichert, John F. "Description and Interpretation in Literary Criticism." *Journal of Aesthetics and Art Criticism*, Vol. 28, 1969.

Rhees, Rush. "Can There Be a Private Language?" *Proceedings of the Aristotelian Society*, Suppl. Vol. 28, 1954. Reprinted

Bibliography

in *Wittgenstein, The Philosophical Investigations: A Collection of Critical Essays*. Ed. George Pitcher. Doubleday, Garden City, N. Y., 1966.

Ricoeur, Paul. "The Model of the Text: Meaningful Action Considered as a Text." *New Literary History*, Vol. 5, 1973.

———. "Writing as a Problem for Literary Criticism and Philosophical Hermeneutics." *Philosophic Exchange*, 1977.

Riffaterre, Michael. "Describing Poetic Structures: Two Approaches to Baudelaire's 'les Chats'." *Yale French Studies*, 1966. Reprinted in *Structuralism*. Ed. Jacques Ehrmann. Doubleday, Garden City, N. Y., 1970.

Rimmon, Shlomith. *The Concept of Ambiguity—the Example of James*. University of Chicago Press, Chicago, Ill., 1977.

Roma, Emilio. "The Scope of the Intentional Fallacy." *The Monist*, Vol. 50, 1966. Reprinted in *On Literary Intention: Critical Essays*. Ed. David Newton-de Molina. Edinburgh University Press, Edinburgh, 1976.

Rorty, Richard. "Realism and Reference." *The Monist*, Vol. 59, 1976.

Rubin, Louis D. *The Teller in the Tale*. University of Washington Press, Seattle, 1967.

Rüdiger, Horst. "Zwischen Interpretation und Geistesgeschichte." *Methodenfragen der deutschen Literaturwissenschaft*. Ed. Reinhold Grimm and Jost Hermand. Wissenschaftliche Buchgesellschaft, Darmstadt, 1973.

Rutherford, Andrew, ed. *Kipling's Mind and Art*. Stanford University Press, Stanford, Calif., 1964.

Ryan, Alan. *The Philosophy of the Social Sciences*. Random House, New York, 1970.

Savigny, Eike von. *Argumentation in der Literaturwissenschaft: Wissenschaftstheoretische Untersuchungen zu Lyrikinterpretationen*. C. H. Beck, München, 1976.

Savile, Anthony. "The Place of Intention in the Concept of Art." *Proceedings of the Aristotelian Society*, Vol. 69, 1968-69. Reprinted in *Aesthetics*. Ed. Harold Osborne. Oxford University Press, London, 1972.

Schiffer, Stephen. *Meaning*. Oxford University Press, Oxford, 1972.

Schmidt, Siegfried. *Elemente einer Textpoetik*. Bayerischer Schulbuch-Verlag, München, 1974.

Bibliography

Schmidt, Siegfried. "Text und Bedeutung." In *Text, Bedeutung, Ästhetik.* Ed. Siegfried J. Schmidt. Bayerischer Schulbuch-Verlag, München, 1970.

Schwartz, Stephen P., ed. *Naming, Necessity, and Natural Kinds.* Cornell University Press, Ithaca, N. Y., 1977.

Scriven, Michael. "The Language of Fiction." *Proceedings of the Aristotelian Society,* Suppl. Vol. 28, 1954.

Searle, John R. "The Logical Status of Fictional Discourse." *New Literary History,* Vol. 6, 1974.

———, ed. *The Philosophy of Language.* Oxford University Press, London, 1971.

———. "Reiterating the Differences: A Reply to Derrida." *Glyph: Johns Hopkins Textual Studies,* Vol. 1. Ed. Samuel Weber and Henry Sussman. The Johns Hopkins University Press, Baltimore, Md., 1977.

———. *Speech Acts: An Essay in the Philosophy of Language.* Cambridge University Press, Cambridge, 1969.

———. "What is a Speech Act?" In *Philosophy in America.* Ed. Max Black. Allen & Unwin, London, 1965. Reprinted in *The Philosophy of Language.* Ed. John R. Searle. Oxford University Press, London, 1971.

Shanks, Edward. *Rudyard Kipling: A Study in Literature and Political Ideas.* Macmillan, London, 1941.

Shwayder, David S. *The Stratification of Behavior: A System of Definitions Propounded and Defended.* Humanities Press, New York, 1965.

Sircello, Guy. *Mind and Art: An Essay on the Varieties of Expression,* Princeton University Press, Princeton, N. J., 1972.

Sirridge, Mary J. "J. R. Tolkien and Fairy Tale Truth." *British Journal of Aesthetics,* Vol. 15, 1974.

———. "The Moral of the Story: A Rejoinder to Pollard." *Philosophy and Phenomenological Research,* Vol. 38, 1977.

———. "Truth from Fiction?" *Philosophy and Phenomenological Research,* Vol. 35, 1975.

Skinner, Quentin. "Hermeneutics and the Role of History." *New Literary History,* Vol. 7, 1975.

———. "Motives, Intentions, and the Interpretation of Texts." *New Literary History,* Vol. 3, 1971-72.

———. "On Performing and Explaining Linguistic Actions." *Philosophical Quarterly,* Vol. 21, 1971.

Smith, Barbara Herrnstein. *On the Margins of Discourse: The*

Bibliography

Relation of Literature to Language. University of Chicago Press, Chicago, Ill., 1978.
———. "Poetry as Fiction." In *New Directions in Literary History.* Ed. Ralph Cohen. The Johns Hopkins University Press, Baltimore, Md., 1974.
Sparshott, Francis E. *The Concept of Criticism.* Oxford University Press, London. 1967.
Spilka, Mark, ed. *Towards a Poetics of Fiction.* Indiana University Press, Bloomington, 1977.
Staiger, Emil. *Die Kunst der Interpretation.* Atlantis Verlag, Zürich, 1963.
Stegmüller, Wolfgang. *Probleme und Resultate der Wissenschaftstheorie und Analytischen Philosophie,* Bd. 1: *Wissenschaftliche Erklärung und Begründung.* Springer Verlag, Berlin, 1969.
———. "Der sogenannte Zirkel des Verstehens." *Natur und Geschichte: X. Deutscher Kongress für Philosophie.* Ed. K. Hübner and A. Menne. Felix Meiner Verlag, Hamburg, 1973.
Steinmann, Martin. "Literature, Knowledge, and the Language of Literature." *College English,* Vol. 34, 1973.
Stevenson, Charles L. *Facts and Values: Studies in Ethical Analysis.* Yale University Press, New Haven, Conn., 1963.
———. "Interpretation and Evaluation in Aesthetics." In *Philosophical Analysis.* Ed. Max Black. Cornell University Press, Ithaca, N. Y., 1950. Reprinted in *Art and Philosophy.* Ed. William E. Kennick. St. Martin's Press, New York, 1964.
———. "On the Reasons That Can Be Given for the Interpretation of a Poem." In *Philosophy Looks at the Arts.* Ed. Joseph Margolis. Charles Scribner's Sons, New York, 1962.
Stierle, Karlheinz. "Die Identität des Gedichts—Hölderlin als Paradigma." *Identität: Poetik und Hermeneutik VIII.* Ed. Odo Marquard and Karlheinz Stierle. Fink Verlag, München, 1979.
Strawson, Peter F. "Intention and Convention in Speech Acts." *Philosophical Review,* Vol. 73, 1964. Reprinted in *The Philosophy of Language.* Ed. John R. Searle. Oxford University Press, London, 1971.
———. "Meaning and Truth." *Logico-Linguistic Papers.* Methuen & Co., London, 1971.
———. "On Referring." *Mind,* Vol. 59, 1950. Reprinted in

Bibliography

Problems in the Philosophy of Language. Ed. Thomas M. Olshewsky. Holt, Rinehart & Winston, New York, 1969.

Szondi, Peter. "Zur Erkenntnisproblematik in der Literaturwissenschaft," *Die Neue Rundschau,* Vol. 73, 1962. Reprinted under the same title in *Universitätstage,* 1962. Reprinted in excerpts in *Einführung in die Neuere deutsche Literaturwissenschaft.* Ed. Karl Otto Conrady. Rowohlt Verlag, Reinbek bei Hamburg, 1966. Reprinted as "Über philologische Erkenntnis." In *Hölderlin Studien. Mit einem Traktat über philologische Erkenntnis.* Suhrkamp Verlag, Frankfurt a. M., 1970. Reprinted under this title in *Methodenfragen der deutschen Literaturwissenschaft.* Ed. Reinhold Grimm and Jost Hermand. Wissenschaftliche Buchgesellschaft, Darmstadt, 1973.

Thorpe, James. "The Aesthetics of Textual Criticism." *Publications of the Modern Language Association,* Vol. 80, 1965.

Tilghman, Benjamin R., ed. *Language and Aesthetics: Contributions to the Philosophy of Art.* University Press of Kansas, Lawrence, 1973.

―――. "The Literary Work of Art." *Language and Aesthetics: Contributions to the Philosophy of Art.* Ed. Benjamin R. Tilghman. University Press of Kansas, Lawrence, 1973.

Todorov, Tzvetan. "How to Read?" *The Poetics of Prose.* Trans. Richard Howard. Cornell University Press, Ithaca, N. Y., 1977.

Tormey, Alan. *The Concept of Expression: A Study in Philosophical Psychology and Aesthetics.* Princeton University Press, Princeton, N. J., 1971.

Trilling, Lionel. *The Liberal Imagination: Essays on Literature and Society.* The Viking Press, New York, 1950.

Vivas, Eliseo. *Creation and Discovery: Essays in Criticism and Aesthetics.* Noonday Press, New York, 1955.

Wain, John. "W. B. Yeats: 'Among School Children'." In *Interpretations: Essays on Twelve English Poems.* Ed. John Wain. Routledge & Kegan Paul, London, 1962.

―――, F. W. Bateson, and W. W. Robson. "'Intention' and Blake's *Jerusalem.*" *Essays in Criticism,* Vol. 2, 1952. Reprinted in *Aesthetics and the Philosophy of Criticism.* Ed. Marvin Levich. Random House, New York, 1963.

Waismann, Friedrich. "Verifiability." *Proceedings of the Aristotelian Society.* Suppl. Vol. 19, 1945. Reprinted in *Logic and*

Bibliography

Language. Ed. Antony Flew. Doubleday, Garden City, N. Y., 1965.
Walton, Kendall. "Categories of Art." *Philosophical Review*, Vol. 79, 1970.
———. "Fearing Fictions." *Journal of Philosophy*, Vol. 75, 1978.
———. "How Remote are Fictional Worlds from the Real World?" *Journal of Aesthetics and Art Criticism*, Vol. 37, 1978.
———. "Pictures and Make-Believe." *Philosophical Review*, Vol. 82, 1973.
———. "Points of View in Narrative and Depictive Representation." *Nous*, Vol. 10, 1976.
Warning, Rainer. "Formen narrativer Identitätskonstitution im Höfischen Roman." *Identität: Poetik und Hermeneutik VIII*. Ed. Odo Marquard and Karlheinz Stierle. Fink Verlag, München, 1979.
Watson, George. "The Literary Past." *The Study of Literature*. Lane Publishers, London, 1969. Reprinted in *On Literary Intention: Critical Essays*. Ed. David Newton-de Molina. Edinburgh University Press, Edinburgh, 1976.
Weinrich, Harald. "Der Leser braucht den Autor." *Identität: Poetik und Hermeneutik VIII*. Ed. Odo Marquard and Karlheinz Stierle. Fink Verlag, München, 1979.
Weitz, Morris. *Hamlet and the Philosophy of Literary Criticism*. University of Chicago Press, Chicago, Ill., 1964.
———, ed. *Problems in Aesthetics*. Macmillan, New York, 1970.
———. "Truth in Literature." *Revue Internationale de Philosophie*, Vol. 9, 1955. Reprinted in *Introductory Readings in Aesthetics*. Ed. John Hospers. The Free Press, New York, 1969.
Wellek, René, and Austin Warren. *Theory and Literature*. Harcourt, Brace & World, New York, 3rd edn., 1956.
Wicksteed, Joseph H. *Blake's Innocence and Experience: A Study of the Songs and Manuscripts*. J. M. Dent & Sons, London, 1928; E. P. Dutton & Co., New York, 1928.
Wienold, Götz. *Semiotik der Literatur*. Athenäum Verlag, Frankfurt a. M., 1972.
Wilson, Edmund. "The Ambiguity of Henry James." *The Triple Thinkers*. Oxford University Press, New York, 1948. Reprinted in *A Casebook on Henry James's* The Turn of the Screw. Ed. Gerald Willen. Crowell, New York, 1960.

Bibliography

Wilson, Edmund. "The Kipling That Nobody Read." *The Wound and the Bow*. London, 1952. Reprinted in *Kipling's Mind and Art*. Ed. Andrew Rutherford. Stanford University Press, Stanford, Calif., 1964.

Wimsatt, William K. "Genesis: A Fallacy Revisited." In *The Disciplines of Criticism: Essays in Literary Theory, Interpretation, and History*. Ed. Peter Demetz et al. Yale University Press, New Haven, Conn., 1968.

———, and Monroe C. Beardsley. "The Intentional Fallacy." *Sewanee Review*, Vol. 54, 1946. Reprinted in William K. Wimsatt and Monroe C. Beardsley. *The Verbal Icon: Studies in the Meaning of Poetry*. University of Kentucky Press, Lexington, 1954.

Winch, Peter. *The Idea of a Social Science and its Relation to Philosophy*. Routledge & Kegan Paul, London, 1973 (1958).

Wittgenstein, Ludwig. *Philosophical Investigations*. Trans. G.E.M. Anscombe. Macmillan, New York, 3rd edn., 1968.

Wollheim, Richard. *Art and its Objects: An Introduction to Aesthetics*. Harper & Row, New York, 1968.

Wright, Georg Henrik von. *Explanation and Understanding*. Cornell University Press, Ithaca, N. Y., 1971.

Zabel, Morton D., ed. *Literary Opinion in America*. Harper & Brothers, New York, 2nd edn., 1951.

Ziff, Paul. "On H. P. Grice's Account of Meaning." *Analysis*, Vol. 28, 1967. Reprinted in Paul Ziff. *Understanding Understanding*. Cornell University Press, Ithaca, N. Y., 1972.

———. *Philosophic Turnings*. Cornell University Press, Ithaca, N. Y., 1966.

———. "What is Said." In *Semantics of Natural Language*. Ed. Donald Davidson and Gilbert Harman. Reidel Co., Dordrecht, Holland, 1972.

Žmegač, Viktor, ed. *Methoden der deutschen Literaturwissenschaft: Eine Dokumentation*. Athenäum Verlag, Frankfurt a. M., 1971.

INDEX

Abel, Theodore, 244n
Abrams, M. H., 19n
'acceptable' interpretations, 197; and a critic's interest or purpose, 209, 211-13; critics disagree about, 209-14, 237
Adorno, Theodor W., 229n
aesthetic considerations, 4, 6, 7, 9, 49, 59, 234; and assertion of propositions expressed by a work, 170; and author's intention, 114-28, 150; coherence, 127; as evidence of intention, 116-21; vs. evidence of intention, 121-26. *See also* coherence
Aiken, Henry David, 46n, 47n, 104n
Aldrich, Virgil, 46n
allusion, 58-62, 148
ambiguity: ambiguous vs. unambiguous sentence, 106-107; and meaning and significance, 30; and the role of context, 91-93; sentence and utterance, 53-58, 205-206; and speaker's statement about his intention, 53-58
Anacker, Heinrich: "Auszug der Schmarotzer," 121-24
Anderegg, Johannes, 155n
Anscombe, G. E. M., 99, 141n, 144
anti-intentionalist thesis, 46, 49-52, 67-69, 151; defined, 45; and interpretive practice, 207-208; and literary work as possible speech act, 288
Aschenbrenner, Karl, 84n, 223n

assertion: and pretended assertion, 167, 172, 174; of propositions expressed by a work, 172, 174, 175, 176, 186, 193, 194; rules of, 167-68. *See also* propositions expressed by a work
associations of a text, and author's attitudes, 135-37
attitudes expressed in literature: author's unrecognized or unacknowledged, 138-40; and Culler's rule of significance, 221; and implied author, 221
Austin, J. L., 167n
author: awareness of implications of details, 128-40; and beliefs expressed by a work, 154, 158; explanatory comments or notes, 101n, 102-104; presumption that he holds beliefs expressed by a work, 187-89; vs. speaker or narrator, 149. *See also* implied author *and* propositions expressed by a work
author's knowledge, and rules of the language, 111-12
autonomy of (fictional) literary works, 163
Ayer, A. J., 145n

Baker, John Ross, 155n
Barnes, Annette, 197n, 201-202
Bateson, F. W., 81n, 125n, 165n, 199-200
Baudelaire, Charles: "Les Chats," 214-18

Index

Beardsley, Monroe C., 8n, 37n, 40n, 46, 86n, 91n, 98n, 100n, 143n, 151, 155n, 162n, 164n, 165n, 207n, 214n, 221n; on change of meaning, 39n; explication as explanation of textual features, 71; on Housman, "1887," 141-42; on internal and external evidence, 67-69; on irony, 123n; on meaning and intention, 50, 52-57, 56-60, 145; on parallel passages, 104; on propositions expressed by a literary work, 167; on Wordsworth, "A slumber did my spirit seal," 70
Beckett, Samuel: *Watt*, 161
Beissner, Friedrich, 269-78
Bennett, Jonathan, 106n
Betti, Emilio, 8n
Beyle, Henri, *see* Stendhal
Bierwisch, Manfred, 108n
biographical approach to literature, 15
biographical facts and textual features: as evidence for an interpretation, 88-89. *See also* textual features
Blake, William, 108n; "Ah! Sunflower," 219-21, 222; "Jerusalem," 124-26; "London," 51, 118-21
Bloom, Harold, 153n, 219-21, 223
Booth, Wayne C., 63n, 64, 89n, 155-59, 163-64, 166, 172, 173, 175, 176, 178, 180-85, 188, 189, 190, 194n, 232n. *See also* implied author
Borges, Jorge Luis: "Pierre Menard, Author of *Don Quixote*," 125, 235-36
Boswell, James: *Life of Johnson*, 57n

Brecht, Bertolt, 123; *Leben des Galilei*, 165-66
Brodbeck, May, 287n
Brooke-Rose, Christine, 67n, 73n, 196
Brooks, Cleanth, 70n, 81n, 86n, 193n, 199-200
Burke, Kenneth, 41n-42n

Camus, Albert: *La Chute*, 159
Cargill, Oscar, 37n-38n
Casey, John, 140n
Cavell, Stanley, 108n, 132n, 134n, 193n, 208n
Céline, Louis-Ferdinand Destouches: *Journey to the End of the Night*, 183
certainty, quest for, and doctrine of the hermeneutic circle, 255, 258-59, 261, 262-65, 279, 300
Cervantes Saavedra, Miguel de: *Don Quixote*, 235-36
chance, text produced by: and concept of a literary work, 83-84; and concept of the meaning of a literary work, 48; and evidence for an interpretation, 77-78; and explanation of textual features, 71-72; interpreting a, 84-86; and literary work as speech act, 288; and speaker or narrator of a work, 76
characters, fictional, *see* speaker (narrator, or character)
Child, Arthur, 198n
Chomsky, Noam, 24n, 54n, 106n, 112n
Cioffi, F., 9n, 67n, 89n, 126n-27n, 141n, 145n, 189n, 293n
Clemens, Samuel L., *see* Mark Twain
Close, A. J., 9n, 14n, 134n, 140n, 166n, 233n

Index

Cohen, L. Jonathan, 41n; and Avishai Margalit, 98n
coherence, as criterion of interpretation, 6, 8, 9, 104; and aesthetic considerations, 117, 127; as criterion of intention, 47-48, 69-81, 82, 83, 87, 88, 149
Coleman, F. X. J., 95n
complexity, as criterion of interpretation, 8, 9; and aesthetic considerations, 117; a criterion of intention, 47-48, 69, 81-82, 87, 88, 149
computer 'poem', 72, 85-86. *See also* chance, text produced by consciousness and intention, 133-35
context: as evidence of author's intention, 47-48, 90-99, 149; and 'retroactive' disambiguation, 92-93; the speaker's view of the situation, 93-94, 99
correct interpretation, the, 196-238; and gaps in the text, 198; (alleged) impossibility of determining, 202, 214, 240-41; and inexhaustibility of literary works, 225-30, 238; intelligibility of concept vs. actual evidence for, 231-32; frequent lack of sufficient evidence for, 232-34, 235, 236; and literary work as speech act, 240-41; vs. many acceptable or admissible interpretations, 196-98, 209; and multiplicity of meaning, 236, 237; as a normative question, 4-6, 12; and partial interpretations, 199-200n; (in principle) possibility of determining, 221, 236, 238; structuralist view of, 197; and survival of literary works, 224-25, 232; Szondi on, 286; and variety of incompatible interpretations, 223-24, 231-38. *See also* evidence
Crane, R. S., 175-80, 188n, 207
criticism and interpretation, 32-34
Crittenden, Charles, 83n
Cruttwell, Patrick, 155n
Culler, Jonathan, 46n, 71n, 151n, 154, 165n, 167n, 177n, 197, 199, 201, 203, 204, 206, 208, 209n, 210, 213n, 218, 219-22, 238

Davis, Walter A., 115n
Derrida, Jacques, 204
details, meanings and implications of: and author's intention, 129-35, 150
Dickie, George, 37n, 46n, 82n, 84n, 90-93, 100n
Dilthey, Wilhelm, 239, 243n
Donagan, Alan, 145n
Donne, John, "Goe, and catche a falling star," 129-34

Eaton, Marcia M., 46n, 104n, 115n, 187n, 208n
Eco, Umberto, 198n
Eichner, Hans, 114n
Eliot, T. S., 15n, 25n, 45n, 186n, 189, 219; "Prufrock," 58-59
Ellis, John M., 14n, 34n, 35, 46n, 61-62n, 67n, 148n, 151-52n, 165n
Empson, William, 86n, 128, 135-37, 151n, 169-75, 180, 188
evidence (objective), 256-59, 277-78, 296-98, 299-300; and certainty, 255, 258-59, 262-65, 266-67, 279; parallel passages, 261-68, 272-76, 289-91; and understanding (*Verstehen*),

325

Index

evidence (*cont.*) 291-92; variant readings, 251-56
Evidenz (self-evidence): as the proper criterion of interpretation, 245-48, 249, 258-59, 263, 265, 286, 299-300; and scientific verification, 246. *See also* Szondi
explanation of textual features, 69-81; and author's intention, 74-76, 78, 87-88
external evidence, 49-50, 147, 235-36; and critical choices among possible interpretations, 207

Farrell, B. A., 235n
fictional and nonfictional narrative: difference between, 161-62
Fiedler, Leslie, 67n
Fielding, Henry: *Tom Jones*, 159, 182
Fodor, Jerry A., and Jerrold J. Katz, 98n
forethought, and doing something intentionally, 133-35
Foulkes, A. P., 3n, 122n, 154n
Fowler, Alastair, 128, 234n
Freedman, Ralph, 155n
Frege, Gottlob, 29n
Frye, Northrop, 15n, 45n, 124, 153, 154, 193

Gabriel, Gottfried, 164-65, 167n, 168n, 187n
Gadamer, Hans-Georg, 7n, 8n, 36n-37n, 46n, 165n, 294-96
Gale, Richard, 83n, 95n
Gang, T. M., 108n
Gardiner, Patrick, 244n
Gardner, Helen, 108n
Geisteswissenschaften and *Naturwissenschaften*, 239, 242n-43n

Gibbon, Edward, 33
Glinz, Hans, 22n
Glover, Jonathan, 235n
Goethe, Johann Wolfgang von: *Faust*, 244n; *Iphigenie auf Tauris*, 226-30
Göttner, Heide, 7n, 298n
Goldsmith, Oliver, "The Traveller," 56n-57n
Gräf, Hans Gerhard, 229n
Graham, Ilse, 192
Grewendorf, Günther, 115n, 118n, 213n-14n
Grice, H. P., 62n, 84-85, 106n, 108n, 145n

Hamburger, Käte, 155n, 186n
Hamburger, Michael, 269n
Hamlyn, D. W., 141n
Hampshire, Stuart, 144n, 198n, 213n, 214n
Hancher, Michael, 14n, 108n, 115n, 134n-35n, 198n, 205n
Hardy, Thomas, 143
Harris, Frank, 141
Hass, H. E., 165n
Hawthorn, Jeremy M., 86n
Heidegger, Martin, 192n
Hempel, Carl G., and Paul Oppenheim, 244n
Hepburn, Ronald, 186n
Hermand, Jost, 15n
hermeneutic circle, doctrine of, 7, 240-41, 249-50, 256-59, 294-98, 299; and misunderstanding, 295-96; and parallel passages, 259-68, 270-73, 276; and variant readings, 250-56, 258. *See also* certainty, quest for
Hermerén, Göran, 63n, 123n
Hirsch, E. D., 3n, 7n, 9n, 15n, Ch. II, 200n, 223n, 233n, 235n, 293n, 297n; basic argu-

Index

ment, 18-19; on Blake's "London," 51, 118, 119; on change of intention, 20-22; on changelessness of meaning, 37-42, 44; on concept of meaning, 18, 43; on the correct interpretation, 18-19, 26; definition of meaning, 16; definition of meaning as recommendation, 12, 19, 38, 43; intention as the only "genuinely discriminating norm," 18-19, 20-23, 24, 25; interpretation and criticism, 32-34; meaning and significance, 12, 21, 27-37, 226; on norms of interpretation, 17-18, 26; "principle of sharability," 17-18

Hogan, Homer, 86n
Hölderlin, Friedrich: "Brod und Wein," 277, 278; "Friedensfeier," 117-18, 268-78; "Patmos," 250-57, 277, 278, 284-85
Homer, 156n; *Iliad*, 33
Horn, András, 198n
Hospers, John, 46n, 54n, 104n, 123n, 143n, 145-46, 187n, 200n
Hough, Graham, 115n-16n, 126-28, 129-40
Housman, A. E.: "1887," 141-43; "With seed the sowers scatter," 169-75, 188
Howell, Robert C., 54n
Hoy, David Couzens, 7n
Hungerland, Isabel C., 4n, 18n, 46n, 104n, 187n, 208n

idiolect, 108, 145
illocutionary acts, recognizing: and implications of details of a text, 129-40

implied author: and anti-intentionalist thesis, 193-94; and assertion of propositions expressed by a literary work, 163-65; attempt to reconcile author's presence with pure fiction, 194; and autonomy of literature, 192-95; demand for an absolute, 193; doctrine of, excludes certain facts in advance, 191-92; fiction and biography, 190-91; and intentionalist thesis, 176; motivation for introducing concept of, 163, 189-94; and narrator, 166-67; and propositions expressed by a literary work, 155-58, 166, 169, 178-79, 186, 221; and real author's beliefs, 157, 166-67, 178-79, 181, 182, 184, 187, 189-90, 191; and sincerity, 181-82
incompatible interpretations, 197, 198, 200, 236, 237; and (logically) compatible interpretations, 199; and different demands imposed on an interpretation, 233-34; not evidence that a work has several meanings, 223, 231-37; and inconsistent intentions, 223n; joint truth and joint plausibilty of, 201-202; and literary work as speech act, 221-23, 238; separate vs. joint plausibility (acceptability) of, 200-202, 210
inexhaustibility of literary works, 36-37, 43-44, 225-30, 234n, 238
Ingarden, Roman, 38n, 154n-55n, 165n, 193
intention: and author's or speaker's statement about his, 52-54, 140-44, 148, 233; concept

Index

intention (*cont.*)
  of, contrasted with planning, 133-35; determining one's, 144-45; evidence of, vs. conclusive evidence of, 103-104; incompatible intentions, 139; vs. plan, motive, textual coherence, 14; rejection of author's statement of, 49, 140-43, 147-48, 150; use of term and evidence of, 14; usefulness of knowledge of author's, 46-47; weight of different kinds of evidence of, 88-89, 152
internal and external evidence, 49-50, 67-69, 88-89, 103
interpretation: constraints on a theory of, 10; expected to satisfy different demands, 233-34; as an explanation of actions, 69-81, 234, 282-85; of facts as evidence, 287-98, 299; and intention, 12-13, and Chs. III-VI *passim*; methods of, and intentionalist thesis, 15; (alleged) subjectivity of, 245-48, 249-50, 252-53, 256, 258-59, 265, 266, 272-73, 286, 299-300. *See also* intention
irony, 62-64, 123, 148
Isenberg, Arnold, 107, 143n, 146-47
Iser, Wolfgang, 155n, 198, 222n

Jakobson, Roman, and Claude Lévi-Strauss, 215-17
James, Henry, 89n; "The Liar," 183-84, 188; *The Turn of the Screw*, 73n, 159, 196, 231, 232
Japp, Uwe, 155n, 198n
Jauss, Hans Robert, 226-30
Johnson, Samuel, 57n
Jones, Alexander, 196
Jones, Peter, 45n, 85n, 230n

Joyce, James: "The Boarding House," 106; *Finnegans Wake*, 108; *A Portrait of the Artist*, 64
Juhl, P. D., 61n, 165n, 293n

Kahn, S. J., 67n
Kaufmann, Walter, 67n
Kayser, Wolfgang, 161n
Kelkar, Ashok R., 165n
Kemp, John, 46n
Kenny, Anthony, 14n
Kermode, Frank, 198n
Kipling, Rudyard: "Loot," 189
Kleist, Heinrich von: *Amphitryon*, 281-86
Knight, G. Wilson, 14n
Krieger, Murray, 194n
Kris, Ernest, and Abraham Kaplan, 6n
Kristeva, Julia, 204
Kuhn, Thomas S., 246n
Kuhns, Richard, 14n
Kunze, Michael, 227n

Lamprecht, Helmut, 122n
Lange, Victor, 100n
language, private, 145
language, rules of the, as a criterion of interpretation, 4, 5, 9, 17-18, 40, 50; and author's intention, 48, 97-98, 106-13, 146, 150
Lardner, Ring: "Haircut," 161-62
Lees, Francis Noel, 145n
Leibfried, Erwin, 46n
Lewis, David, 160, 161n
Linsky, Leonard, 95n
literary competence, 204
literary work as a speech act, 218-19, 220-23, 233, 240, 288
literature and fiction, 159
Lohner, Edgar, 15n
Lyas, Colin, 84n, 208n

Index

Macdonald, Margaret, 187n
MacIntyre, Alasdair C., 134n, 141n
Mackie, J. L., 214n
Malcolm, Norman, 145n
Man, Paul de, 155
Margolis, Joseph, 104n, 197, 200-210, 208n, 213n
Marsh, Robert, 151n
Martinez-Bonati, Felix, 187n
Marvell, Andrew: "To his Coy Mistress," 58-59
Matthews, Robert J., 67n, 198n
meaning of a literary work: and author's beliefs, 119-21; change of, 37-42, 227-30; complexity of considerations in determining the, 232, 235; concept of, and author's intention, 47; critical choices, 206-208; evidence of, as evidence of intention, 150-51; and meaning of a sentence *in abstracto*, 203-206, 223, 238; and meaning of an utterance (speech act), 204-206, 238; and reference, 29, 82-83n; and significance, 12, 27-37, 226-30, 234n; and understanding, 230; view of, as always richer than any one reading, 222-23. *See also* literary work *and* variety of meanings
Meggle, Georg, and Manfred Beetz, 213n, 235n
Meiland, Jack, 26n, 223n
Melden, A. I., 99n, 144n
Melville, Herman: *White Jacket*, 128
Mew, Peter, 186n-87n
Milton, John: *Paradise Lost*, 138-40
Mink, Louis O., 225n

misunderstanding, and doctrine of hermeneutic circle, 295-96
Mörike, Eduard: "Auf eine Lampe," 192-93
Montherlant, Henry de, 184-85

Nabokov, Vladimir, *Pale Fire*, 162
Nagel, Ernest, 244
narrator: reliable and unreliable, 159, 161-62; unreliable, and implied author, 166-67. *See also* speaker
Nathan, Daniel O., 115n
nonassertion thesis, 154, 172; and connection between literature and life, 158; and intentionalist thesis, 176; and view that meaning of a work may change, 165-66

objectivity, 23, 26, 43. *See also* evidence *and* correct interpretation
Ohmann, Richard, 155n, 161n, 167n
Orwell, George, 189n

palimpsest, theory of text as, 137-40
Palmer, Richard E., 7n, 46n
Panofsky, Erwin, 9n
Pap, Arthur, 19n
parallel passages: and contextual features, 261-63; (objective) evidence, 265-68, 289-91; evidence vs. certainty, 264-65; and facts about the author, 268, 277-78; and literary work as speech act, 214-19, 223, 238; and relation between speaker and author, 104-105; and the rules of the language,

329

Index

parallel passages (*cont.*) 110-12; Szondi on, 259-61, 262-63, 264, 265-66, 272-76
Patton, T. E., and D. W. Stampe, 108n, 147n
Picasso, Pablo: *Mother and Child*, 68
piece of language, interpretation of, 86
planning and intending, 150
plausible interpretations, *see* 'acceptable' interpretations *and* possible interpretations
playwright vs. historian, 60-61
Plenzdorf, Ulrich: *Die neuen Leiden des jungen Werther*, 227
Pleydell-Pearce, A. G., 83n
poem, concept of, 83-84
Politzer, Heinz, 192n
Pollard, D. E. B., 186n
Pope, Alexander, 179, 180; "Elegy to the Memory of an Unfortunate Lady," 135-37
possible interpretations: vs. correct interpretation, 213-14, 223; and critical choices, 206-209, 237. *See also* 'acceptable' interpretations, *and* variety of interpretations
Pratt, Mary Louise, 186n, 205n
Price, Kingsley B., 187
propositions expressed by a literary work: asserted, 158; and the author's beliefs, 162-63, 171-75, 176-89, 194-95; author committed to the truth of the, 169, 172-74, 177-78, 185, 186, 194-95; examples of, 153; presumption that author holds beliefs corresponding to the, 187-89; vs. propositions expressed by the narrator (or a character), 159

Quine, W. V. O., 29n

Racine, Jean Baptiste: *Iphigénie*, 227
Rader, Melvin, 81n
Redpath, Theodore, 6n, 46n
Reichert, John F., 198n
Rhees, R., 145n
reinterpretation of literary works, 36-37, 44; and Goethe's *Iphigenie*, 226-30
Richards, I. A., 169
Ricoeur, Paul, 46n, 198n, 204n
Riffaterre, Michael, 123n, 215-18
Rimmon, Shlomith, 71n, 93n, 202n
Roma, Emilio, 67n
Rorty, Richard, 95n
Rubin, Louis D., 155n, 157n, 190-93, 194n
Rüdiger, Horst, 242n-43n
Ryan, Alan, 239n

Savigny, Eike von, 115n, 117, 118n, 213n-14n
Savile, Anthony, 8n, 46n
Schiffer, Stephen, 106n
Schiller, Friedrich, 229n
Schmidt, Siegfried, 203n-204n
Schwartz, Stephen P., 95n
Scriven, Michael, 186n
Searle, John R., 83n, 84n, 95n, 106n, 109n, 134, 167n, 186n, 187n, 223n, 288n
sentence-meaning, and utterance-meaning, 54-58, 204-205
Shakespeare: *Hamlet*, 164; *King Lear*, 232
Shanks, Edward, 189n
Shelley, Percy Bysshe, 126-28
Shwayder, David S., 144n, 145n, 167n, 187n
Sidney, Sir Philip, 219
Sircello, Guy, 158n, 187n

330

Index

Sirridge, Mary J., 186n
Skinner, Quentin, 14n, 67n, 89n, 112n, 115n
Smith, Barbara Herrnstein, 45n, 125, 155n, 198n, 203n
Sparshott, F. E., 140n
speaker (narrator, or character): and author's beliefs, 105, 183-84, 185; and author's intention, 48, 62-63, 75-76, 100-105; and beliefs expressed by a literary work, 158-59, 188-89, 221; and historical person, 60; in fiction and author's pretense, 159-60; in fiction and nonfiction, 161-62
stage directions, and distinction between speaker and author, 100-102
Staiger, Emil, 192n, 242n
Stegmüller, Wolfgang, 7n, 145n, 235n, 243n-44n, 293
Steinmann, Martin, 187n
Stendhal, 192
Stevens, Wallace, 219
Stevenson, Charles L., 4n, 5n, 18n, 19n, 46n, 115n, 198
Stierle, Karlheinz, 155n
Strawson, P. F., 95n, 106n, 108n
survival of literary works, 34-36, 37, 43-44, 224-25
Swift, Jonathan: "A Modest Proposal," 34-36, 124, 230n; *Gulliver's Travels*, 175-80, 188n, 207
Szondi, Peter, 7n, 46n, 240-46, 248, 249, 299-300; arguments against Beissner (on "Friedensfeier"), 268-79; on author's intention, 280-81; on correct and incorrect interpretation, 286; on evidence for an interpretation, 258-59; implicit conception of the meaning of a literary work, 282-84; on interdependence of evidence and understanding, 249-50, 299, 300; on interpretation of facts as evidence, 287-89, 299; on parallel passages, 256-61, 262-63, 264, 265-66; on philological knowledge, 242-43, 249-50; on variant readings, 250-56, 258; on verification of interpretive claims, 244-46, 248, 249

text: appeal to the, as appeal to intention, 66-89, 151; concept of, 83-84; and statement of intention, 141-43, 147-48
textual features: and biographical facts, 67-69, 88-89, 149; as evidence for an interpretation, and intention, 76-81, 88, 149; explanation of, as explanation of actions, 69-81, 87-88, 149
theory of interpretation, task of ·a, 10, 207-208
Thoreau, Henry David, 146-47
Thorpe, James, 46n, 128n
Tilghman, B. R., 101n-102n
Todorov, Tzvetan, 137n, 198n
Tormey, Alan, 158n, 159n, 198n
Trilling, Lionel, 45n
truth-claims, *see* assertion *and* propositions expressed by a literary work
Twain, Mark: *Adventures of Huckleberry Finn*, 190-92

understanding and meaning, 63-64, 230
utterance-meaning and sentence-meaning, 54-58, 204-205

variety of meanings: claim that a literary work has, 197, 200-202; (logically) compatible and incompatible meanings, 199-200; and context, 101n-102n; and external evidence, 235-36; and inexhaustibility of a literary work, 226-30; and interpretive disagreements, 209-14, 223; and one correct interpretation, 236, 237; and poem as speech act, 222-23; and variety of incompatible interpretations proposed, 201; and doctrine of *Verstehen*, 286-87. See also meaning of a literary work; interpretation; hermeneutic circle

Verstehen (understanding), 239-40, 241, 242; and *Erklären* (explaining), 239; of facts as evidence, 287-98, 299-300; as involving a certain experience, 239-40, 242-46; and knowledge of a literary work, 242-43; and verification of interpretive claims, 243-48, 258-59, 299. See also hermeneutic circle

Vivas, Eliseo, 192n

Wain, John, 103n, 124-25
Waismann, Friedrich, 265n, 287n
Walton, Kendall, 110n, 115n, 159n, 161n, 224-25
Warning, Rainer, 155n
Watson, George, 125n, 134n
Weil, Simone, 33
Weinrich, Harald, 155n-56n
Weitz, Morris, 71n, 186n
Wellek, René, and Austin Warren, 14n, 36n, 40, 45n, 151n, 165n, 292n
Wicksteed, Joseph H., 120
Wienold, Götz, 3n
Wilson, Edmund, 189, 196
Wimsatt, William K., 46n, 47n, 50-52, 56n-57n, 67n, 102n, 118-21, 142-43, 151, 189n; and Monroe C. Beardsley, 46n, 49-51, 58-59, 67n, 102, 104, 105n, 161
Winch, Peter, 99n, 239n, 287n
Wittgenstein, Ludwig, 57n, 134n, 144-45
Wollheim, Richard, 9n, 224n
Wordsworth, William: "A slumber did my spirit seal," 70ff., 199-202, 206, 211
Wright, Georg Henrik von, 141n, 144n, 239n, 287n

Yeats, William Butler: "Among School Children," 103

Ziff, Paul, 30n, 53n, 94n, 96, 97, 108n, 110n, 111

Library of Congress Cataloging in Publication Data

Juhl, Peter D.   1946-
  Interpretation, an essay in the philosophy of literary criticism.

  Bibliography: p.
  Includes index.
  1. Hermeneutics.   2. Criticism.   I. Title.
PN81.J83   801'.95   80-7534
ISBN 0-691-07242-6